KEN BARBIER, the author of *CP/M Assembly Language Programming* (Prentice-Hall, 1982), has more than 30 years of experience in electronics and computers. In addition to writing numerous articles on computer hardware, software, and applications, he has been involved in the systems integration of microcomputers and in designing, constructing, and programming real-time data acquisition and control systems.

Ken Barbier

CP/M TECHNIQUES

A SPECTRUM BOOK

PRENTICE-HALL, INC., Englewood Cliffs, New Jersey 07632

Library of Congress Cataloging in Publication Data

BARBIER, KEN.
  CP/M techniques.

  "A Spectrum book."
  Includes index.
  1. Electronic digital computers—Programming.
2. Operating systems (Computers) 3. Assembler language
(Computer program language) 4. Structured programming.
I. Title. II. Title: C.P./M. techniques.
QA76.6.B3574 1984   001.64'2   83-24689
ISBN 0-13-187865-4
ISBN 0-13-187857-3 (pbk.)

This book is available at a special discount when ordered
in bulk quantities. Contact Prentice-Hall, Inc., General
Publishing Division, Special Sales, Englewood Cliffs, N.J. 07632.

Editorial production/supervision and interior design by Jane Zalenski
Manufacturing buyer: Joyce Levatino
Cover illustration © 1984 by Jeannette Jacobs

ISBN 0-13-187857-3 {PBK.}

ISBN 0-13-187865-4

Prentice-Hall International, Inc., *London*
Prentice-Hall of Australia Pty. Limited, *Sydney*
Prentice-Hall Canada Inc., *Toronto*
Prentice-Hall of India Private Limited, *New Delhi*
Prentice-Hall of Japan, Inc., *Tokyo*
Prentice-Hall of Southeast Asia Pte. Ltd., *Singapore*
Whitehall Books Limited, *Wellington, New Zealand*
Editora Prentice-Hall do Brasil Ltda., *Rio de Janeiro*

Contents

APPENDIXES

Preface

Intended for the experienced programmer with some background in writing assembly language programs under CP/M or some similar operating system, this book presents three main topics: an understanding of the structure of the CP/M operating system, guidelines on writing well documented and structured assembly language programs, and details on how instructions are linked together to perform tasks within a program. The reader is assumed to have some knowledge of the CP/M operating system and 8080 assembly language programming. Beginners are advised to start with *CP/M Assembly Language Programming*, published in 1983 by Prentice-Hall.

Readers who have worked their way through that book will recognize some of the I/O subroutines at first appeared there and are included in this book as well. Other than this minor duplication, the subject matter here is all new and is on a more advanced level. Although this is a logical sequel, this book contains no subject matter that requires familiarity with the contents of that beginners level text. Any of the introductory texts on CP/M and assembly language programming will serve as background for following the examples in this book.

The reader is assumed to have access to a microcomputer running a standard version of the CP/M operating system. Access to the Digital Research CP/M manuals will also be required, and the reader is advised to have a copy of the *8080/8085 Assembly Language Programming Manual* published by Intel Corporation. An equivalent coverage of the details of the 8080 instruction set can also be found in many of the introductory texts on assembly programming, and can substitute for the Intel manual.

Section 1 provides an overview of CP/M and the facilities it provides for the assembly language programmer. The first five chapters may be largely review for experienced CP/M programmers. Chapters 6 and 7 introduce advanced input/output, investigative, and structured programming techniques.

Section 2 covers techniques for determining the characteristics of your disk mass storage from the operator's console or from within a program, as well as techniques for accessing directories and the data stored on disks. Instruction is provided on the new Winchester hard disks, and the steps necessary to incorporate them into floppy disk based computers. Techniques for cataloging disks and the modules within programs are covered, and a complete module cataloging program is included.

Section 3 is devoted to writing a complete customized BIOS, as well as techniques for installing operating system interfaces for new hardware added to an existing computer. The use of an extended bootstrap program permits generating complicated versions of the operating system for handling more massive storage, and the system generation process is automated by using a SUBMIT program.

Exercises are integrated within the subjects discussed, in the form of subroutines to be added to a library of program modules that are then used in example programs. It is recommended that all of these routines and programs be keyed into your computer, assembled, and run as they are encountered in the text. Other exercises are suggested that will help the reader flex his programming muscles on his own schedule.

Acknowledgments

Most of the blame for the existence of this book falls squarely on the shoulders of George Resch and his "TOY 12" computer that got me started working with little machines back in the days before 1970. Poor George was still around and got trapped into reviewing the manuscript of this book. Some people will never learn, and I appreciate his help with this project.

I would also like to thank Kwok Ong, Herb Siegel, and the rest of the crew at Action Computer for their encouragement and the opportunity to work with lots of new Winchester hard disks.

Notes on CP/M Documentation

The documentation for the first releases of the CP/M operating system from Digital Research, Inc. consisted of a set of five individual manuals. Later releases combined these into a single book, but retained the original individual titles as section titles within the book.

In this book we will be concerned with the interfacing of programs with the CP/M operating system, and with customizing the operating system. References will be made to the *Interface Guide* and the *Alteration Guide* which were originally individual manuals and later became sections within the *CP/M Operating System Manual*.

The documentation for CP/M Plus has changed the names of the two guides that we will be concerned with. Program interfacing is now documented in the *Programmer's Guide* and system customizing is now covered in the *System Guide*.

Depending on the CP/M version in use, the reader may have to mentally translate *Interface Guide* to *Programmer's Guide* and *Alteration Guide* to *System Guide* where references are made to Digital Research documentation in this book.

part 1

The CP/M operating system

chapter 1

The computer system

Back in the good old days a couple of decades ago all cars had tail fins and all computers looked alike, as far as their hardware organization was concerned. They all had a **C**entral **P**rocessing **U**nit (CPU), their memory was in a separate package, and **I**nput/**O**utput (I/O) channels were connected to terminals and tape drives and punched card readers and line printers. Although their sizes varied greatly, those were the common hardware components.

These days most small microcomputers have all their components in a single desktop-sized package, and anyone can afford to pay for the electric power they consume. Since the traditional block diagram of a computer system found in all the early textbooks no longer applies, we should take a quick look at a microcomputer system in its general form to make sure that we are using common terms for all of the components of a system.

HARDWARE COMPONENTS

The microcomputer system you will be using to perform the exercises in this book may be the minimum practical configuration for a general purpose program development system. To insure that all readers can perform all of the exercises, only the smallest microcomputer will be required, and only the simple tools provided with all standard versions of the CP/M operating system will be used. This will provide the basis on which you can branch out to more capable systems after finishing this text.

8080 CPU

So that no reader will chance stumbling over any incompatibilities in instruction sets, we will begin by assuming that the computer you are using runs the Intel 8080 microprocessor. It probably doesn't, unless you are an antique collector. The Intel 8085, the Zilog Z-80 and Z-800, and the National NSC800 are more advanced micros, and execute more opcodes than the 8080 does, but they will also each execute the basic 8080 instruction set, so we will be working with that common subset of opcodes exclusively.

Main Memory

The **R**andom **A**ccess read/write **M**emory (RAM) in your computer probably provides 64 K bytes of storage, but it may be as little as 16 K if you are running CP/M version 1.4; 20 K if you have CP/M 2.2; or may be more than 64 K if you are so fortunate as to have a system with bank-switched RAM and CP/M Plus (version 3). All of the exercises in this book will run properly on any 1.4 or 2.2 system, and the minor incompatibilities with version 3 will be noted as they occur.

Peripheral Devices

The computer operator's **CON**sole (CON:) may be built into your one-piece microcomputer, or it may be connected to the computer by a cable plugged into an RS-232C serial I/O port. Either configuration will appear the same to the programs in this book until we get into Part 3, where we have to assume that the CON: is serviced through a serial port. The interfacing to built-in keyboards and CRT displays is beyond the scope of this book, and unless you are building such a system from scratch, or plan to modify that portion of your existing system, the differences won't affect anything we are going to attempt here.

Your system may have a line printer for the **Li**S**T** device (LST:), possibly connected through a Centronics compatible parallel interface. Optionally, LST: could be serviced through an RS-232C serial port. Both cases will be covered when the time comes later on, and for most of our work the difference will be invisible to the programmer.

The existence on your system of one other peripheral device will be assumed, but we won't need it until we start writing a Customized **B**asic **I**nput/**O**utput **S**ystem (CBIOS) in Chapter 12. That auxiliary device will be plugged into another RS-232C serial port on your computer, and it could be a modem for telephone communications or just a cable for intercomputer data transfer. While either of these interconnects could support bidirectional data transfers, ancient microcomputers had one output device, a paper tape **PUN**ch (PUN:), and one input device, a paper tape **R**ea**D**e**R** (RDR:). When the time comes to worry about this peripheral, we will consider it to be a single bidirectional **AUX**iliary (AUX:) device of some sort.

Mass Storage

Version 1 of CP/M assumed the existence of two 8-inch, single-sided, single-density floppy disk drives as its standard mass storage configuration. System integrators were able to fake that version of the operating system into believing that it was accessing disks configured as 26 sectors of 128 bytes each on 77 tracks on each of two disks, while it was actually servicing other floppy and minifloppy disk configurations. However, that required some monstrous programming.

Version 2 permits more flexible disk configurations to be specified, and is the first version to support the massive storage provided by hard disks in a practical manner, but even 2.2 has its limitations. Version 3, also known as CP/M Plus, is even more powerful, and we will be looking at the capabilities of all three versions in Part 2 and Part 3.

While the more advanced techniques for handling mass storage will be covered later, the minimum configuration necessary for performing the tasks laid out in this book is the two floppy disk setup, using any size or capacity of disks.

Those are the only hardware components we will discuss in this book. You might like to supply some more of your own, such as a desk, chair, coffee cup, etc.

FIRMWARE COMPONENTS

When you first turn on your computer, or press the front panel RESET switch, one of two things will occur. Either the bootup program stored in a **P**rogrammable **R**ead **O**nly **M**emory (PROM) will automatically load CP/M from the first disk drive (A:), or it will display a prompting message on the CON: and let you load CP/M when you have inserted the right disk in the A: drive.

This software in PROM (firmware) may also allow you the option of entering a monitor program instead of loading the operating system. Monitors provide the capabilities for testing hardware and software components even when the mass storage devices are inoperative. If you are fortunate enough to have a fully capable monitor in PROM, and if that program can co-exist with CP/M, occupying memory space above the disk operating system, then you are fortunate indeed.

Since we will be working intimately with the operating system, and in particular with the device drivers in CBIOS, being able to bail out to an unerasable monitor program would be a great help in troubleshooting. It is not indispensable, of course, and DDT can be used in its place, but it is nice if you have it for the kind of systems development work we will be doing.

THE OPERATING SYSTEM

The bootup program in PROM in your computer will load the **O**perating **S**ystem (OS), in our case some version of CP/M, at power up or in response to an operator's instruction. Since the PROM accomplishes this by reading in one sector from the first track of the first disk drive, and then executing the loader program stored on that sector, different OSs on different removable disks can be loaded by the same program in PROM.

Our computer will load one of the standard versions of the CP/M operating system, however, and we will look at the capabilities of that OS in the next two chapters. For now, just keep in mind that CP/M will be loaded as high up in the computer's RAM as possible, to make room for the application programs that are serviced by the OS. While CP/M does a lot for us, the real purpose for its existence is to provide an environment in which other programs can run. These other programs are what provide us with the working ability of the computer. The OS just provides them with support services.

APPLICATION PROGRAMS

These are the programs that actually perform the functions that make the computer a useful tool. Included in the application programs are some of the programs supplied with the operating system: the text editor, assembler, loader, and debugger. But most application programs are those most useful to the end user of the computer: the word processing, accounting, data base management, and game programs.

The operating system was loaded as high up in memory as possible to make room for the application programs. Once booted up, the OS resides permanently (we hope!) in RAM, and loads and executes the application programs in whatever RAM space is left below it. Since the application programs come and go, they are called transient programs, even if they never cross a border on their way to your computer.

CP/M loads transients into the Transient Program Area (TPA) below it in RAM. One of the features of CP/M is that it is a very compact operating system, maximizing the memory available for the TPA. This produces an environment that permits the maximum capabilities in application programs, by limiting the bells and whistles (and size) of the operating system. Since it is within these programs in the TPA that we want the most bells and whistles, we want the operating system to be as small as possible, and this is one of the finest features of CP/M.

To prove this, let's take a look at operating systems in general and CP/M in particular.

chapter 2

Operating systems

There seem to be two types of operating systems: those for computer users and those for computer programmers. All OSs are written by programmers, and some have such simplified commands, consisting of only a couple of letters, that only a programmer with a good memory and intimate knowledge of the computer's innards can operate them properly without endangering the security of stored data.

Other OSs were obviously designed to be operated by the end users: secretaries, accountants, writers, executives, etc. Their commands are more like plain English words and the operator can be pretty sure what they mean. Secondary command verification before execution, like "DO YOU REALLY WANT TO ERASE ALL OF YOUR FILES?", prevents disasters. And takes up a lot of program space in memory.

Happily, CP/M falls somewhere between the two extremes. Although it was originally written by and for programmers, it is sufficiently user friendly to permit it to be operated by end users who could care less what ED, ASM, and DDT do.

OS FUNCTIONS

Operating systems in general provide a number of services in any computer system, large or small. These include

1. Processing of operator commands
2. Loading and execution of tasks in response to commands
3. Task support through system service calls
4. Operator information services at the command level
5. System programming support by editors, assemblers, and debuggers

Command Processing

When initially loaded, all OSs begin by issuing some kind of sign-on message that may include the day and date, if the computer hardware provides a battery-operated calendar clock. Next, the OS will prompt the computer operator for a command.

Input line editing is usually provided at this level to permit the operator to make corrections to the command line before it is executed. The OS will read in the command from the operator's console and parse it, determining the desired action.

The action requested will be either a system support function or some service provided by a program named in the command input line. If the request is for a system service, that will be executed and the operator will be prompted for another command. Otherwise, the named program will be loaded and executed, if the operating system can find the program on the mass storage devices.

Task Execution

If the operator requests a named program that the OS can find on disk, that program is loaded into memory, some operating system information is passed to it, and it is set into operation. The information passed to the task, which might be done passively by merely supplying a fixed system service call address, enables the program to avail itself of all of the resource allocation and control provided by the OS.

Task Support

The physical resources of the computer system, such as the main memory and peripheral devices, are made available to the running program through service calls issued to the operating system. If the OS can only support one task at a time, this servicing becomes simple. All the OS needs to do is decode the service call function code and connect the calling program with the requested resource. In multitask operating systems, however, the OS must also prevent more than one task from trying to access the same resource at the same time, by "locking" the resource the first time the first task requests it, and unlocking it only when the task releases the resource.

Operator Information

The operating system has the responsibility to answer operator inquiries about the status of system resources and tasks, and to allow the operator to change resource allocations. The OS should be able to tell the operator how many different hard copy devices are available to be used as the LST: device, for example, and allow the operator to attach the particular device chosen.

Other information the operator might request includes the status of mass storage: how much is available on each different drive, and what files are locked by other users or other tasks.

Programming Support

The operating system should provide the user with the ability to prepare and execute strings of commands automatically, allowing the processing of tasks in batches. This batch processing is best provided
through the use of a simple executive language, or job control language,
that the end user can learn in a minimum of time.

More complicated language support should also be provided to the
system programmers through the inclusion of a programming language
(preferably the native assembly language of the host computer) that is
fully compatible with the operating system itself, so that the system user
can provide customization and expansion of the operating system.

These are, in general terms, the functions provided by operating
systems. Before looking at CP/M in particular, we should look at some of
the more important OS functions in a little more detail.

SEPARATING USERS FROM HARDWARE

Neither the computer user as operator nor the computer user as programmer should be concerned with the details of the computer and
peripheral hardware, other than knowing what resources are available
and how to allocate them. The details of the hardware (baud rates, busy
status bits, I/O port addresses, driver subroutine memory addresses,
etc.) should not be of any concern to the computer user.

Peripheral Interfacing

Expanding on the simple example above, the computer user should
know that two types of hard copy device are available to use as the LST:
device—a letter-quality printer and a high-speed dot matrix printer, for
example. The OS should provide the mechanism to allow the user to
attach either of these physical devices as the logical LST: device, and to
send data to it through a system call to the single logical LST: device.

This physical device to logical device mapping should be readily
available to the operator through the CON: and to the programmer
through a system call. The logical AUX: device might also have more
than one physical peripheral device that could be assigned to it: a
modem for communicating over the telephone system, or a paper tape
punch and reader subsystem for communicating with antique compu-

ters in the Smithsonian, or an interface to a satellite dish on the roof for sending secrets to the Russians.

No matter how many physical devices may be connected to each logical device, the operating system should handle those assignments and provide the software routines to interface with each peripheral. The OS should also provide the user with the means to write new peripheral drivers and incorporate them into the operating system in an orderly and uncomplicated manner as new hardware is added to the computer system.

Mass Storage Interfacing

The concept of logical to physical device mapping can be extended to the mass storage devices as well. The simple system described in Chapter 1, with two floppy disks, would not have any need for any complicated mapping. That system has only two disk drives of limited capacity, and the physical disks are accessed as logical drives A: and B:.

Systems with more massive storage may find the need to divide up a single physical hard disk drive into a number of smaller logical disk drives. An extreme example occurred when an early 5 million-byte (M byte) hard disk drive was connected to a computer running CP/M version 1.4. Since 1.4 believed all disk drives could only access 256 K bytes, the hard disk had to be divided up into 256 K byte logical drives A:, B:, C:, etc., until the system ran out of logical drive addresses before the hard disk ran out of storage!

There are less unfortunate reasons for dividing a physical disk drive up into logical drives. CP/M 2.2 knows that disks can be larger than 256 K bytes, but draws the line at 8 M bytes. So 26 M byte drives, for example, have to be broken up into 3 logical disks for version 2.2. CP/M Plus has once again solved this rapidly expanding hard disk capacity problem, at least until disk drives larger than 512 M bytes become commonplace.

Other than being unable to address all of the data on a physical disk drive, users might want to break up a physical disk into a number of logical drives for other reasons. Multiuser systems might need to assign different logical drives to different users. Even single-user systems might want to establish logical drives assigned to particular tasks or particular user passwords.

Whatever the reason, the operating system should provide the user with the ability to break physical disks up into logical segments, and make provisions for restricting who can access certain logical segments.

TASK INVOCATION
AND CONTROL

When the operating system is first loaded into RAM, it may automatically invoke one or more tasks that will run continuously, invisible to the computer user. The most common of these is servicing a **R**eal **T**ime **C**lock (RTC) that will be used to monitor and control user tasks that are in execution. Even a single-user, single-task OS may have an RTC-driven interrupt service routine that does things unbeknownst to the computer operator.

The computer operator, by entering a command line through the CON:, will ask the operating system to load and execute an application program. The OS then has the responsibility to find the requested program on disk, determine that it will run properly within the memory available to it, load it into memory, provide it with hooks into OS services, and start it executing.

Multitasking systems can then allow the user to invoke other tasks as well, and the OS will see that each task gets a chance to execute in turn, all scheduled in response to ticks from the RTC. With more than one task in execution, the OS must supervise the allocation and use of system resources, preventing two tasks from printing on the LST: device at the same time, for instance.

Foreground/Background

Although most of us will be working on a single-user, single-task computer that probably doesn't have an RTC among its hardware resources, it is possible for more than one thing to be going on at any one time. Every time a user application program makes a service call to the operating system requesting a character from the CON:, many hours (in computer time) pass between each operator keystroke. This is because, as far as any computer is concerned, we human operators are incredibly slow.

A computer executing a million instructions a second has time to run a 50 K byte program between each operator keystroke. You can imagine how slow we appear to that computer! Since that computing time is wasted, some programs, such as print spoolers, can co-reside with user application programs, and execute a second task in the time available between operator keystrokes.

A spooler is a program that, in response to an operator command, will be loaded up at the top of the TPA, right below the OS, and transfer data from a disk file to the LST: during those time slices when the computer is waiting for the operator to press a key on the console.

Since it is the OS that provides the interface to the CON: device even when an application program is running, it is a simple matter for the system to provide for the incorporation of this second task, and most do provide that capability. When a system runs two jobs at once like this it is often said that one is running in the "foreground," and the other in the "background." Which is which?

From the operator's point of view, he or she is foreground, and the printer spooler is in the background. From the LST: device's point of view it is the other way around. There seems to be no hard and fast rule for deciding which task is foreground and which is in the background. Operating systems written by human-oriented programmers would say it the first way, if there are any human-oriented programmers in the real world.

In the process of taking a look at operating systems in general, we have covered some of the features offered by the various versions of CP/M, and also some that are only available through extensions to the CP/M operating system. These extensions are available from a number of software sources, and when we look at CP/M and see that it doesn't provide all of the fancy bells and whistles of the fancier OSs, keep in mind that after you become a CP/M programming expert, you can add features available from other sources as well as those you will write yourself.

chapter 3

The control
program for
microcomputers

The Control Program for Microcomputers (CP/M), a product of Digital Research, Inc. (DRI), was originally developed on the Intel Microprocessor Development System (MDS), from which it has inherited some characteristics. The MDS is an expensive, industrial-quality system that has also run Intel's own ISIS operating system, and FDOS from iCOM.

Anyone who has ever used ISIS loves FDOS. Anyone who has ever used ISIS and FDOS worships CP/M. ISIS is still around on Intel's MDS, since both are Intel products, like the original 8080 microprocessor itself. Whatever happened to FDOS?

CP/M, meanwhile, since its inception in those early days around 1975, has migrated into just about every other microcomputer ever built by any other manufacturer. This is evidence of the portability, moderate size, and user friendliness of CP/M.

A LITTLE HISTORY

In the beginning, a floppy disk was 8 inches in diameter, stored data in 128-byte sectors, had 26 sectors per track, and 77 tracks per disk. Two drives were packaged together so that users could make backups of their programs and data without having to resort to the use of the slow paper tape punches or unreliable audio cassette recorders that preceded floppies as the mass storage devices for micros.

Early CP/M Versions

The earlier versions of CP/M (1.3 and 1.4) were written with the characteristics of that 8-inch disk built into the Basic Disk Operating System (BDOS). In spite of this, independent system integrators, such as Lifeboat Associates, were able to adapt CP/M to just about any configuration of mass storage device, including hard disks and disk emulators consisting of masses of RAM memory.

This adaptation required the remapping of calls to the disk access primitive driver software. CP/M would try to access a 128-byte record, insisting that the first 26 of these were on disk track 0, the second 26 on track 1, etc. Since CP/M would tell the driver software, "Go to track 3 and give me sector 14," the remapping algorithm would have to multiply 3 × 26 to get to the start of the fourth track (track 3, counting from zero), then add 14 to determine the absolute sector address referenced to the first sector on the first track.

The remapping software would then have to convert this absolute sector number into the track and sector address relative to its own disk configuration. For instance, the first North Star computers used mini-floppy disks with 256 bytes per sector and 10 sectors per track. So the absolute sector computed would have to be divided by 20 (the number of 128 byte half-sectors per track) to give the track number, with the remainder equal to the number of the half-sector on that track. The 256-byte sector containing the desired half-sector would then be fetched from the disk, and the proper half sent to CP/M if it was a read operation that was requested.

If CP/M had requested a write operation, the remapper would have to first read in the proper 256-byte North Star sector, merge in the 128-byte half sent by CP/M, and write the result back to the disk. Of course, all of this is an oversimplification. There was also that skew factor on the 8-inch disks to be factored out as well. We will cover *that* in Chapter 8.

As you can imagine, system programmers adapting early versions of CP/M got pretty proficient at juggling things. All of this serves to illustrate the great advance made from version 1.4 to version 2.2, and also illustrates some of the techniques you will be learning that are necessary to handle physical disk sectors that are two, four, eight, or more times the size of the CP/M 128-byte logical record. There are lessons to be learned from history.

Newer and Better

When version 2 of CP/M was released, the first thing the computer operator noticed was that the display of the disk directory would fit on the CRT terminal screen, because it was now shown with four file names per line instead of only one, which had caused version 1 DIR displays to scroll off the top of the screen before the user could read them.

Inside version 2 was the real improvement that was not so obvious. The tables of values that define the characteristics of the floppy disk were moved into the user customizable area of the program. Digital Research now supplies the complete documentation, and any system integrator can easily adapt CP/M to just about any possible disk format.

Other Great Versions

Not directly in the mainstream of the evolution of CP/M are other versions available from Digital Research. MP/M attempts to make 8-bit microcomputers look like mainframes by permitting more than one user to work on the system at the same time. This requires some special hardware. MP/M won't run on just any computer.

CP/M-86 is the version that runs on the Intel 8086 16-bit microprocessor. It uses the same disk and file formats as 8-bit versions of CP/M, and some computers include both 8-bit and 16-bit CPUs to allow the user to run software written for either processor under either version of CP/M without moving from one computer to another.

Since the 8086 runs faster and is able to address more memory than any 8-bit microprocessor, Concurrent CP/M-86 allows multitasking. The operator can start more than one task and have up to four running at the same time, monitoring their progress by switching the CON: from one task to another under software control, a technique known as the virtual terminal. MP/M-86 permits multiple terminals and multiple users on 8086-based microcomputers.

But these are versions of CP/M that are outside the scope of this book. They are mentioned here so that you will keep in mind that expertise learned in any version of CP/M can be applied to other versions. You just can't waste any time or effort because the whole product line preserves common characteristics, making the transition from one version to another easier on the operator and programmer.

Newest and Best

While CP/M was developing through all of the versions mentioned above, other 8-bit operating systems have come along, and some have already gone away. There are those derived directly from CP/M under license, but with a different name, and others that try to make 8-bit micros look like mainframes. These provide so many services, and such detailed operator messages, that there isn't much room left in memory for user programs.

To cure the memory crunch, bank switched memory was developed and operating systems written to make use of it. Bank switching allows an 8-bit microcomputer to address more memory than the 64 K bytes that its 16-bit registers can access directly. External hardware is controlled by the microprocessor to select from among multiple banks of RAM. Only 64 K can be accessed at one time, but more than one bank of memory can exist, and the OS can select which one it wants at a particular time.

We will be looking at this technique in detail in Chapter 15. It allows most of the OS to reside in one memory bank, while the application programs get to fill up almost all of their own 64 K byte bank. This permits the OS to incorporate many more bells and whistles, such as file secrecy through user passwords, date and time stamping of files, automatic system generation to support hardware reconfigurations, and much more user friendly CON: communications and system services.

CP/M Plus, version 3, was developed to take advantage of bank switched memory, although a subset of its features can be made to run on a computer with only 64 K of RAM. Obviously, this new operating system is much more complicated than any previous version, and installing it on a new computer is much more difficult than installing the smaller versions.

How Big Are They?

A look at the relative sizes of all of these versions of CP/M will illustrate their progression. Table 3.1 shows how much memory the operating system versions would occupy in a 64 K RAM microcomputer and how much user workspace is available. These sizings assume that the disk and I/O driver software has been kept to a minimum, so that a 64 K size version of CP/M was installed in each case.

The evolution from 1.3 to 1.4 to 2.2 illustrates how the OS grew slowly as features were added, and the user workspace shrank accordingly. The great leap in OS memory requirements from the earlier versions to CP/M Plus shows how the advent of inexpensive RAM permitted the addition of many more features to version 3, including expanded user friendliness. By taking advantage of bank-switched memory, the workspace available to the user has expanded as well. Almost like getting something for nothing—except the additional hardware costs something.

CP/M Version	*1.3*	*1.4*	*2.2*	*3.0*
CP/M size including dedicated RAM.	6 K	6 K	7¼ K	21¼ K
Resident in main RAM.	6 K	6 K	7¼ K	2¼ K
User workspace	58 K	58 K	56¾ K	61¾ K
Including CCP	60¼ K	60 K	58½ K	61¾ K

Table 3.1 Relative sizes of 8-bit versions of CP/M. The size of the operating system has increased constantly while the space available for the user has shrunk. The use of bank-switched main random access memory (RAM) permits CP/M Plus (Version 3) to increase greatly in size and capability while still providing an increase in user workspace.

This then, is a quick look at the history of the development and evolution of this most popular of operating systems. Next, we will examine its features in detail.

This has been kind of a funny history. It didn't even mention Gary Kildall, the nice guy who brought us CP/M. It didn't mention how Digital Research came into being, or who has gotten wealthy in the meantime selling computers, software, or books. Well, this is a history written for programmers. We are all just a bunch of computerheads. All we care about is wares: hard-, soft-, and firm-. We don't care about people. Or money.

ORGANIZATION OF CP/M

The internal organization of CP/M, as is true for all operating systems, has been dictated partly by the constraints imposed by the computer hardware and partly by the logical breakdown of its functions. Some aspects of CP/M were forced upon it by the environment in which it was developed: the Intel MDS development system. We have already mentioned some of the building blocks of CP/M. Some more organizational details of each of these follow.

Dedicated RAM

The lowest 256 bytes (100 in hexadecimal) of main memory in a CP/M computer have been set aside for dedicated uses. This is partly a hand-me-down from the MDS, and partly dictated by the organization of the 8080 CPU and its descendants. The functions of the first eight memory locations are discussed in detail in Chapter 5. Following those are 56 bytes reserved for hardware interrupt vectors, as dictated by the architecture of the 8080. From just above the highest interrupt vector location, and on up through the first 256 byte "page" of memory, CP/M sets aside some standard usage buffer workspaces.

These buffers have been organized to make the most efficient use of the first memory page so that user application programs can all start at the same easy-to-remember location: hexadecimal 100, the start of the TPA. These buffers also permit the **C**onsole **C**ommand **P**rocessor (CCP) portion of CP/M to leave data behind so that CCP itself can be overwritten by transient programs, giving the user more workspace.

Console Command Processor

This OS functional block is the software that communicates with the computer operator, inputs a command line, provides simple editing functions as the line is being typed in, sets up buffers with data derived from the command line, and instructs BDOS to load and execute named programs, unless the operator requests a built-in CCP function.

The built-in functions are DIR, ERA, REN, SAVE, TYPE, and USER. Any other command input by the operator as the first word in the command line is assumed by CCP to be the name of a transient program, and CCP will tell BDOS to load and execute the named program as soon as the rest of the command line has been decoded.

The buffers set up by CCP include a copy of the command line typed by the operator, so that transient programs can be aware of instructions that the operator has placed on that line following the program name. If the operator has specified the names of disk data files that the transient program is to operate on, CCP also sets up default File Control Blocks (FCBs) for the first one or two named files.

Once CCP has input the operator's command, parsed it, set up the command line and FCB buffers, and told BDOS what transient program to execute, its work is done, and the space originally occupied by CCP can be reused by the transient program. If this happens, CCP must be reloaded from disk at the termination of the transient program.

Table 3.1 shows that the user workspace (TPA) can be expanded by overwriting CCP, which picks up a couple of extra K bytes for the user. CP/M Plus shows no increase in TPA space, because the version 3 CCP is loaded into the bottom of the TPA (at location 100H) instead of at the top, as was true for earlier versions. This means that the V3 CCP is *always* overwritten by the transient, and what was an optional user accessible feature (available with some overhead) has now become a part of the operating system.

Basic Disk Operating System

The first time the computer operator becomes aware of BDOS is when the program named in the command line is loaded from disk. BDOS handles all of the disk file operations, as its name implies. This includes the allocation of disk space, the structuring of data into named disk files, and the maintenance of those files.

BDOS does all of this for the operator through commands passed to it from CCP, and does it for the writers of transient programs through function codes passed to it through one dedicated BDOS CALL memory location. BDOS functions that are available to transient programs include system controls, disk file accesses, and the transfer of data to and from peripheral devices.

BDOS itself receives and decodes all of these function codes and handles those that concern the system operating parameters, but disk and I/O accesses at the most primitive level are passed through BDOS to the final building block of CP/M, the BIOS. Knowing the intricacies of BDOS will enable you to write programs that take full advantage of the functions provided by CP/M while maintaining program portability. Part II explains how BDOS handles disks and disk files.

Basic Input/Output System

BIOS is a bit of a misnomer for this building block because in every CP/M installation other than the original some customization of the BIOS has been necessary to adapt it to the particular computer environment in which it will be executing. That is why "CBIOS" is used exclusively in this book, for Customized **BIOS.** Much of what you will be learning in this book is concerned with customizing the BIOS so that you can install CP/M on a new computer or add new hardware features to an existing computer.

The fact that all hardware-specific programming is contained in the CBIOS is one of the great features of CP/M, allowing it to be moved from computer to computer, and allowing the operator of any CP/M-based computer to easily operate any other without retraining. All of Part III of this book is devoted to teaching you all you will have to know about CBIOS.

CP/M VS. THE COMPETITION

Version 1 of CP/M first ran on a microcomputer that had only 16 K bytes of RAM, and even then allowed the user to write transient programs that occupied 12 K of that 16 K. This was the most outstanding feature of CP/M in the early days when computer memory was a very expensive commodity.

As RAM prices dropped, so did the cost of disk storage. Minifloppy disks storing a megabyte of data have become common. CP/M version 2 doesn't run on a 16 K system anymore, but it permits the easy customization of the system to accommodate more and larger disk storage, and will still allow a user to use up to 14.5 K bytes of RAM on a 20 K computer.

This small size and the adaptability of the CBIOS are what permitted CP/M to become the most widely used microcomputer operating system. Even microcomputers that did not originally have an 8080 compatible CPU have been retrofitted with "CP/M cards," a plug-in hardware adaptation that allows them to run CP/M. There must be a reason for this. There is. Users demanded it.

Comparing these small, early versions of CP/M to operating systems such as UNIX, OASIS, the Pascal p-System, or other minicomputer-like OSs that require a minimum of 64 K bytes of RAM, is a bit like comparing apples to orchards. CP/M is *tiny* in comparison, while still providing enough disk and I/O handling capability along with sufficient user friendliness.

Now that lots of RAM and masses of disk storage are inexpensive, with 64 K now costing a fraction of what 16 K used to five years ago, Digital Reseach has accepted the challenge of the sellers of the other OSs, and produced a version that will match the competition in almost every feature they offer. CP/M Plus will make your micro look like a mini. And along with CP/M the user gets the documentation that permits ease of customization offered by no other competitive 8-bit operating system.

MISSING DOCUMENTATION

Maybe someday Ralph Nader will get into the act. All of the nice things said about CP/M in the preceding paragraphs do not apply to every CP/M installation out there in the real world. But the deficiency is not on the part of CP/M or Digital Research.

When you buy CP/M from its creators, DRI, you get all the documenation you need to install it on any computer, along with sample program listings and even the source code for the CBIOS and programs that support customization. Some computers that come with CP/M already installed are delivered with some of this supporting documentation missing.

Perhaps the sellers should discriminate between a computer that "includes" CP/M (and all of its support) and a computer that "runs" CP/M simply as a means of loading programs. Sometimes these systems do not include the Digital Research CP/M manual set, and often they do not include the necessary details about the hardware of the computer that would allow the user to add new disks or peripheral devices and customize the software system.

In order to complete the exercises in Part II, you should have a set of the CP/M manuals from Digital Research, and for Part III you really need to know about the I/O interface hardware in your computer. If the sellers of your computer have shortchanged you, let your displeasure be known. You could even hit them over the head with this book.

chapter 4

The CP/M programmer's tools

There are two areas of programming that we will cover in this book: the writing of application programs that execute in the TPA and the writing of a complete new CBIOS. Some of the tools that are available to the programmer will be used for both types of programming, while others will be used only for CBIOS generation.

All of the software tools required are supplied by Digital Research with all standard versions of CP/M. Other nice tools are available, like more advanced debuggers and relocatable macro assemblers with their linking loaders, but since they don't come with every version of CP/M, and do cost extra, we won't be needing them here. But feel free to use them if you have them.

ALL CP/MS
ARE NOT EQUAL

Since one of the goals that we are pursuing is an understanding of the intricacies of how CP/M handles disk and I/O accesses, some of our investigative application programs will be sensitive to different versions (1.4, 2.2, 3) of CP/M. Programs designed for the end user can be written to be compatible with all versions, but when you use programs to investigate the innards of the operating system itself, as we will be doing, they will not be portable.

Whenever possible we will detect the version number of CP/M and adjust our programs automatically, so that they can execute under any version. This is not always possible, so we will look at the reasons for the differences whenever we are not able to write a completely portable program.

CP/M Plus (Version 3) is so different from earlier versions that some of our investigative programming will not be compatible with it. But all of the lessons learned in Part III, on writing a CBIOS from scratch, can be used when you start working with CP/M Plus.

And finally, not all of the programmer's tools are the same from one version to another. While minor differences exist within PIP, ED, ASM, and MOVCPM, we won't even bother to mention them here because the Digital Research manuals cover them in detail. Other differences, like the nonexistence of XSUB with the original version 1.4, can't be ignored, but will be noted where appropriate.

SOFTWARE TOOLS

Here we find the tools necessary to generate assembly language programs in general, and some additional tools needed to generate a new-size system and to modify it for new hardware additions or to install it on a new computer.

Program Generation

All we need here are ED, ASM, LOAD, and DDT to edit our source code, assemble it, load it into memory, and debug any possible problems. PIP will also be required to handle files and printing. You may want to use a word processor program to replace the text editor ED, and that is fine so long as it provides for the insertion of blocks of text with ".LIB" file types that are stored separately on disk.

CP/M Plus replaces ASM with MAC, and DDT with SID, but for our purposes you won't notice the differences once you learn the new names. In particular, the basic commands are the same in SID as in DDT, and the advanced features of SID are not required for the work you will be doing.

Beginning in the next chapter, we will use these tools to generate the first of the example programs in this book. Techniques included in all of our exercises are mainly oriented to the generation of software modules usable by a programmer working intimately with the operating system, but those same techniques are applicable to programs intended for the unsophisticated end user. We will be careful to separate the general purpose from the for-experts-only programs and their building blocks.

System Generation

To modify CBIOS, or to generate a new one, you will also require the use of MOVCPM and SYSGEN, and SUBMIT and XSUB can be used to make things easier on the programmer. Some customized versions of CP/M have changed the names of MOVCPM and SYSGEN to reflect the fact that they have been modified by the customizer. Other than the name change, they should work the same as the standard Digital Research versions.

One word of caution here. Some system disks have been sold by smaller suppliers of customized CP/M systems that include the original

MOVCPM and SYSGEN utilities, but the use of these will cause the generation of an incompatible operating system image on the disk system tracks. This should be punishable by the death, dismemberment, and chastisement (in that order?) of the sellers, but since instant justice isn't readily available, you have to make sure that you are working with a copy of your system disk and not the original.

The unfortunate situation described in the preceding paragraph does not occur very often and shouldn't be allowed to occur at all, but since you are an experienced programmer, you should be able to detect the problem if it happens. And you can correct it provided you received the necessary documentation with your system.

DOCUMENTATION TOOLS

Since you are assumed to have served an apprenticeship as an assembly language programmer working with CP/M or some other OS, it is also assumed that some reference book is available that describes the details of the 8080 microprocessor instruction set. You must have the documentation and knowledge necessary to figure out how things work within the programs listed in this book because, although a general discussion of program flow will be included, details of how each instruction executes are not included. You aren't a beginner, presumably.

The Digital Research CP/M *Interface Guide* will be necessary for the exercises in Part II, and the *Alteration Guide* is required for Part III. Particularly for Part III, it is assumed that you have been supplied with documentation that explains what your computer hardware looks like as seen by the CP/M operating system, CBIOS in particular.

This could be in the form of the complete schematic diagrams of your computer's hardware, or just lists of memory addresses of subroutines if your disk and I/O driver routines are in a PROM, or even the complete assembly listing of the PROM. Alternatively, you may have received lists of I/O port addresses used by the peripheral device driver Integrated Circuits (ICs), and you may need to acquire data sheets explaining the software interfacing to these ICs.

CBIOS Source Code

Ideally, if you are very fortunate, you have been supplied with both the assembly listing and the source code on disk of the BIOS that is actually installed in your computer. Don't confuse this with the sample BIOS supplied by Digital Research on all of its CP/M distribution disks. That one is written for the Intel MDS and probably is not what is installed in your computer. You may have to look at all of the .ASM source code files on your system disk to determine which one, if any, is right for your computer.

Assembling that source and using the .PRN output and DDT to compare the result with what is found in the CBIOS area of your own operating system may be necessary to verify that the source code supplied is exactly that used to generate your system. You can't make changes or additions if it is not the correct source to begin with.

Go Ahead Anyway

Even if every one of the tools listed in this chapter is not under your finger at this very moment, go ahead and proceed with the next chapter or two and work through the exercises. You will need a CP/M based computer and ED, ASM, PIP, etc., of course.

Following that, Part II includes programs that show how CP/M handles disk drives and files. If you don't have a need to understand how these programs work in detail, you can simply copy them on to your system and see what comes out. The programs will still show you how CP/M works, even if you don't understand every line.

Only in writing your very own CBIOS, the subject of Part III, will you really need all of the documentation listed here. And even if some of that is missing, Part III can be read as a guide to what some other programmer went through to make your computer run the CP/M operating system.

chapter 5

Programming under CP/M

Except for special purpose investigative and diagnostic utilities, assembly language programs and assembly language subroutines callable from higher level languages can be written to be compatible with any standard version of CP/M running on any make and model of computer. This is possible only if the programmer adheres to strict procedures defined by the structure of the operating system.

While this seems obvious, it is stressed here because there are a number of valuable free programs available from the **CP/M User's Group (CPMUG)** and other sources that have been around for a long time and that were not written in such a manner as to make them compatible with all versions of CP/M. Some of these programs can be fixed up by a technique we will cover in the next chapter, while others require more extensive reprogramming using information you will be learning throughout this book.

To prevent our own programs from ever becoming incompatible with future releases of CP/M, we have to obey some simple rules for programming under CP/M. We will also look at some common-sense programming and documentation practices that will make it easier to keep track of all the bits and pieces of software that we create, and that will make our programs more easily adaptable to other operating systems. To do this we have to examine the environment in which our programs will run and the means for interfacing them with the operating system.

DEFINING OUR PROGRAMMING ENVIRONMENT

We already know that our programs will run in the Transient Program Area (TPA) and will interface with CP/M through system calls handled by BDOS. A more detailed understanding will result from examining some of the dedicated memory locations at the bottom of our computer's RAM, looking at what is in these locations and how we use them.

Location 0

A jump instruction (JMP WBOOT) is written into the first 3 bytes of memory by the routines in CBIOS that load and initialize CP/M. This jump is to the warm start entry into CBIOS, which is the second entry in a list of 3-byte jump instructions at the very start of the CBIOS.

WBOOT itself is used to restart CP/M after a transient program has completed operation. WBOOT will reload the CCP, that may have been overwritten by programs in the TPA, and will reestablish CP/M's stack pointer. Any of our programs that overlay CCP or lose track of the CP/M stack should exit by performing a jump to location zero.

The contents of locations 1 and 2 are the address field of the JMP WBOOT instruction, and this tells us exactly where in memory the CBIOS is located. A transient program could use this address to determine the size of the particular version of CP/M under which it is running. This address is also used by programs that make direct BIOS calls, a dangerous technique that we will look at in Chapter 11.

Location 3

The IOBYT is stored in this memory location, providing that IOBYT is implemented on your computer. Unless your computer is loaded up with lots of I/0 devices, IOBYT may not be implemented. It is not required by CP/M, and there are other methods for implementing selectable I/0 devices. CP/M Plus, for example, uses a different method and does not use the IOBYT or location 3 at all.

We will look at IOBYT, what it can do, and how to implement it, in Chapter 12. Even if you don't expect to modify your CBIOS or install CP/M on a new computer, you might be interested in reading about it anyway. It may convince you to implement IOBYT on your computer to take advantage of the power it can provide. This is one of the reasons for being an assembly language programmer.

Location 4

This memory location is referred to symbolically by the label **DRIVE**. It contains the binary address of the "current" disk drive. The word current is quoted here because it does not always mean the same on every computer. Experience with a number of different implementations of CP/M has shown that the use of DRIVE is not always the same in every CBIOS.

We will use a technique in this chapter that should make our programs fully compatible with any CBIOS that uses DRIVE in a nonstandard manner. More details on DRIVE are also included in Chapter 14. Note once again that CP/M Plus does not use DRIVE or this location in memory.

Location 5

After CP/M has been loaded and initialized, this memory location contains a JMP instruction to the entry point for BDOS. All of our system control functions, and I/0 device and disk file accesses, will be performed by loading the C register with a BDOS function code, optionally loading register DE with an address value, and then performing a CALL BDOS, after defining BDOS as being equal to location 5.

The address field (locations 6 and 7) of this JMP instruction points to the highest memory address that is available to our programs running in the TPA. But it may or may not point to the actual entry into the BDOS code itself. DDT and other **R**esident **S**ystem e**X**tensions (RSXs), such as printer spoolers, menu systems, and XSUB, are initially loaded into the TPA beginning at location 100H, but they relocate themselves up in memory before beginning execution, to free the bottom of the TPA for our programs.

Since we use the address at locations 6 and 7 to determine the highest memory address available to our programs, RSXs will change the contents of that address to point to their own entry point. The RSXs will then pass along to BDOS any system calls received through that entry that they are not to execute directly. More than one RSX can be in operation at the same time. Each will load itself below the current address contained in locations 6 and 7, and then readjust that value to point to the lowest address that they occupy. Successive RSX loads therefore fill the TPA memory from the bottom of BDOS down, each loading below its predecessor, and setting the address field of location 5 to its own lowest address.

This then defines the environment in which our programs are to execute. They will be loaded into the TPA beginning at location 100H, will avoid using any memory address below 100H or equal to or greater than that contained in locations 6 and 7, will access all I/O devices and disk files through a system call to location 5, and when finished will return to CP/M by a jump to location zero.

There are both legal and illegal possible variations to the rules stated in the last paragraph, and we will be looking at them throughout the rest of this book, as they become appropriate. For now, though, we should stick with the basic environment defined by these memory locations. So now let's take a detailed look at how we will communicate with I/O devices through location 5.

ALL INPUT/OUTPUT THROUGH BDOS

The functions available through the jump instruction at memory location 5 are divided into three categories: operating system controls, disk file accesses, and peripheral device I/O. For a program to be completely compatible with all versions of CP/M on all computers, two things are necessary: the program must make all external accesses through the BDOS entry in compliance with the rules specified in the CP/M *Interface Guide*, and the computer system integrator must have installed CP/M properly, in accordance with the rules spelled out in the CP/M *Alteration Guide*.

Unless you have installed CP/M on your own computer yourself, you have no control over how accurately the system integrator followed the rules. One of the purposes of this book is to point out inconsistencies discovered in various CP/M installations and provide you with the background necessary to correct or modify the installation to suit your own needs and preferences. But since most of the necessary details are not covered until Part III, for now we will limit the discussion to how to use BDOS calls properly.

Table 5-1 lists all of the BDOS function codes that are used in program examples in this book. There are many more. All are spelled out in detail in the *Interface Guide*, and this book will not replace that document entirely. Although each function listed in the table will be explained as it occurs in the following programs, you may want to refer to the CP/M manuals for the definitive decriptions of them.

BDOS FUNCTION	*NUMBER*	*DESCRIPTION*
RCONF	1	Read a Con: Character into (A)
WCONF	2	Write a Character in (A) to Console
RBUFF	10	Read a Buffered Console Line
CSTAF	11	Check Con: Status for Character Ready
VERSF	12	Test CP/M Version Number
DSELF	14	Select a Disk Drive
OPENF	15	Open a File for Read or Write
SFRSF	17	Search for First File Matching FCB
SNXTF	18	Search for Next File Matching FCB
READF	20	Read One Disk Record into DMA
GCURF	25	Get the Current Disk Drive Number
SDMAF	26	Set the Direct Memory Address
GALVF	27	Get an Allocation Vector Address
GDPBF	31	Get a Disk Parameter Block Address

Table 5.1 BDOS call functions. This subset of the available BDOS functions is a complete list of the functions used in the programming examples in this book. Many other functions are available but are not required for most programming tasks.

I/O access functions test the state of, and pass data to or from, the computer console and other peripheral devices. Disk access functions transfer data to or from disk files. System control functions affect the CP/M environment in which our programs execute. There is some arbitrariness in the categorization of disk access and system control functions, because the categories sometimes overlap.

Application programs that are intended for use by nonprogrammers can be made completely portable by restricting all of their data I/O to the most simple BDOS functions. Diagnostic programs may have to resort to techniques that would not be legal or desirable in portable programs. We will be looking at both kinds of programs in this book, so the techniques that bend the rules will be carefully noted as not the kind of programming to include in programs for the usual computer user.

Just keep in mind that virtually all of the BDOS functions will operate the same on all CP/M computers. That is one of the features that a standard operating system provides.

A LIBRARY OF SUBROUTINES AND MODULES

Although it wasn't a programmer who first said "Don't do as I do, do as I say," we all have been guilty of violating the programming standards that we advocate. Sometimes there just isn't enough time to do it right. Often a program will be thrown together in a hurry to do a one-time job. You can easily recognize those. They run on for page after page without a break. They are devoid of comments and other supporting documentation. And sometimes they get into the hands of beginning programmers who then believe that this is the right way to do things.

Sloppy programming may appeal to the laziness in all of us, and we may excuse it when there is a severe time constraint. But our sins will catch up with us eventually, when we need just a little piece out of the middle of one of those "temporary" programs, and we can't find it in the expanse of uncommented code. Or when we do find the desired procedure we can't use it because we can't remember the register or memory variable usage required to support it.

There is a way to avoid this. Always write each program in the form of stand-alone building blocks. Entire languages, such as Pascal, have been created in an attempt to force us to structure our programs properly. But a clever programmer can still violate all the rules and write incomprehensible code, even in Pascal. Structuring can't be handed down by edict; it comes from within. That does not mean to imply that there are no edicts in this book. On the contrary, it is full of them. But they don't have the force of law, so it is up to the reader to adopt them and make them a part of every programming effort. It will pay off in the long run.

Building Blocks

The basic building block in an assembly language program is the subroutine, with a single entry point, that performs a single task, and exits through a single return instruction, meanwhile using registers and memory variables in a standardized manner.

While that goal is always achievable in theory, the rule can be bent slightly to take advantage of the power of the conditional return instructions available to users of the CP/M assembler. Sometimes two different entries into a subroutine can save a lot of code. The single-entry, single-return edict is often violated without disastrous results, provided adequate commenting is included in the source code.

The single-function edict, however, is one you should stick with. This permits the building up of a library of subroutines that can be used in many programs without alteration. We will see examples of this in the next few pages.

First, we will create a few subroutines that provide communication with the computer operator's console. These subroutines will be grouped into a module, named CPMIO.LIB. The .LIB file type implies that this group of subroutines constitutes a library file accessible to ED (or any other text editor) that can be merged with other .LIB files into a complete program. Other library files will be added to the collection, until future programming efforts can be largely limited to picking out and linking the proper sets of subroutines, and writing a main program that is largely a series of subroutine calls.

STANDARD MODULE HEADER

Since we will be writing subroutines that are each a single building block, but we will be grouping them into modules that contain related subroutines, we will need a method for keeping track of the modules so that they can be easily found when we want to include them in future programs. The standard module header shown below is used for that purpose:

Listing 5-1

```
;  MODULE NAME: xxxxxxxx.LIB
;  LAST UPDATE: 11 FEB 84      BY: KMB
;  FUNCTION:
;  REQUIRES:
;===========================================================
```

Use your text editor or ED to key in an exact duplicate of this header image and name it HEADER.LIB. It will be appended to the beginning of every program module you will ever create. It serves a number of purposes.

First, by requiring you to fill in the module name (replacing the xxx's), the date the module was created or updated, the purpose of the module ("FUNCTION"), and a list of other modules required to support it, it forces you to document what you are doing and why. Each programmer working on your system should use his or her own header source file with his or her own initials following the "BY:" prompt, so that everyone's modules can be kept together on one system but still be separated by programmer.

Whenever you sit down to write a new subroutine or combine several into a new module, read in this file first before keying in your source code. Immediately fill in the blanks. The examples in this book use the military method of date stamping consisting of a day number, a three-letter month abbreviation, and the year. You can use the commercial format 2/11/84 or any other you choose, but be consistent throughout your programming.

Cataloging Modules

The reason for consistency is that later in this book we will generate a module cataloging program (PGMCAT) that will be a great help in keeping track of things, and that program will want a consistent header format at the top of each source code file. Starting with HEADER.LIB and appending it to the beginning of each module will provide an image that PGMCAT can find and decipher.

Maintaining consistency in the entry of the data contained on these three little lines will put you way ahead of the overwhelming majority of programmers, amateur or professional. An examination of many program listings from many programmers will prove that point. There isn't that much data that is really vital for keeping track of various versions of programs, but without a standard header like this one all of the required information will seldom be found in practice.

HEADER.LIB will force you to enter WHO, WHAT, WHEN, and WHY every time you sit down to enter or update a program. If you like, add a line telling WHERE. And the bottom line in the header will help you avoid another common programmer error: entering comments that wander off the right side of the program listings after assembly.

Get It All on the Page

Since ASM.COM uses 15 character positions on the left side of the .PRN output file, you have to restrain your enthusiasm for long comment lines when keying in your source program. The examples in this book assume you have a console terminal with at least 64 character positions per line, and that your line printer can handle 8½-inch-wide paper and print 80 columns. If the bottom line on your HEADER.LIB file is 60 characters long, and you use it as a line-length guide while keying in source programs, your .PRN outputs will not include any comments printed off the edge of the paper, and your program listings will always look as nice as those in this book.

This HEADER.LIB edict is not the last edict you will encounter in this book. There are more edicts concerning programming style and practices just ahead. They are included here to help you learn as painlessly as possible lessons that others (no names mentioned!) spent many years and many tears in learning. There is a reason for it all. We are not doing it just to slow down your programming efforts. Proper practices will save time in the future. But now it's time to do some actual programming before you fall asleep.

CPMIO AND A TEST PROGRAM

In keeping with the practice of directing all I/O operations through the BDOS call at location 5, the console input and output subroutines in this module guarantee program portability. These subroutines provide for single-line input from the computer operator and single-line output to the operator.

Since it is assumed that you have served an apprenticeship as an assembly language programmer and are familiar with the instruction set recognized by ASM.COM, no detailed discussions are included here of how each instruction in each subroutine works. Only unusual techniques are explained in detail.

In the course of displaying messages on the operator's console and inputting responses from it, the programs that call the I/O routines should not have to keep track of what registers are used by the subroutines and should not have to be concerned with changes in the register contents during the time the operating system is servicing the BDOS calls. By preserving all register contents (except the accumulator), these subroutines give the appearance, to the calling program, of not using any registers, making their use as easy as possible for the programmer writing the main program.

Listing 5-2

```
; MODULE NAME:    CPMIO.LIB
; LAST UPDATE: 11 FEB 84     BY: KMB
; FUNCTION: CONSOLE INPUT/OUTPUT SUBROUTINES
; REQUIRES:
;==============================================================

; ASCII CHARACTERS

CR      EQU     0DH             ; CARRIAGE RETURN
LF      EQU     0AH             ; LINE FEED

; CP/M BDOS FUNCTIONS AND ADDRESSES

WCONF   EQU     2               ; WRITE (A) TO CON:
RBUFF   EQU     10              ; READ A CONSOLE LINE
BDOS    EQU     5               ; SYSTEM CALL ENTRY

; MESSAGE POINTED TO BY STACK OUT TO CONSOLE
SPMSG:  XTHL                    ; GET "RETURN ADDRESS" TO HL
        XRA     A               ; CLEAR FLAGS AND ACCUMULATOR
        ADD     M               ; GET ONE MESSAGE CHARACTER
        INX     H               ; POINT TO NEXT
        XTHL                    ; RESTORE STACK FOR
        RZ                      ; RETURN IF DONE
        CALL    CO              ; ELSE DISPLAY CHARACTER
        JMP     SPMSG           ; AND DO ANOTHER

; CARRIAGE RETURN, LINE FEED TO CONSOLE
TWOCR:  CALL    CCRLF
CCRLF:  MVI     A,CR
        CALL    CO
        MVI     A,LF
; FALL THROUGH INTO CO:

CO:     PUSH    B               ; SAVE REGISTERS
        PUSH    D
        PUSH    H
        MVI     C,WCONF         ; SELECT FUNCTION
        MOV     E,A             ; CHARACTER TO E
        CALL    BDOS            ; OUTPUT BY CP/M
        POP     H
        POP     D
        POP     B
        RET
```

Listing 5-2 (*continued*)

```
; INPUT CONSOLE MESSAGE INTO BUFFER
CIMSG:  PUSH    B               ; SAVE REGISTERS
        PUSH    D
        PUSH    H
        LXI     H,INBUF+1       ; ZERO CHARACTER COUNTER
        MVI     M,0
        DCX     H               ; SET MAXIMUM LINE LENGTH
        MVI     M,80
        XCHG                    ; INBUF POINTER TO DE PAIR
        MVI     C,RBUFF         ; SET UP READ BUFFER FUNCTION
        CALL    BDOS            ; INPUT A LINE
        LXI     H,INBUF+1       ; GET CHARACTER COUNTER
        MOV     E,M             ; INTO LSB OF D,E REGISTER
        MVI     D,0             ; ZERO MSB
        DAD     D               ; ADD LENGTH TO START
        INX     H               ; PLUS ONE POINTS TO END
        MVI     M,0             ; INSERT TERMINATOR AT END
        POP     H               ; RESTORE ALL REGISTERS
        POP     D
        POP     B
        RET

; GET YES OR NO FROM CONSOLE
GETYN:  CALL    SPMSG           ; PROMPT FOR INPUT
        DB      ' (Y/N)?: ',0
        CALL    CIMSG           ; GET INPUT LINE
        CALL    CCRLF           ; ECHO CARRIAGE RETURN
        LDA     INBUF+2         ; FIRST CHARACTER ONLY
        ANI     01011111B       ; CONVERT LOWER CASE TO UPPER
        CPI     'Y'             ; RETURN WITH ZERO = YES
        RZ
        CPI     'N'             ; NON-ZERO = NO
        JNZ     GETYN           ; ELSE TRY AGAIN
        CPI     0               ; RESET ZERO FLAG
        RET                     ; AND ALL DONE

; MESSAGE POINTED TO BY HL OUT TO CONSOLE
COMSG:  MOV     A,M             ; GET A CHARACTER
        ORA     A               ; ZERO IS THE TERMINATOR
        RZ                      ; RETURN ON ZERO
        CALL    CO              ; ELSE OUTPUT THE CHARACTER
        INX     H               ; POINT TO NEXT ONE
        JMP     COMSG           ; AND CONTINUE

INBUF:  DS      83              ; LINE INPUT BUFFER
```

Output to the Console

The first subroutine, SPMSG:, works like the BASIC language PRINT statement. To display a message on the console device, the main program invokes SPMSG: with a CALL followed by the message text, which is terminated by a zero:

```
CALL        SPMSG
DB          'Message text',0
```

This permits messages to be embedded within a program at the point in the logic of the program where they are to be displayed, just as is true for the BASIC PRINT statement.

For message texts that are located elsewhere, as in a message list or some buffer, COMSG: is used to display the text, again terminated by a zero. The HL register pair are used to point to the location of the message text:

```
LXI       H,MESSAGE
CALL      COMSG
```

Since the HL register is used as a pointer by the main program, its contents are not preserved by the subroutine, because the programmer knows it will be used.

All of the output to the console is passed through subroutine CO:, which begins by saving the contents of the BC, DE, and HL register pairs, so that the main program is protected from any possible changes to their contents that might occur during the time the operating system is processing the system call. The only system call function used for output is WCONF, which stands for **W**rite to the **CON**sole **F**unction.

Input from the Console

CIMSG: inputs a message text, terminated by zero, from the computer operator. The calling program will find the text in INBUF beginning at INBUF + 2. The first two locations in INBUF contain the maximum number of characters allowed in the input line, and the number actually received, as is detailed in the discussion of the buffered console input function (RBUFF) in the CP/M *Interface Guide*.

In addition to using that BDOS function, CIMSG: also forces the zero terminator at the end of the input line, relieving the main program of the task of keeping a character count as the input line is parsed.

This message terminated by zero convention is therefore standardized here for both input and output messages. This makes more sense than the CP/M technique of terminating output messages with "$" because that prohibits the use of that character within a message text.

Note that the only input function BDOS call occurs within subroutine CIMSG:, and it saves all the registers before calling BDOS and restores them before returning to the main program. RBUFF, for **R**ead **BUF**fered input **F**unction, is the only BDOS call function used for input, so all of CPMIO operates with only two system calls.

Subroutine Support

Two additional routines are included here to help the main program writer handle input and output messages. CCRLF: writes a carriage return, line feed sequence to the console. TWOCR: does it twice. GETYN: displays a prompt asking for a yes or no response from the operator and returns with the zero flag set for yes, not set for no. The subroutine insists on receiving an upper case or lower case "y" for yes or "n" for no as the first character typed in response to the prompt. Both CIMSG: and GETYN: permit the computer operator to use the line editing controls described in the CP/M manuals and require that the input be terminated with a carriage return.

XTHL Tricks

The only unusual technique employed in the CPMIO routines is in SPMSG:, which stands for **S**tack **P**ointer **M**e**S**sa**G**e. Since the message text immediately follows the CALL SPMSG instruction, the address of the first text character is the address pushed onto the stack by the CALL opcode. SPMSG opens with an XTHL opcode, which gets that address from the top of the stack and puts it into the HL index register, while simultaneously saving the original contents of HL on the top of the stack. HL now points to the first text character in memory. That character is fetched, HL is incremented, and is then placed back on the top of the stack by the second XTHL.

As each character is fetched and sent to the console, the address value, which is the contents of the top of the stack (the "return address"), is incremented by one. When the zero terminator has been fetched, the address on the top of the stack will have been incremented to the next address following the message text. SPMSG will return there, and main program execution will resume at that point.

Note that in this process the original contents of the HL register were preserved by the XTHL operations, so the subroutine call doesn't seem to change any register contents except the accumulator, which will always contain zero following a call to SPMSG.

Using CPMIO

When you have keyed in CPMIO.LIB exactly as shown in Listing 5.2, key in the test program TESTC5.LIB as is shown in Listing 5.3. This test routine includes at least one call to each of the CPMIO subroutines,

Listing 5-3

```
; MODULE NAME: TESTC5.LIB
; LAST UPDATE: 12 FEB 84    BY: KMB
; FUNCTION: TEST CPMIO SUBROUTINES
; REQUIRES: CPMIO.LIB
;==========================================================
            ORG     100H             ; ASSEMBLE FOR TPA

TEST:       CALL    TWOCR
            CALL    SPMSG
            DB      'Testing CPMIO Subroutines',0
            CALL    CCRLF
            CALL    SPMSG
            DB      'Enter a line of text terminated by RETURN',0
            CALL    CCRLF
            CALL    CIMSG
            CALL    CCRLF
            CALL    SPMSG
            DB      'Your line was:',0
            CALL    CCRLF
            LXI     H,INBUF+2
            CALL    COMSG
            CALL    CCRLF
            CALL    SPMSG
            DB      'Want to do it again',0
            CALL    GETYN
            JZ      TEST
            RET
```

providing an adequate test of every line of programming thus far entered.

The test program shows how your main programs will use the subroutines and also illustrates that a main program will consist mostly of subroutine calls. The absence of comments within the test program attests to the power of the SPMSG subroutine. Since the message texts appear in the program listing at their logical places in the program flow, they serve to document what the main program is doing as it executes. Meaningful subroutine names help in the self-documenting of the program listing.

To run the test program, merge TESTC5.LIB followed by CPMIO.LIB into a source program named TESTC5.ASM. This can be done using PIP:

PIP TESTC5.ASM = TESTC5.LIB,CPMIO.LIB

or by using the "R" directive in ED, or by using the file append instructions in your text editor program.

Assembling TESTC5 should produce a .PRN file as is shown in Listing 5.4. Examination of this file should help you debug your own version of the test program, in the unlikely event that your version doesn't run properly. All right, what did you do wrong?

Listing 5-4

```
                        ; MODULE NAME: TESTC5.LIB
                        ; LAST UPDATE: 12 FEB 84    BY: KMB
                        ; FUNCTION: TEST CPMIO SUBROUTINES
                        ; REQUIRES: CPMIO.LIB
                        ;============================================================

0100                          ORG     100H              ; ASSEMBLE FOR TPA

0100 CDA101     TEST:    CALL    TWOCR
0103 CD9501              CALL    SPMSG
0106 5465737469          DB      'Testing CPMIO Subroutines',0
0120 CDA401              CALL    CCRLF
0123 CD9501              CALL    SPMSG
0126 456E746572          DB      'Enter a line of text terminated by RETURN',0
0150 CDA401              CALL    CCRLF
0153 CDB801              CALL    CIMSG
0156 CDA401              CALL    CCRLF
0159 CD9501              CALL    SPMSG
015C 596F757220          DB      'Your line was:',0
016B CDA401              CALL    CCRLF
016E 210602              LXI     H,INBUF+2
0171 CDFA01              CALL    COMSG
0174 CDA401              CALL    CCRLF
0177 CD9501              CALL    SPMSG
017A 57616E7420          DB      'Want to do it again',0
018E CDD701              CALL    GETYN
0191 CA0001              JZ      TEST
0194 C9                  RET

                        ; MODULE NAME:    CPMIO.LIB
                        ; LAST UPDATE: 11 FEB 84    BY: KMB
                        ; FUNCTION: CONSOLE INPUT/OUTPUT SUBROUTINES
                        ; REQUIRES:
                        ;============================================================

                        ; ASCII CHARACTERS

000D =          CR       EQU     0DH               ; CARRIAGE RETURN
000A =          LF       EQU     0AH               ; LINE FEED

                        ; CP/M BDOS FUNCTIONS AND ADDRESSES

0002 =          WCONF    EQU     2                 ; WRITE (A) TO CON:
000A =          RBUFF    EQU     10                ; READ A CONSOLE LINE
0005 =          BDOS     EQU     5                 ; SYSTEM CALL ENTRY

                        ; MESSAGE POINTED TO BY STACK OUT TO CONSOLE
0195 E3         SPMSG:   XTHL                      ; GET "RETURN ADDRESS" TO HL
0196 AF                  XRA     A                 ; CLEAR FLAGS AND ACCUMULATOR
0197 86                  ADD     M                 ; GET ONE MESSAGE CHARACTER
0198 23                  INX     H                 ; POINT TO NEXT
0199 E3                  XTHL                      ; RESTORE STACK FOR
019A C8                  RZ                        ; RETURN IF DONE
019B CDAB01              CALL    CO                ; ELSE DISPLAY CHARACTER
019E C39501              JMP     SPMSG             ; AND DO ANOTHER

                        ; CARRIAGE RETURN, LINE FEED TO CONSOLE
01A1 CDA401     TWOCR:   CALL    CCRLF
01A4 3E0D       CCRLF:   MVI     A,CR
01A6 CDAB01              CALL    CO
```

44

```
01A9 3E0A                  MVI     A,LF
                   ; FALL THROUGH INTO CO:

01AB C5            CO:     PUSH    B               ; SAVE REGISTERS
01AC D5                    PUSH    D
01AD E5                    PUSH    H
01AE 0E02                  MVI     C,WCONF         ; SELECT FUNCTION
01B0 5F                    MOV     E,A             ; CHARACTER TO E
01B1 CD0500                CALL    BDOS            ; OUTPUT BY CP/M
01B4 E1                    POP     H
01B5 D1                    POP     D
01B6 C1                    POP     B
01B7 C9                    RET


                   ; INPUT CONSOLE MESSAGE INTO BUFFER
01B8 C5            CIMSG:  PUSH    B               ; SAVE REGISTERS
01B9 D5                    PUSH    D
01BA E5                    PUSH    H
01BB 210502                LXI     H,INBUF+1       ; ZERO CHARACTER COUNTER
01BE 3600                  MVI     M,0
01C0 2B                    DCX     H               ; SET MAXIMUM LINE LENGTH
01C1 3650                  MVI     M,80
01C3 EB                    XCHG                    ; INBUF POINTER TO DE PAIR
01C4 0E0A                  MVI     C,RBUFF         ; SET UP READ BUFFER FUNCTION
01C6 CD0500                CALL    BDOS            ; INPUT A LINE
01C9 210502                LXI     H,INBUF+1       ; GET CHARACTER COUNTER
01CC 5E                    MOV     E,M             ; INTO LSB OF D,E REGISTER
01CD 1600                  MVI     D,0             ; ZERO MSB
01CF 19                    DAD     D               ; ADD LENGTH TO START
01D0 23                    INX     H               ; PLUS ONE POINTS TO END
01D1 3600                  MVI     M,0             ; INSERT TERMINATOR AT END
01D3 E1                    POP     H               ; RESTORE ALL REGISTERS
01D4 D1                    POP     D
01D5 C1                    POP     B
01D6 C9                    RET


                   ; GET YES OR NO FROM CONSOLE
01D7 CD9501        GETYN:  CALL    SPMSG           ; PROMPT FOR INPUT
01DA 2028592F4E            DB      ' (Y/N)?: ',0
01E4 CDB801                CALL    CIMSG           ; GET INPUT LINE
01E7 CDA401                CALL    CCRLF           ; ECHO CARRIAGE RETURN
01EA 3A0602                LDA     INBUF+2         ; FIRST CHARACTER ONLY
01ED E65F                  ANI     01011111B       ; CONVERT LOWER CASE TO UPPER
01EF FE59                  CPI     'Y'             ; RETURN WITH ZERO = YES
01F1 C8                    RZ
01F2 FE4E                  CPI     'N'             ; NON-ZERO = NO
01F4 C2D701                JNZ     GETYN           ; ELSE TRY AGAIN
01F7 FE00                  CPI     0               ; RESET ZERO FLAG
01F9 C9                    RET                     ; AND ALL DONE

                   ; MESSAGE POINTED TO BY HL OUT TO CONSOLE
01FA 7E            COMSG:  MOV     A,M             ; GET A CHARACTER
01FB B7                    ORA     A               ; ZERO IS THE TERMINATOR
01FC C8                    RZ                      ; RETURN ON ZERO
01FD CDAB01                CALL    CO              ; ELSE OUTPUT THE CHARACTER
0200 23                    INX     H               ; POINT TO NEXT ONE
0201 C3FA01                JMP     COMSG           ; AND CONTINUE

0204               INBUF:  DS      83              ; LINE INPUT BUFFER
```

chapter 6

CP/M
programming
techniques

In addition to compliance with the edicts contained in the last chapter, there are some other techniques you can use to make your programming more consistent, readable, maintainable, and portable, and therefore more valuable. We will look at some of these on the way to producing a program preprocessor that has been used to rescue some nonportable programs from extinction.

PROGRAMMING STYLE

Hemingway wrote short sentences. Other writers in that era, in an effort to project the image of intellectualism on a more exalted plane, composed lengthy sentences, full of subordinate clauses, wandering about the main subject while interjecting peripheral thoughts that might better have been relegated to another sentence, or even paragraph, or even the wastebasket, all the while distracting the reader from the main theme and thereby negating the best efforts of the author, all in the name of compliance with the flowery writing style of the day.

Software authors also have their individual styles. One whom I used to work with seemed to feel that labels should contain no more than two characters, preferably beginning with "X" or "Q," and that comments were for dummies. Having to pick up where he left off and update his software products reinforced my belief that labels should be meaningful without being overly long, and that comments should be included in program listings.

There are some elements of my personal style visible in the listings in this book. This is not the place to attempt to dictate programming style, but there are some very good reasons for doing things the way they are done in this book. The basic reason for following a particular style is that your programs may someday have to be read and understood by another programmer. There are some things you can do to help out those who follow you.

Comments

Look back at Listing 5.4, where right below the second module header there appears the comment line:

; ASCII CHARACTERS

followed by the definitions of CR and LF, complete with their own comments. In this case all those comments amount to overkill, since we all know the codes for CR and LF and we all know that code is ASCII. But if there were many more codes in many more categories defined right there, the comment line would set the block of ASCII codes off from other blocks of definitions above and below it.

The comments accompanying the BDOS function definitions are not overkill because Digital Research did not establish a list of mnemonic labels for all of the system call functions, and those found in this book may vary from those found in other programs by other authors. So there are times when it doesn't hurt to make sure your programs are adequately commented. No comments at all make for a program that will have a short life.

Upper case

Somewhere along the way some new programmers decided it was cute to write assembly language programs in lower case. Old-timers never did that, because a decade ago most terminals didn't have lower-case letter capability. So is the selection of upper case or lower case just a personal preference? Not at all! Look at the difference between the digit one (1) and the lower-case letter "L" (l) in any program listing. Sure, the computer can tell the difference between 31H (ASCII for the number) and 6CH (ASCII for the letter), but can you tell the difference between "1" and "l" when you see them in a listing? A lot depends on the printer and your optometrist.

Even insisting that program source code be written all in upper case will not help to discriminate between the number zero (0) and the letter "Oh" (O) now that most printers no longer use the slashed (Ø) that was obviously not an "Oh." To avoid confusion here it is best to avoid the use of zero in labels.

Absolute Values

As a general rule, always define all absolute values by setting some mnemonic label equal to the value at the very beginning of a program module. Then, if the environment that the program is to be used in ever changes, only the absolute value in the definition ever needs to be changed. While it is unreasonable to expect that ASCII, for example, will ever change, you might want to adapt your program to run on a computer using EBCDIC character codes. It is easier to change the "ODH" in "CR EQU ODH" one time than it is to find every occurrence of the value within a program.

Much more changeable are memory addresses and system call codes. In Part III we will be working with absolute memory addresses, hardware port addresses, and bit patterns. Define them all one time at the beginning of each module and updates become not only possible, but easy.

A sharp-eyed reader might already have discovered that this rule has been violated in Listing 5.4. The rest of you can search for the place in that listing where an absolute value has been defined within a program module, when it might have been better to do so at the top of the module.

All of these elements of programming practice and style, from always remembering to update the date field in the header through defining absolute values one time, contribute to the readability, maintainability, and portability of computer software. And that's about enough on that topic!

Except for one more element. Listing 5.4 starts off with a module header, implying that it is the listing of only a part of a program. But we assembled TESTC5 as a complete program. We need to differentiate between a module and a program. A standard program header will do just that, and a standard program beginning will contribute to program portability.

Standard Program Header

The print file output by ASM (Listing 5.4) is the listing of a complete program, but you can't tell it from the header. Obviously, we need a different header that will be appended to the beginning of all programs. Just as was true for the module header, the program header will force the programmer to identify WHO, WHAT, WHEN, and WHY. Forgetting these is only one common programmer error we are trying to eliminate here.

Programmer Errors

With the need for adequate program documentation automatically taken care of by the use of a standard header, it is time to try to correct some other common programmer errors. Two common ones are forgetting to specify the program start address (100H) at the beginning of the TPA, and forgetting to set up enough stack space and a stack pointer.

BEGIN: and DONE:

A program header isn't enough here, so we will use a complete and standardized program startup routine right at the beginning of every program. BEGIN.LIB (Listing 6.1) is designed to cure most of the

common programmer errors as well as some hardware and system
implementation errors. Since we are incorporating a standard program
startup routine (BEGIN:), we will also include a standard program ending routine (DONE:).

Listing 6-1

```
***************************************************************
*                                                             *
*   PROGRAM NAME:   TESTC6.ASM                                *
*                                                             *
*   LAST UPDATE:  18 FEB 84   BY: KMB                         *
*                                                             *
*   FUNCTION: TEST BEGIN/DONE                                 *
*                                                             *
***************************************************************

              ; ASCII CHARACTERS

000D =          CR     EQU   0DH          ; CARRIAGE RETURN
000A =          LF     EQU   0AH          ; LINE FEED
001A =          CTRLZ  EQU   1AH          ; OPERATOR INTERRUPT

              ; CP/M FUNCTIONS AND ADDRESSES

0001 =          RCONF  EQU   1            ; READ CON: INTO (A)
0002 =          WCONF  EQU   2            ; WRITE (A) TO CON:
000B =          CSTAF  EQU   11           ; CHECK CON: STATUS
0004 =          DRIVE  EQU   4            ; CURRENT DRIVE NUMBER
0005 =          BDOS   EQU   5            ; SYSTEM CALL ENTRY
0080 =          TBUFF  EQU   80H          ; TRANSIENT DEFAULT BUFFER

0100                   ORG   100H         ; TRANSIENT PROGRAM AREA

0100 210000    BEGIN: LXI   H,0          ; SAVE CP/M STACK
0103 39               DAD   SP
0104 229701           SHLD  CPMSP
0107 310002           LXI   SP,STAK      ; SET UP LOCAL STACK
010A 3A0400           LDA   DRIVE        ; SAVE CURRENT DISK
010D 329601           STA   DRSAV
0110 0E0B             MVI   C,CSTAF      ; CHECK CONSOLE STATUS
0112 CD0500           CALL  BDOS         ; FOR ANY INPUT
0115 B7               ORA   A
0116 CA1E01           JZ    BEGIN1       ; CONTINUE IF NONE
0119 0E01             MVI   C,RCONF      ; READ AND IGNORE CON:
011B CD0500           CALL  BDOS         ; (DEBOUNCE KEYS)
011E CD5701    BEGIN1: CALL  CCRLF
0121 CD4801           CALL  SPMSG        ; SIGN-ON MESSAGE
0124 7369676E62D      DB    'sign-on message and date here',0
0142 CD5701           CALL  CCRLF
0145 C30002           JMP   START        ; RUN THE PROGRAM

              ; COMMON SUBROUTINES

              ; MESSAGE POINTED TO BY STACK OUT TO CONSOLE
0148 E3       SPMSG: XTHL                ; GET "RETURN ADDRESS" TO HL
0149 AF              XRA   A             ; CLEAR FLAGS AND ACCUMULATOR
```

```
014A 86                       ADD     M               ; GET ONE MESSAGE CHARACTER
014B 23                       INX     H               ; POINT TO NEXT
014C E3                       XTHL                    ; RESTORE STACK FOR
014D C8                       RZ                      ; RETURN IF DONE
014E CD5E01                   CALL    CO              ; ELSE DISPLAY CHARACTER
0151 C34801                   JMP     SPMSG           ; AND DO ANOTHER

                    ; CARRIAGE RETURN, LINE FEED TO CONSOLE
0154 CD5701         TWOCR:  CALL    CCRLF
0157 3E0D           CCRLF:  MVI     A,CR
0159 CD5E01                 CALL    CO
015C 3E0A                   MVI     A,LF
                    ; FALL THROUGH INTO CO:

015E C5             CO:     PUSH    B               ; SAVE REGISTERS
015F D5                     PUSH    D
0160 E5                     PUSH    H
0161 0E02                   MVI     C,WCONF         ; SELECT FUNCTION
0163 5F                     MOV     E,A             ; CHARACTER TO E
0164 CD0500                  CALL    BDOS            ; OUTPUT BY CP/M
0167 E1                     POP     H
0168 D1                     POP     D
0169 C1                     POP     B
016A C9                     RET

                    ; SHOW SPACES = CONTENTS OF A

016B C5             SPACES: PUSH    B               ; SAVE TEMPORARY REGISTER
016C 4F                     MOV     C,A             ;   FOR COUNT
016D B7                     ORA     A               ; TEST FOR NONE
016E CA7A01                 JZ      SPACE2          ; QUIT IF NONE
0171 3E20           SPACE1: MVI     A,' '           ; SHOW A SPACE
0173 CD5E01                 CALL    CO
0176 0D                     DCR     C               ; COUNT DOWN
0177 C27101                 JNZ     SPACE1          ; SHOW MORE TIL ZERO
017A C1             SPACE2: POP     B               ; RESTORE
017B C9                     RET                     ;   AND RETURN

                    ; CONSOLE OPERATOR INTERRUPT

017C 0E0B           OPINT:  MVI     C,CSTAF         ; CHECK FOR OPERATOR
017E CD0500                 CALL    BDOS            ; INTERRUPT = CTRL Z
0181 B7                     ORA     A
0182 C8                     RZ                      ; RETURN IF NONE
0183 0E01                   MVI     C,RCONF         ; CHARACTER AVAILABLE
0185 CD0500                 CALL    BDOS            ; READ IT IN
0188 FE1A                   CPI     CTRLZ           ; ABORT PROGRAM IF
018A C0                     RNZ                     ; ELSE RETURN TO PROGRAM
                    ; FALL THROUGH INTO END-OF-PROGRAM ROUTINE

                    ; END OF PROGRAM EXECUTION

018B 3A9601         DONE:   LDA     DRSAV           ; RESTORE "CURRENT" DISK
018E 320400                 STA     DRIVE
0191 2A9701                 LHLD    CPMSP           ; RESTORE CP/M STACK
0194 F9                     SPHL
0195 C9                     RET                     ; RETURN TO CP/M
```

Listing 6-1 (*continued*)

```
                    ; LOCAL STORAGE

0196 00             DRSAV   DB      0               ; CURRENT DRIVE NUMBER
0197 0000           CPMSP   DW      0               ; CP/M STACK POINTER

0200                        ORG     200H

                    STAK:                           ; LOCAL STACK TOP
                    START:                          ; PROGRAM FOLLOWS HERE

0200 CD7C01                 CALL    OPINT           ; BACK TO CP/M?
0203 C30002                 JMP     START           ; NO, LOOP FOREVER
```

Now all programs will automatically include instructions for saving the CP/M system stack pointer (the first three lines in BEGIN:), and setting the stack pointer to the top of a reserved stack area within our program workspace. At BEGIN1: we force the programmer to identify the program currently executing, if he will only fill in the blanks. If you are careful and keep the sign-on message length constant, which is easy using a word processor in the noninsert (overlay) mode, the assembled addresses that follow it within BEGIN.LIB will never change. If you use the "11 Feb 84" date format, you can always overlay "date here" in that line, since both strings contain 9-character positions.

Finally, after skipping over the common subroutines and the stack and DRSAV storage space, we jump to the real start of the program, which will begin at a constant standard address, 200H.

System Errors

Right after we set up the stack pointer at BEGIN:, the contents of memory location 4 (DRIVE) are saved, for reasons we will not get into in detail until Chapter 14, but that has proved to be necessary because some improper implementations of CP/M have been discovered lurking around waiting for the unwary programmer. Some programs also cause DRIVE to change improperly, and we can fix them by appending BEGIN.LIB to the start of their source code, if it is available.

Also waiting to trip up our program right at the start is a common hardware fault: terminal key bounce. When a program is first loaded from disk, there should be no operator keystrokes waiting for it. Checking the console status (Console **STA**tus Function, CSTAF) and reading in (**Read CON**sole Function) and ignoring any waiting characters ensures that the program execution will begin in a clean environment.

Utility Subroutines

Every program should begin with a sign-on message giving the program name and version. To enable this to be done within BEGIN:, we have to include some of the subroutines from CPMIO. When you are ready to key in BEGIN.LIB, start by extracting SPMSG: through CO: from CPMIO.LIB, and then insert them into BEGIN.LIB after BEGIN:, as shown in the listing.

What is left of CPMIO will include the **CON**sole **BUFF**ered Input routines CIMSG: and GETYN: along with INBUF:, so rename these remnants of the file CONBUFFI.LIB and set it aside for future use. The subroutines we need for BEGIN are now available for use by all our programs. They have been included in BEGIN to help fill up the first 100H locations so our main programs can all start at exactly 200H.

A new subroutine included here to help fill some of this space is SPACES:, one we won't be needing until Chapter 7, but there was room to put it in BEGIN.LIB. Also included here is an operator interrupt subroutine that can be called from various places in the main program to enable an orderly program abort if the operator finds it necessary. OPINT: will check for a console character, return a zero if none is ready, or return the character if it is not the operator interrupt character specified, in this case CTRL Z.

An Orderly Exit

Whenever OPINT: detects a CTRL Z, it will fall through into DONE:. Whenever the main program is finished, it should terminate by a jump to DONE:, provided that the program has not overwritten CCP. DONE: provides the code for a fast return to CP/M, rather than the time-consuming jump to WBOOT through memory location 0. This is possible because the contents of the CP/M stack pointer were saved at the beginning of BEGIN: and are restored by DONE:.

When a transient program is loaded following a CCP command, CP/M doesn't just jump to the program in the TPA, but it CALLs it so that a fast RETurn to CP/M is possible if CCP doesn't get overwritten by the transient program. DONE: implements this fast return.

TESTC5 also included this fast return to CP/M, but during its execution it used the CP/M stack. Since this stack is limited in size when the transient program is CALLed, longer programs should set up their own stacks, as we have done in BEGIN:. As Listing 6.1 shows, our local stack includes all the space from the end of LOCAL STORAGE to the START: of the main program at 200H.

This 67H (103 decimal) byte block of stack space should provide more than enough room for PUSHes and CALLs in any main program. The CP/M stack space allocated for transient programs is limited to eight levels, which was all right for our test program, but will not be relied upon for future, more complicated, main programs.

How Much Stack Space?

The 103 bytes of stack space left over in BEGIN.LIB would permit the nesting of 51 subroutine calls or register pushes: more than enough. So, some space is available for expansion of the code below the stack space, as would happen if the sign-on message got longer

It is up to the programmer writing the main program to make sure that the stack area is big enough. An easy way to tell is to allocate more than enough space, use DDT to fill the space with some fixed value, such as 11H, and then let DDT run the program with a trap set at the RET instruction in DONE:. When the trap is encountered, DDT will be reentered, and can be used to dump the stack area. The 11H fill is useful because then the stack contents that pushed down from 1FFH will be easily visible in the dump, and you can see exactly how much stack space your program used.

Testing BEGIN:

The program listing for BEGIN.LIB is actually the .PRN listing of TESTC6.ASM, which is BEGIN.LIB plus the two-line test program:

```
CALL        OPINT
JMP         START
```

added at START:. When you key in BEGIN.LIB, leave the PROGRAM NAME: field empty, as in:

```
xxxxxxxx.ASM
```

and leave out the two-line test program and the END statement. Make a copy of BEGIN.LIB, name it TESTC6.ASM, and add the test program lines. When you assemble it, your .PRN file should be identical to Listing 6.1. The program will sign on and then simply loop, echoing all CON: input until you enter CTRL Z, at which time you will instantly return to CP/M without the warm boot disk access.

WHAT CAN IT ALL DO?

Since the claim was made that BEGIN/DONE can make programs more portable, there had better be some experience to back that up. There is. Some early users' group programs that did funny things on different computers have been patched up by the inclusion of these orderly startup and return routines.

There was nothing wrong with the programs to begin with except that they were written to run under CP/M 1.4 on single-density, 8-inch floppy disks. When they were moved to CP/M 2.2 and asked to handle other disk formats, funny things happened. Some of the trouble was because the program authors couldn't see into the future, and some problems were caused by improper installations of CP/M.

If you have had funny things happen to programs when they were moved from a 1.4 system to one running 2.2, give BEGIN/DONE a try. It will not always work miracles, but it will sometimes salvage an older program.

WHAT DOES IT ALL MEAN?

If you are an experienced CP/M assembly language programmer, you should have found these first chapters to be mostly a review of knowledge already acquired, sprinkled with a few glimpses of new information and loaded with the rantings of the opinionated author. But something useful has been accomplished.

We have been setting the stage for what follows. The newer programmers among you will now have a feel for the approach to programming under CP/M that is to follow and will be ready to start investigating the intricacies of the operating system. You experienced programmers now know the viewpoint from which we will attack the more interesting tasks that follow.

All of you should now be sure that copies of HEADER.LIB, BEGIN.LIB, and CONBUFFI.LIB are ready for the tasks to follow. As was true for Listing 6.1, future modules will be printed only in their .PRN format to prevent having to list them all twice, in their source and .PRN formats. You will have to pick out the parts of the listings that you have to add to your library. For example, CONBUFFI.LIB will look like Listing 6.2 when it is assembled as part of a program in the next chapter.

Up to this point we have completed an overview of CP/M and have completed a couple of programming exercises in a form compatible with

all the good stuff to come. Now it is time to look deeper inside CP/M
and see how it works.

Listing 6-2

```
          ; MODULE NAME: CONBUFFI.LIB
          ; LAST UPDATE: 19 FEB 84      BY: KMB
          ; FUNCTION: BUFFERED CONSOLE INPUT SUBROUTINES
          ; REQUIRES: BEGIN.LIB
          ;=========================================================

          ; CP/M BDOS FUNCTIONS
000A =    RBUFF    EQU     10                 ; READ A CONSOLE LINE

          ; INPUT CONSOLE MESSAGE INTO BUFFER
0305 C5   CIMSG:   PUSH    B                  ; SAVE REGISTERS
0306 D5            PUSH    D
0307 E5            PUSH    H
0308 214803        LXI     H,INBUF+1          ; ZERO CHARACTER COUNTER
030B 3600          MVI     M,0
030D 2B            DCX     H                  ; SET MAXIMUM LINE LENGTH
030E 3650          MVI     M,80
0310 EB            XCHG                       ; INBUF POINTER TO DE PAIR
0311 0E0A          MVI     C,RBUFF            ; SET UP READ BUFFER FUNCTION
0313 CD0500        CALL    BDOS               ; INPUT A LINE
0316 214803        LXI     H,INBUF+1          ; GET CHARACTER COUNTER
0319 5E            MOV     E,M                ; INTO LSB OF D,E REGISTER
031A 1600          MVI     D,0                ; ZERO MSB
031C 19            DAD     D                  ; ADD LENGTH TO START
031D 23            INX     H                  ; PLUS ONE POINTS TO END
031E 3600          MVI     M,0                ; INSERT TERMINATOR AT END
0320 E1            POP     H                  ; RESTORE ALL REGISTERS
0321 D1            POP     D
0322 C1            POP     B
0323 C9            RET

          ; GET YES OR NO FROM CONSOLE
0324 CD4801 GETYN: CALL    SPMSG              ; PROMPT FOR INPUT
0327 2028592F4E    DB      ' (Y/N)?: ',0
0331 CD0503        CALL    CIMSG              ; GET INPUT LINE
0334 CD5701        CALL    CCRLF              ; ECHO CARRIAGE RETURN
0337 3A4903        LDA     INBUF+2            ; FIRST CHARACTER ONLY
033A E65F          ANI     01011111B          ; CONVERT LOWER CASE TO UPPER
033C FE59          CPI     'Y'                ; RETURN WITH ZERO = YES
033E C8            RZ
033F FE4E          CPI     'N'                ; NON-ZERO = NO
0341 C22403        JNZ     GETYN              ; ELSE TRY AGAIN
0344 FE00          CPI     0                  ; RESET ZERO FLAG
0346 C9            RET                        ; AND ALL DONE

0347      INBUF:   DS      83                 ; LINE INPUT BUFFER
```

chapter 7

Input/output techniques

The input/output subroutines used in the last two chapters provided easy access to the computer console for plain text messages to and from the operator. In this chapter we will develop subroutines for handling numeric I/O in three formats: binary, hexadecimal, and decimal.

What happened to octal? Good question, since the 8080 instruction set is most easily decoded by breaking up the 8-bit opcodes into the three octal fields of 3, 3, and 2 bits each. Before octal caught on with 8080 programmers, hexadecimal was forced upon us by common usage of the first available 8080 assemblers, from Intel and Processor Technology, back in 1975. So octal will not be covered in this book.

There will be enough to cope with without octal. In this chapter we will develop what appears at first glance to be a staggering array of subroutines for I/O in three number-base formats. There are a large number of subroutines because we want to be able to handle both 8-bit and 16-bit unsigned integer values in each of three number bases for both input and output. That makes for lots of subroutines, and we have to choose labels for them carefully so that we can remember what each one does.

The usual treatment of this subject in programming books gives examples that are greatly simplified by using character-by-character console I/O. Since CP/M provides the operator with powerful input line editing, we will use the buffered console input facilities that we first saw in Chapter 5, to allow the operator to edit input as typed. We will input numbers from either the buffered console input or the command line input buffer set up by CCP. That will be true even for the input of a single numeric value. That helps to make our programs more user-friendly, because the user can correct mistakes before entering that final carriage return.

To fetch numbers from these buffers, we will have to be able to search through the buffers to find the proper numeric fields, and then convert the ASCII character strings we find into the 8-bit or 16-bit values we can work with in assembly language.

All of these number base and I/O options will produce a large array of subroutine entries, but the labels used will tell you what each subroutine does. There is consistency in register use and error reporting throughout all of the routines for each of the number bases.

NUMBER SYSTEMS

Assembly language programmers have to cope with values expressed in different bases, like the binary representation of the lower-case to upper-case conversion mask used in GETYN:. In addition to binary, it is common practice to display addresses in hexadecimal. Coping with these bases is simple, because we break up 8-bit or 16-bit register contents into individual bits for binary display, or into 4-bit nibbles for hex input or output.

The decimal system used by ten-fingered humans is the only thing complicating our I/O techniques. But since we have to communicate with human operators, we need the tools to input decimal numbers typed by the operator and convert them into binary values in working registers.

Limited Numeric Range

While all memory and I/O hardware addresses will be expressed in hex, we will need to communicate decimal values to the operator also, as in displaying disk track and sector numbers. We can limit the programming complication by restricting our I/O to the 0 through 65,535 range of numbers contained in a 16-bit register.

Handling larger numbers, and operating on them mathematically, is not a proper subject for this book, and there is little reason for assembly language programmers to be concerned with such complications. Higher-level languages are now readily available for such operations, and most of those permit calls to assembly language subroutines when necessary. So we will leave number-crunching to BASIC, Fortran, and the newer languages, and restrict our number handling to 16 bits.

All of the subroutines that are developed in this book will handle 8-bit values in the A register, or 16-bit values in the HL register pair. All will use the carry flag to report illegal input patterns, and all will preserve the contents of all the registers except the accumulator.

The only violation of this orthogonality of our array of subroutines will be the lack of subroutines for inputting values in binary, which should never be necessary. We will input 8-bit or 16-bit numbers in hex or decimal, and display them in binary, hex, or decimal.

DISPLAYING NUMBERS

The example CP/M memory maps shown in Figure 7.1 were produced by CPMMAP.ASM, which is used to test and illustrate the number display subroutines developed next. You can use CPMMAP to display the significant CP/M locations in your own computer.

As mentioned before, the program listings in this chapter will be derived from CPMMAP.PRN, and will show the absolute memory addresses and their contents to the left of the source code that you will be entering into your computer. CPMMAP consists of BEGIN. LIB, CPMMAP.LIB, and SHOWNUMB.LIB. We will examine SHOW-NUMB first to understand how the numeric fields in the displays in Figure 7.1 were produced. Later we will see how CPMMAP figures out the various memory addresses.

Binary Displays

To output the contents of the 8-bit accumulator (A) or 16-bit index (HL) registers in binary, we use subroutines CO8BIN: or CO6BIN: respectively. The mnemonic labels stand for **Console Output** in **BIN**ary, with the 8 or 16 bits designated by "8" or "6" ("16" would make the labels too long). These subroutine entry points are listed in Table 7.1, along with those for the other number bases and combinations of these.

The binary display subroutines are actually two entries into the first subroutine in SHOWNUMB.LIB, Listing 7.1, which is part of the complete .PRN file resulting from the assembly of CPMMAP.ASM. Note that CO6BIN: starts at memory address 02BFH. We already know that BEGIN:, etc., occupies 0100H through 01FFH, and you can guess that the main CPMMAP program fills 0200H through 02BEH.

CO8BIN: is the second entry into the subroutine, and takes the contents of A and shifts it out as 8 binary characters ("0" or "1") as counted down by register C. The bits are shifted into the carry bit by the rotate left through carry instruction RAL, the proper character is

	CONSOLE OUTPUT DISPLAY SUBROUTINES	
	8 bits from A	16 bits from H,L
Binary	CO8BIN:	CO6BIN:
Hexadecimal	CO8HEX:	CO6HEX:
Decimal	CO8DEC:	CO6DEC:
Bin, Hex & Dec	CO8BHD:	CO6BHD:
Hex & Dec	CO8HD:	CO6HD:
Requires:	BEGIN.LIB	BEGIN.LIB

Table 7.1 Numeric display subroutines. These ten subroutine entries are all part of module SHOWNUMB.LIB and provide for displaying 8-bit or 16-bit values in binary, hexadecimal, or decimal format. Combination displays of all three number bases (xxx-BHD) or hex and decimal only (xxxHD) can be generated through single subroutine calls.

decided by a test for carry, and it is output to the console by a call to CO: down in BEGIN.LIB.

CO6BIN: uses CO8BIN: to display the 16-bit contents of the HL register pair one register at a time. Note that the original contents of HL are not changed, and that the original contents of the BC registers are saved on the stack, so that the only register contents to be affected by either subroutine call are the contents of the accumulator A. Subroutines that save all of the registers except A should be anticipated by any subroutine call, so that the calling programs don't have to worry about their registers getting garbaged.

Figure 7.1 CPMMAP address displays. A 44 K version of CP/M V1.4 installed in a computer with 48 K of RAM produced the map shown in (a), where extra RAM space has been reserved above the BIOS. A 48 K version 2.2 installed in the same computer produces the map in (b). Map (c) shows CP/M V2.2 in a 64 K computer, and the address errors in (d) illustrate the problems that can arise with programs that attempt to calculate system addresses when DDT or some other resident system extension is in operation.

```
CP/M System Map   23 Feb 84

RAM TOP:   1011111111111111B     BFFFH     49151D
CBIOS:     1010111000000000B     AE00H     44544D
BDOS:      1010000100000000B     A100H     41216D
CCP:       1001100100000000B     9900H     39168D

                     (a)


CP/M System Map   23 Feb 84

RAM TOP:   1011111111111111B     BFFFH     49151D
CBIOS:     1011101000000000B     BA00H     47616D
BDOS:      1010110000000000B     AC00H     44032D
CCP:       1010010000000000B     A400H     41984D

                     (b)


CP/M System Map   23 Feb 84

RAM TOP:   1111111111111111B     FFFFH     65535D
CBIOS:     1111101000000000B     FA00H     64000D
BDOS:      1110110000000000B     EC00H     60416D
CCP:       1110010000000000B     E400H     58368D

                     (c)


CP/M System Map   23 Feb 84

RAM TOP:   1111111111111111B     FFFFH     65535D
CBIOS:     1111101000000000B     FA00H     64000D
BDOS:      1101101111111010B     DBFAH     56314D
CCP:       1101001111111010B     D3FAH     54266D

                     (d)
```

Listing 7-1

```
                    ; MODULE NAME: SHOWNUMB.LIB
                    ; LAST UPDATE: 19 FEB 84    BY: KMB
                    ; FUNCTION: DISPLAY IN BINARY, HEXADECIMAL, OR DECIMAL
                    ; REQUIRES: BEGIN.LIB
                    ;================================================================

                    ; DISPLAY 16 ("..6...:") OR 8 ("..8...:") BITS IN BINARY
                    ; AS 16 OR 8 "0" OR "1" CHARACTERS, LEFT JUSTIFIED

02BF 7C       CO6BIN: MOV    A,H              ; DISPLAY 16 BITS FROM H,L
02C0 CDC402           CALL   CO8BIN
02C3 7D               MOV    A,L
02C4 C5       CO8BIN: PUSH   B                ; DISPLAY 8 BITS FROM A
02C5 0E08             MVI    C,8              ; BIT COUNTER
02C7 17       CO8BI1: RAL                     ; SHIFT MS BIT INTO CARRY
02C8 47               MOV    B,A              ; SAVE REMAINDER
02C9 3E30             MVI    A,'0'            ; DISPLAY ZERO
02CB D2D002           JNC    CO8BI2           ;   IF NO CARRY
02CE 3E31             MVI    A,'1'            ; ELSE DISPLAY ONE
02D0 CD5E01   CO8BI2: CALL   CO               ; OUTPUT THE CHARACTER
02D3 78               MOV    A,B              ; RESTORE REMAINDER
02D4 0D               DCR    C                ; COUNT THE BIT
02D5 C2C702           JNZ    CO8BI1           ; DO ANOTHER IF NOT DONE
02D8 C1               POP    B                ; ELSE RESTORE
02D9 C9               RET                     ; AND RETURN

                    ; DISPLAY 16 OR 8 BITS IN HEXADECIMAL
                    ; AS 4 OR 2 "0-9, A-F" CHARACTERS, LEFT JUSTIFIED

02DA 7C       CO6HEX: MOV    A,H              ; DISPLAY H,L IN HEX
02DB CDDF02           CALL   CO8HEX
02DE 7D               MOV    A,L
02DF F5       CO8HEX: PUSH   PSW              ; DISPLAY A IN HEX
02E0 E6F0             ANI    0F0H             ; MASK 4 MS BITS
02E2 0F               RRC                     ; SHIFT TO 4 LS BITS
02E3 0F               RRC
02E4 0F               RRC
02E5 0F               RRC
02E6 CDEC02           CALL   CO4HEX           ; DISPLAY THE FOUR BITS
02E9 F1               POP    PSW              ; RESTORE INPUT
02EA E60F             ANI    0FH              ; MASK 4 LS BITS
02EC FE0A     CO4HEX: CPI    10               ; GREATER THAN 9?
02EE FAF302           JM     CO4HE1           ; CONTINUE IF NOT
02F1 C607             ADI    7                ; ADD OFFSET, "9" TO "A"
02F3 C630     CO4HE1: ADI    '0'              ; CONVERT TO ASCII, ZERO UP
02F5 C35E01           JMP    CO               ; AND DISPLAY THE CHARACTER
```

Hexadecimal Displays

The hex display subroutines are similarly simple. Here CO8HEX: displays the contents of A as two 4-bit nibbles, converting the 00H through 0FH nibble contents into ASCII characters for "0" through "9" and "A" through "F." If the nibble contains any value from 0 through 9, it can be converted to ASCII by adding the base value 30H, which is ASCII for the number zero (see Appendix A).

If the nibble contents are 10 through 15 (0AH through 0FH), an additional value of 7 has to be added to convert to the proper ASCII character. This can be seen from the ASCII character codes in Appendix A, where there is a gap of seven character codes between "0" and "A".

These simple explanations, along with the comments in the program listings, should be enough to allow you to figure out how all this code works. We won't be getting into any more detailed handholding in this book, at least on such straightforward code segments.

Decimal Displays

Decimal numbers are freaks, and if you have ever wondered why the flying saucer crews never stop to talk with us earthlings, maybe it is because the decimal system is enough to drive off any intelligent life forms, no matter how many fingers they have. But we are stuck with it, so here goes.

Since the binary displays will always show 8 or 16 characters, and hex shows 2 or 4, we want all our decimal displays to show the same number of characters so that tables of values, like those in Figure 7.1, will have their columns aligned properly. We will right-justify our decimal displays and allow for five characters to be displayed for any value from 0 through 65,535. That way either an 8-bit (0 through 255) or 16-bit display will align properly.

To make the decimal numbers look right, we have to suppress leading zeros, except in the case where the display is simply zero. These considerations, and the conversion to decimal itself, complicate the CO8DEC: and CO6DEC: subroutines (Listing 7.2). We can make things a little more understandable with the flowchart in Figure 7.2.

Back in the good old days, the rules for programming stated that you must always draw a flowchart for every program before beginning to write the code. Up to now, for the programs in this book, the flowcharts would have been trivial because the programs and subroutines just started at the top and ran straight through to the bottom with only single-level (unnested) loops along the way.

But here we have a routine that includes three successive conditional branches that may have to be taken when the value to be displayed is zero. You experienced programmers could probably follow the logic of the decimal display subroutines without the flowchart, but it is included to make it easier for you to modify the code if you want to display leading zeros or change the width of the displayed field.

Listing 7-2

```
                    ; DISPLAY 8 OR 16 BITS IN DECIMAL
                    ; AS FIVE "0-9" CHARACTERS, RIGHT JUSTIFIED
                    ; AS IN 'PRINT USING "#####"' IN BASIC

02F8 E5       CO8DEC: PUSH    H             ; SAVE H,L REGISTER
02F9 2600             MVI     H,0           ;  FOR USE AS 8 BIT VALUE
02FB 6F               MOV     L,A
02FC C30003           JMP     CO6DE1
02FF E5       CO6DEC: PUSH    H             ; SAVE ALL REGISTERS
0300 D5       CO6DE1: PUSH    D
0301 C5               PUSH    B
0302 AF               XRA     A             ; CLEAR LEADING ZERO FLAG
0303 325303           STA     ZFLAG
0306 0E05             MVI     C,5           ; DISPLAY 5 CHARACTERS
0308 225403           SHLD    VALUE         ; STORE CURRENT VALUE
030B 215803           LXI     H,TTHOU       ; POINT TO FIRST "DIVIDER"
030E 225603           SHLD    INDEX         ;  SO WE CAN
0311 2A5603   CO6DE2: LHLD    INDEX         ; GET "DIVIDER" VALUE
0314 5E               MOV     E,M           ;  INTO D,E
0315 23               INX     H
0316 56               MOV     D,M
0317 23               INX     H             ; POINT INDEX TO NEXT
0318 225603           SHLD    INDEX         ;  "DIVIDER" VALUE
031B 0600             MVI     B,0           ; CHARACTER STARTS AT ZERO
031D 2A5403           LHLD    VALUE         ; GET CURRENT INPUT VALUE
0320 19       CO6DE3: DAD     D             ; SUBTRACT "DIVIDER"
0321 D22B03           JNC     CO6DE4        ;  UNTIL "BORROW"
0324 225403           SHLD    VALUE         ; SAVE CURRENT VALUE
0327 04               INR     B             ; COUNT # OF SUBTRACTS
0328 C32003           JMP     CO6DE3        ; AND CONTINUE "DIVIDE"
032B 78       CO6DE4: MOV     A,B           ; IS COUNT ZERO?
032C B7               ORA     A
032D CA4103           JZ      CO6DE7        ; YES, INHIBIT LEADING ZEROS
0330 325303           STA     ZFLAG         ; NO, FLAG FIRST NON-ZERO
0333 78       CO6DE5: MOV     A,B           ; GET COUNT
0334 C630             ADI     '0'           ; CONVERT TO ASCII
0336 CD5E01   CO6DE6: CALL    CO            ; DISPLAY IT
0339 0D               DCR     C             ; COUNT CHARACTERS
033A C21103           JNZ     CO6DE2        ; LOOP TIL DONE
033D C1               POP     B             ; ELSE RESTORE AND
033E D1               POP     D
033F E1               POP     H
0340 C9               RET                   ;  RETURN

0341 3A5303   CO6DE7: LDA     ZFLAG         ; SUPPRESS LEADING ZERO?
0344 B7               ORA     A
0345 C23303           JNZ     CO6DE5        ; NO, DISPLAY ZERO
0348 79               MOV     A,C           ; LAST CHARACTER?
0349 FE01             CPI     1             ;  AND ALL ZEROS?
034B CA3303           JZ      CO6DE5        ; YES, DISPLAY A ZERO
034E 3E20             MVI     A,' '         ; NO, DISPLAY A SPACE
0350 C33603           JMP     CO6DE6

0353          ZFLAG   DS      1             ; LEADING ZERO FLAG
0354          VALUE   DS      2             ; CURRENT VALUE
0356          INDEX   DS      2             ; INDEX INTO
0358 F0D8     TTHOU   DW      0-10000       ;  "DIVIDER" VALUES
035A 18FC     UTHOU   DW      0-1000
035C 9CFF     HUNDS   DW      0-100
035E F6FF     TENS    DW      0-10
0360 FFFF     UNITS   DW      0-1
```

Figure 7.2 Flowchart of Listing 7.2. The subroutines for console output display in decimal are complicated by the requirement for suppressing leading zeros in the five-character display space, except for the case where the total value is zero. An otherwise simple logic flow now needs the extra decision diamonds shown in the center and right columns to implement the leading zero suppresion.

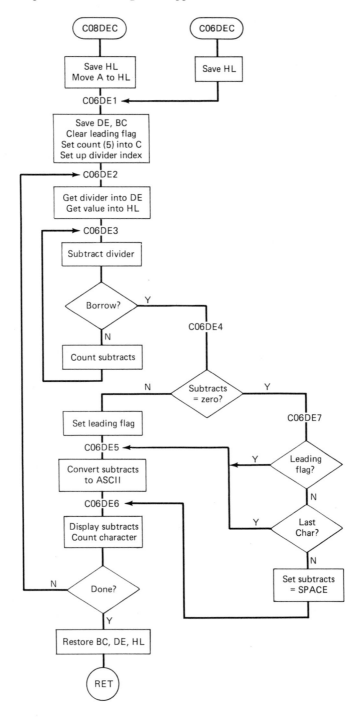

Decimal Conversion

Converting a binary value to decimal is somewhat complicated in a CP/M program because, for compatibility, we can only use the 8080 instruction set. C06DEC: could be a lot shorter if we had either 16-bit divide or subtract opcodes and a couple more index registers. The chances are your CPU is a Z-80. We could really make use of its double precision subtract opcode and extra index registers, but that would violate the portability edict, so we have to do it the hard way.

If you look at the top value in the right-hand column in Figure 7.1, you will see that CPMMAP converted 0BFFFH into the decimal value 49151. Using the decimal system positional notation, we know that this string of characters stands for the sum of:

$$
\begin{array}{rrrr}
4 \times & 10,000 \times & 40000 \\
9 \times & 1,000 \times & 9000 \\
1 \times & 100 \times & 100 \\
5 \times & 10 \times & 50 \\
1 \times & 1 \times & 1 \\
\hline
\text{or} & & 49151
\end{array}
$$

which tells us how 49151 was put together. To take 0BFFFH apart, to display it in decimal, we have to start by dividing it by 10,000 to find out how many 10,000's there are in it, which is then the first (most significant) decimal digit.

Since our opcode set does not include a 16-bit divide, we have to successively subtract 10,000 until our remainder is less than 10,000, and the number of subtractions is then equal to the first decimal digit. But we don't even have a 16-bit subtract opcode!

Fortunately, the quantities we are going to have to subtract are all constants rather than the variable contents of some other register. This simplifies things because subtraction is the same as adding the complement of a number, and we do have a 16-bit add instruction (DAD). We can also use the assembler to calculate the complements of 10,000, 1,000, etc.

The Tens of **THOU**sands complement (TTHOU in Listing 7.2) is calculated when we tell the assembler to **D**efine a **W**ord (16 bits) equal to 0-10,000, and so on. ASM.COM provides us with the table of values that we will be successively subtracting. We then count the subtractions and stop when we have to borrow, which emulates a division. With nine possible subtractions for each of five digit positions, this process would be ridiculous to do longhand, but computers can perform the repetitive operations simply, and CO6DEC: does it for us in no time at all.

Along the way we run out of registers, and have to store VALUE and INDEX in RAM now and then. This serves to illustrate that no matter what computer you are using and no matter how many registers it has, you will always want more. Even displaying only the 8-bit contents of A in CO8DEC: uses up all the registers. We cheated with this one and used CO6DEC: to display only 8 bits by setting H to zero and going through the whole 16-bit conversion anyway. Why? Because it makes one subroutine do the job of two, with only a few extra operations.

COMBINING SUBROUTINES

Doing more with just a few lines of code makes programming easier, and the bottom four subroutines shown in Table 7.1 and listed in Listing 7.3 are just combinations of the console display routines with a few extra characters and some strings of spaces thrown in, as the CPMMAP display shows.

Listing 7-3

```
; DISPLAY 16 BITS IN BINARY, HEX, AND DECIMAL

0362 CDBF02    CO6BHD: CALL    CO6BIN      ; SHOW BINARY
0365 3E42              MVI     A,'B'       ;   AND FLAG IT
0367 CD5E01            CALL    CO
036A 3E05              MVI     A,5         ; SPACE OVER
036C CD6B01            CALL    SPACES
036F CDDA02    CO6HD:  CALL    CO6HEX      ; SHOW HEXADECIMAL
0372 3E48              MVI     A,'H'       ;   AND FLAG IT
0374 CD5E01            CALL    CO
0377 3E05              MVI     A,5         ; SPACE OVER
0379 CD6B01            CALL    SPACES
037C CDFF02            CALL    CO6DEC      ; SHOW DECIMAL
037F 3E44              MVI     A,'D'       ;   AND FLAG IT
0381 C35E01            JMP     CO          ; AND RETURN

; DISPLAY 8 BITS IN BINARY, HEX, AND DECIMAL

0384 CDC402    CO8BHD: CALL    CO8BIN      ; SHOW BINARY
0387 3E42              MVI     A,'B'       ;   AND FLAG IT
0389 CD5E01            CALL    CO
038C 3E05              MVI     A,5         ; SPACE OVER
038E CD6B01            CALL    SPACES
0391 CDDF02    CO8HD:  CALL    CO8HEX      ; SHOW HEXADECIMAL
0394 3E48              MVI     A,'H'       ;   AND FLAG IT
0396 CD5E01            CALL    CO
0399 3E05              MVI     A,5         ; SPACE OVER
039B CD6B01            CALL    SPACES
039E CDF802            CALL    CO8DEC      ; SHOW DECIMAL
03A1 3E44              MVI     A,'D'       ;   AND FLAG IT
03A3 C35E01            JMP     CO          ; AND RETURN
```

It was just as easy to put these combinations in SHOWNUMB.LIB than in the main program, so now we have one library file providing us with ten useful display subroutines. To generate SHOWNUMB.LIB, combine the source code in Listings 7.1, 7.2 and 7.3 into one library file. And now that we've got it, let's use it.

CPMMAP MAPS THE OPERATING SYSTEM

This program will test almost all of the subroutines in SHOW-NUMB.LIB, will finally test SPACES: in BEGIN.LIB, and will show you the memory map of CP/M in your computer, provided you are not running MP/M or CP/M Plus, that is.

Listing 7-4

```
; MODULE NAME:    CPMMAP.LIB
; LAST UPDATE: 23 FEB 84     BY: KMB
; FUNCTION: DISPLAY THE CP/M SYSTEM MEMORY MAP
; REQUIRES: SHOWNUMB.LIB, BEGIN.LIB
;============================================================

000C =          VERSF    EQU     12              ; TEST CP/M VERSION
0030 =          VERS3    EQU     30H             ; CP/M PLUS VERSF RETURN

0200 CD5701     CPMMAP: CALL    CCRLF
0203 CDA102             CALL    RAMTOP           ; GET TOP OF RAM
0206 CD4801             CALL    SPMSG            ; SHOW IT
0209 52414D2054         DB      'RAM TOP: ',0
0214 CD6203             CALL    CO6BHD           ; IN BIN, HEX, AND DEC
0217 CD5701             CALL    CCRLF
021A 0E0C               MVI     C,VERSF          ; CHECK CP/M VERSION
021C CD0500             CALL    BDOS             ; WE CAN ONLY SHOW 1 OR 2
021F 7C                 MOV     A,H              ; FILTER OUT MP/M
0220 B7                 ORA     A
0221 C27A02             JNZ     CPMERR           ; SHOW UNABLE TO SHOW
0224 7D                 MOV     A,L
0225 FE30               CPI     VERS3            ; CHECK FOR CP/M PLUS
0227 D27A02             JNC     CPMERR
022A 2A0100             LHLD    1                ; GET CBIOS ENTRY
022D 2B                 DCX     H                ;   THREE LESS THAN
022E 2B                 DCX     H                ;     JMP BOOT
022F 2B                 DCX     H
0230 CD4801             CALL    SPMSG            ; SHOW IT
0233 4342494F53         DB      'CBIOS: ',0
023E CD6203             CALL    CO6BHD
0241 CD5701             CALL    CCRLF
0244 2A0600             LHLD    6                ; GET BDOS ENTRY
0247 11FAFF             LXI     D,0-6            ; BDOS STARTS 6 BELOW
024A 19                 DAD     D                ;   SO SUBTRACT 6
024B CD4801             CALL    SPMSG            ; SHOW IT
024E 42444F533A         DB      'BDOS: ',0
```

```
0259  CD6203              CALL    CO6BHD
025C  CD5701              CALL    CCRLF
025F  1100F8              LXI     D,0-800H          ; CCP IS 800H BELOW BDOS
0262  19                  DAD     D
0263  CD4801              CALL    SPMSG             ; SHOW IT
0266  4343503A20          DB      'CCP:      ',0
0271  CD6203              CALL    CO6BHD
0274  CD5701              CALL    CCRLF
0277  C38B01              JMP     DONE

027A  CD5701      CPMERR: CALL    CCRLF             ; GIVE THE BAD NEWS
027D  CD4801              CALL    SPMSG
0280  554E41424C          DB      'UNABLE TO MAP THIS VERSION',0
029B  CD5701              CALL    CCRLF
029E  C38B01              JMP     DONE

02A1  210020      RAMTOP: LXI     H,2000H           ; START ABOVE THE PROGRAM
02A4  110004              LXI     D,1024            ; TEST 1 K BYTE INCREMENTS
02A7  0E38                MVI     C,56              ; TEST TO 64 K ONLY
02A9  46          RAMTO1: MOV     B,M               ; SAVE THIS CONTENTS
02AA  AF                  XRA     A                 ; TRY TO WRITE ZEROS
02AB  77                  MOV     M,A
02AC  BE                  CMP     M                 ; THEN TEST ZEROS
02AD  70                  MOV     M,B               ; RESTORE LOCATION
02AE  C2BD02              JNZ     RAMTO3            ; FAILED ZEROS?
02B1  3D                  DCR     A                 ; TEST ONES
02B2  77                  MOV     M,A
02B3  BE                  CMP     M
02B4  70                  MOV     M,B               ; RESTORE MEMORY
02B5  C2BD02              JNZ     RAMTO3            ; FAILED ONES?
02B8  19          RAMTO2: DAD     D                 ; NO, AHEAD ONE BLOCK
02B9  0D                  DCR     C
02BA  C2A902              JNZ     RAMTO1
02BD  2B          RAMTO3: DCX     H                 ; BACK UP ONE LOCATION
02BE  C9                  RET                       ; AND THAT IS LAST RAM
```

RAMTOP Maps the Main Memory

As is true for all properly structured main programs, CPMMAP consists mostly of subroutine calls. A new one here is RAMTOP:, which is part of CPMMAP.LIB, but you might want to separate it from the main program and use it elsewhere in your programming. When called, RAMTOP: will return with HL containing the address of the highest RAM location in the main memory of your computer. It tests RAM beginning at 2000H on up through 64 K bytes in 1 K byte increments until it finds a location that it can't write ones and zeros into.

The first byte of each 1 K block is saved, 00H and then 0FFH are written into each location, the writes are verified, and the original contents restored. RAMTOP: could blow itself up if it tried to write into its own code, so the initial 2000H offset prevents that. When the top of contiguous RAM is found, CPMMAP calls SPMSG: and then CO6BHD: to display the first data line shown in the map displays in Figure 7.1.

A Version-Specific Program

CPMMAP is written as an investigative tool to show you how the main memory in your computer is used, and not as a transportable end-user program. It will work with CP/M versions from 1.3 through 2.2, but not for MP/M or CP/M Plus. The program therefore calls BDOS with function code 12 to get the version number of the CP/M currently running. BDOS returns a zero in the H register for all 8-bit versions of CP/M and ten times the version number (in hex) in the L register. CPMMAP tests for zero in H and less than 30H in L, and quits if either test fails.

CP/M Boundaries Are Mapped

We know from Chapter 5 that memory location 0 contains a JMP instruction to the WBOOT entry in CBIOS. The CP/M *Alteration Guide* points out that the WBOOT entry is the second in a list of 3-byte JMP instructions that must reside at the beginning of CBIOS. Fetching the address field (locations 1,2) and decrementing three times gives us a pointer to the bottom of CBIOS, and we display that address.

We can find BDOS because its address is in locations 6 and 7, the address field of the BDOS entry at location 5. So we fetch that address, subtract 6 to point to the real bottom address of BDOS, and then display it, too. The display will be correct, provided that DDT or some resident system extension (RSX, see Chapter 5) hasn't been loaded below BDOS and changed the address at location 6. We can see what happens in that case, as the map in Figure 7.1(c) is correct for a 64 K CP/M V2.2, but that in Figure 7.1(d) is incorrect, because DDT was used to load and execute CPMMAP.

The location for CCP is also wrong in Figure 7.1(d). In fact, CCP has been overwritten by DDT and doesn't even exist in the computer. The normal location for CCP has been calculated from the BDOS start address by subtracting 800H, the size of CCP in all CP/M versions from 1.3 through 2.2. But there are no simple means to detect DDT or RSXs, so CPMMAP remains a simple-minded, fallible demonstration program.

WHY CPMMAP MAY SURPRISE YOU

When you run the program on your own computer, you may detect that the space from the beginning of your CBIOS to the top of your RAM is larger than the "standard" values of 512 bytes (V1.3 and V1.4) or 1536 bytes (V2.2) as determined by your map display and your trusty old (decimal) calculator. The map in Figure 7.1(a) shows this sort of discrepancy. Here a 44 K version of CP/M 1.4 was installed in a computer with 48 K of RAM, to allow extra space for a background processor.

There are other reasons for having extra RAM above the CBIOS start. Large hard disks take up more space in RAM for various reasons explained in Part III. Some computers with built-in displays need RAM space for the display buffer. Some implementors can't write compact code, so their CBIOSs grow and grow, and they have to install versions of CP/M that are smaller than would normally be permitted by the amount of RAM that is available in the computer.

EXERCISES

Once you have entered SHOWNUMB.LIB and CPMMAP.LIB, linked them with BEGIN.LIB into CPMMAP.ASM, assembled the program, and tested it, there are some changes you can make to exercise your programming prowess.

First, you might want to eliminate the binary part of the display, since it is of doubtful usefulness in this particular program. Then you might want to calculate and display the differences between CBIOS and RAM TOP, BDOS and CBIOS, and CCP and BDOS. This requires a 16-bit subtract, and you now know that all you have to do is complement and add. With the low address of each pair in DE, you can use the accumulator to complement each register (D and E) in turn, and then DAD. This also means that you should save the last displayed address while calculating the next (save CBIOS while calculating BDOS, for example) and that will require more temporary storage in memory.

Note that all of the subroutines shown in Table 7.1 are completely stand-alone, requiring only the support of the common subroutines in BEGIN.LIB. They are all quite usable in other programs. Some more complicated situations are coming up shortly, however.

INPUTTING NUMBERS

When we wanted subroutines to display 8-bit or 16-bit numbers in each of three bases, we ended up with six general-purpose, stand-alone subroutines, and another four that made use of them in combinations. In this chapter we will develop subroutines to input numbers from the computer operator, and we will have even more options.

While there will never be much need to input numbers in binary, and we can drop that requirement, we are going to add options for inputting numbers from three different sources. Those three, times the remaining two number bases, times two number lengths (8 or 16 bits) produce twelve different subroutines we could write. But we will add one more selection and end up with twenty-four options!

Twenty-four Options

This is not as confusing as you might think, after we study Table 7.2 a little. The four columns are self-explanatory. They show the base and length options.

The rows in the table list the input options. It is easy to understand that we might want to input numbers from three sources: the console buffered input like we used in GETYN:, the command line that CCP leaves us when we invoke a transient program, or any other ASCII string that contains one or more numeric values expressed as strings of digits.

Since these three optional sources of inputs can contain any number of input values, in the form of ASCII character substrings separated by delimiters, with the whole string terminated by a zero (remember that standard?), we need one subroutine call to point to the start of the input buffer and fetch the first value, and another subroutine entry to continue from there and get the next value(s), if any. For example, in a program to add two hex numbers we could enter:

HEXADD 1234, 0dbcaH

to illustrate some of the variations we will have to handle.

HEXADD will be the main program that will expect to find two hex number strings in the command line buffer. It will input the numbers, convert them to 16-bit binary, add them, and display the total. Since the program knows that the two inputs are hex numbers, our subroutines will not need the "H" designator after each number, and won't even need the leading zero for a number that begins with a letter. Human nature being what it is, we'd better be able to handle either upper case or lower case for the "A" through "F" hex digits, and even the optional suffix "H." We will also permit any kinds of delimiters between the numeric fields: commas, spaces, or any other punctuation or combinations thereof. The human computer operator will not have to perform with machine-level accuracy.

Since HEXADD gets the numbers from the CCP command line buffer (TBUFF at location 80H), it would call LI6HEX (Table 7.2) to initialize the pointer into TBUFF and fetch the first value. Successive

| | 8 bits into A | | 16 bits into H,L | |
	HEX	DEC	HEX	DEC
Console Buffered Input				
First Value	CI8HEX	CI8DEC	CI6HEX	CI6DEC
Next Value(s)	BI8HEX	BI8DEC	BI6HEX	BI6DEC
Command Line Input				
First Value	LI8HEX	LI8DEC	LI6HEX	LI6DEC
Next Value(s)	BI8HEX	BI8DEC	BI6HEX	BI8DEC
Any ASCII String				
First Value	— — — — — SUPPLIED BY USER — — — —			
Next Value(s)	BI8HEX	BI8DEC	BI6HEX	BI6DEC
Requires:	— — — —	CONBUFFI.LIB NICOMMON.LIB BEGIN.LIB	— — — —	

Table 7.2 Numeric input subroutines. Numbers can be input to a program in hex-adecimal or decimal, as either 8- or 16-bit values. The numeric input subroutines can get the values from any of three sources: the operator's console, a CCP command line, or from a disk file. Various subroutine entries provide for the input of the first numeric field in an input line and then for any number of subsequent fields in the same line.

values would be fetched by successive calls to BI6HEX until the called subroutine signals end-of-line by returning with the flag register carry bit set.

If HEXADD instead wanted to prompt for inputs, as in:

HEXADD

Hexadecimal add   3 Mar 84

Enter two hex numbers:——

then CI6HEX would be called first, and BI6HEX subsequently. Other programs, such as assemblers or compilers, might want to fetch hex or decimal values from ASCII strings in input files, so Table 7.2 shows a row for the user to specify first-value subroutines that would set up their own initial input buffer pointer. You could name these UI8HEX, etc.

Decipherable Labels

Just as was true for the output routines listed in Table 7.1, all of the input entries have mnemonic labels that tell what they are doing, once you first learn that the "CI" prefix stands for Console Buffered Input, and "LI" designates Command Line Buffered Input, and "BI" indicates Specified Buffer Input. You will soon see how easy it will be for you to add those subroutines.

Since the BI-prefix subroutines are used repeatedly in Table 7.2, you can see that there are nowhere near twenty-four subroutines required, and some of the twelve that are necessary are only two lines long. Let's look at the code and see how we can reduce all of this to just a few software routines. We will start with hexadecimal input and write that HEXADD program to demonstrate how the subroutines work.

Listing 7-5

```
          ; MODULE NAME: HEXNUMBI.LIB
          ; LAST UPDATE: 28 FEB 84     BY: KMB
          ; FUNCTION: INPUT HEXADECIMAL NUMBERS
          ; REQUIRES: CONBUFFI.LIB, NICOMMON.LIB, BEGIN.LIB
          ;============================================================

          ; INPUT 2 HEX CHARACTERS FROM COMMAND LINE AS 8 BITS IN A

0245 218100   LI8HEX: LXI    H,TBUFF+1      ; POINT TO TRANSIENT BUFFER
0248 C35102           JMP    CI8HE1         ; USE THAT FOR INPUT

          ; INPUT 2 HEX CHARACTERS FROM CONSOLE AS 8 BITS IN A

024B CD0503   CI8HEX: CALL   CIMSG          ; GET AN INPUT LINE
024E 214903           LXI    H,INBUF+2      ; POINT INTO IT
0251 22AF02   CI8HE1: SHLD   IBPNT          ; INITIALIZE BUFFER POINTER

          ; FALL THROUGH INTO BI8HEX:

          ; INPUT 1 OR 2 HEXADECIMAL DIGITS POINTED TO BY IBPNT INTO A
          ;   RETURNS WITH NO CARRY IF INPUT IS LEGAL
          ;   RETURNS WITH CARRY AND A = 0 IF NO DIGITS BEFORE E.O.L.
          ;   RETURNS WITH CARRY AND A = FF IF OVERFLOW

0254 E5       BI8HEX: PUSH   H              ; SAVE TEMPORARY REGISTER
0255 CD7802           CALL   BI6HEX         ; USE 16 BIT INPUT
0258 DA6502           JC     BI8ERR         ; IMMEDIATE ERROR
025B 7C               MOV    A,H            ; ELSE CHECK 8 BIT OVERFLOW
025C B7               ORA    A
025D C26502           JNZ    BI8ERR         ; IS H NOT ZERO
0260 37               STC                   ; NO ERROR, CLEAR CARRY
0261 3F               CMC
0262 7D       BI8HE1: MOV    A,L            ; GET 8 INPUT BITS TO A
0263 E1               POP    H              ; RESTORE TEMPORARY
0264 C9               RET                   ; AND ALL DONE

0265 37       BI8ERR: STC                   ; FLAG ERROR
0266 C36202           JMP    BI8HE1         ; RESTORE AND RETURN

          ; INPUT 4 HEX CHARACTERS FROM COMMAND LINE AS 16 BITS IN H,L
```

Listing 7-5 (*continued*)

```
0269 218100    LI6HEX: LXI     H,TBUFF+1       ; POINT TO TRANSIENT BUFFER
026C C37502            JMP     CI6HE1          ; USE THAT FOR INPUT

                       ; INPUT 4 HEX CHARACTERS FROM CONSOLE AS 16 BITS IN H,L

026F CD0503    CI6HEX: CALL    CIMSG           ; GET AN INPUT LINE
0272 214903            LXI     H,INBUF+2       ; POINT INTO IT
0275 22AF02    CI6HE1: SHLD    IBPNT           ; INITIALIZE BUFFER POINTER

                       ; FALL THROUGH INTO BI6HEX:

                       ; INPUT UP TO 4 HEX DIGITS POINTED TO BY IBPNT INTO H,L
                       ;   RETURNS WITH NO CARRY IF INPUT IS LEGAL
                       ;   RETURNS WITH CARRY AND H,L = 0 IF NO DIGITS BEFORE E.O.L.
                       ;   RETURNS WITH CARRY AND H,L = FFFF IF OVERFLOW

0278 C5        BI6HEX: PUSH    B               ; SAVE WORKING REGISTERS
0279 D5                PUSH    D
027A 2AAF02            LHLD    IBPNT           ; GET INPUT BUFFER POINTER
027D EB                XCHG                    ;    INTO D,E
027E 210000            LXI     H,0             ; START WITH ZERO
0281 CDE502            CALL    HFIELD          ; FIND HEXADECIMAL FIELD
0284 DAA002            JC      BI6HE4          ; ABORT IF NONE IN BUFFER
0287 1A        BI6HE1: LDAX    D               ; GET AN INPUT DIGIT
0288 CDB102            CALL    CHKHEX          ; VALIDATE AND CONVERT
028B DA9E02            JC      BI6HE3          ; DONE IF NOT 0-9, A-F
028E 13                INX     D               ;    NOT DONE, POINT AHEAD
028F 0E04              MVI     C,4             ; 4 ADDS = TIMES 16
0291 29        BI6HE2: DAD     H               ; DOUBLE THE RESULT
0292 DAA802            JC      BI6ERR          ; ABORT IF OVERFLOW
0295 0D                DCR     C               ; COUNT DOWN
0296 C29102            JNZ     BI6HE2          ; LOOP TIL DONE
0299 B5                ORA     L               ; ADD IN NEW 4 BITS
029A 6F                MOV     L,A
029B C38702            JMP     BI6HE1          ; AND GET ANOTHER DIGIT

029E 37        BI6HE3: STC                     ; NORMAL EXIT,
029F 3F                CMC                     ;   CLEAR CARRY
02A0 EB        BI6HE4: XCHG                    ; UPDATE BUFFER POINTER
02A1 22AF02            SHLD    IBPNT
02A4 EB                XCHG
02A5 D1                POP     D               ; RESTORE AND
02A6 C1                POP     B
02A7 C9                RET                     ;   RETURN

02A8 21FFFF    BI6ERR: LXI     H,-1            ; OVERFLOW ERROR EXIT
02AB 37                STC
02AC C3A002            JMP     BI6HE4

                       ; SET IBPNT TO THE INPUT BUFFER TO BE PARSED

02AF           IBPNT   DS      2               ; INPUT BUFFER POINTER
```

Input in Hexadecimal

Taking the listing of HEXNUMBI.LIB (Listing 7.5) right from the top, you can see from the header that this module requires support from CONBUFFI.LIB, which reads an input line from the console; NICOMMON.LIB, which contains common subroutines for the Numeric Input modules for hex and decimal input; and good old BEGIN.LIB, which shouldn't need to be listed, since it is always there in all of our programs.

Next we see that the LI8HEX: entry takes the address of the default transient buffer TBUFF plus 1 (skipping the character count) and puts it into the Input Buffer PoiNTer (IBPNT) memory location at the bottom of the listing. The CI8HEX: entry does the same with the address of the first input character in the console input buffer, skipping the maximum character count and actual character count that are stored at the beginning of that buffer.

Both of these entries then use BI8HEX: to input the 8-bit value, but do it in a sneaky way by calling for the 16-bit input (CI6HEX:), ignoring the upper 8-bit byte (H) if it is zero. If H is not zero, the carry is set, indicating an 8-bit overflow.

An identical trio of entries exists for the 16-bit subroutines, but only in BI6HEX: do we actually get around to inputting numbers from the input buffer pointed to by IBPNT. Since we first have to find a valid numeric field in the input buffer, BI6HEX: calls HFIELD: (find a Hexadecimal **FIELD**), which is part of the common subroutine module NICOMMON.LIB, so we will look at it in detail later. HFIELD: increments the contents of the DE register pair until it finds a valid hex character ("0" through "9" or "A" through "F").

The Carry Flags Errors

Note that immediately after the call to HFIELD:, BI6HEX: will return with 0 in HL if HFIELD: returned with the carry bit in the flag register set. The carry is our standard error flag for all these subroutines. If there is no valid hex field of characters in the input buffer, HFIELD returns a carry to BI6HEX, which just passed it back to whatever routine had called it. That could have been LI8HEX: or CI6HEX:, or the main program, etc., and the same error flag is simply propagated back to the originating program segment for final processing, as we will see later.

Shifting in the Numbers

BI6HE1: begins a loop that will fetch characters from the input buffer and test them by a call to CHKHEX: (**CH**ec**K HEX**adecimal character), also in NICOMMON.LIB. Since HFIELD: already found a valid hex field, the carry bit returned by CHKHEX: will be used to indicate the end of that field of hex characters, so of course it will never occur at the first fetch.

As each hex character is fetched and converted to its 4-bit binary value by CHKHEX:, the DE buffer pointer is incremented, and the previous contents of HL are multiplied by 16 in the loop at BI6HE2:. Adding HL to itself four times carries out the multiplication, which has the effect of shifting the previous contents of the HL pair left 4 bits before the current hex character value is added by the ORA L and MOV L,A instructions.

This input of a hex character, testing and conversion of it to binary, shifting of the previous 16-bit value, checking for overflow with each shift, and finally adding in the new 4 bits continues through the hex character field. At the end of the field, BI6HE3:, BI6HE4:, or BI6ERR: will update the buffer pointer, restore DE and BC, and return to the calling program (or subroutine) with the carry flag indicating any errors.

ADDING USER INPUT IN HEX

Since the 8-bit and 16-bit entries consist of only a couple of lines of code before BI6HEX: is reached, it is easy to see that your own programs can specify some other input buffer by merely setting the start address of the buffer into IBPNT and then jumping into BI8HEX: or BI6HEX:, as was done for the console or command line buffers. Then, successive calls to the BI subroutines will produce subsequent values in A or HL, with the carry flag indicating end of line (carry set and value = 0) or overflow (carry set and value = all one bits).

COMMON SUPPORT SUBROUTINES

NICOMMON.LIB (Listing 7.6) contains subroutines that support the hex and decimal buffered inputs and can also be useful to other programs or subroutines. All use the standard register conventions and error flagging by the carry bit. CHKHEX: and CHKDEC: verify that the A register contains a valid ASCII hex or decimal character and convert it to its binary equivalent.

Listing 7-6

```
                    ; MODULE NAME: NICOMMON.LIB
                    ; LAST UPDATE:  1 MAR 84    BY: KMB
                    ; FUNCTION: NUMBERS BUFFERED INPUT COMMON SUBROUTINES
                    ; REQUIRES: NO SUPPORT
                    ;===============================================================

                    ; THIS MODULE SUPPORTS SUBROUTINES IN HEXNUMBI.LIB
                    ;  AND DECNUMBI.LIB

                    ; CHECK FOR A VALID HEX CHARACTER, CONVERT TO BINARY

007F =              ASMASK  EQU     01111111B       ; STRIP PARITY BIT FOR ASCII
005F =              UCMASK  EQU     01011111B       ; CONVERT TO UPPER CASE

02B1 C5             CHKHEX: PUSH    B               ; SAVE WORKING REGISTER
02B2 E67F                   ANI     ASMASK          ; INSURE 7 BIT ASCII
02B4 FE3A                   CPI     '9'+1           ; IS IT A NUMBER?
02B6 DACA02                 JC      CHKDE1          ; MAYBE, TRY DECIMAL
02B9 E65F                   ANI     UCMASK          ; NO, CONVERT TO UPPER CASE
02BB 0E41                   MVI     C,'A'           ; CHECK LOWER LIMIT
02BD 0646                   MVI     B,'F'           ;  AND UPPER LIMIT
02BF CDDF02                 CALL    LIMITS
02C2 DADA02                 JC      CHKERR          ; NOT A-F, FLAG ERROR
02C5 D637                   SUI     '0'+7           ; CONVERT TO BINARY
02C7 C1                     POP     B               ; RESTORE AND RETURN
02C8 C9                     RET

                    ; CHECK FOR A VALID DECIMAL CHARACTER, CONVERT TO BINARY

02C9 C5             CHKDEC: PUSH    B               ; SAVE WORKING REGISTER
02CA E67F           CHKDE1: ANI     ASMASK          ; INSURE 7 BIT ASCII
02CC 0E30                   MVI     C,'0'           ; CHECK LOWER LIMIT
02CE 0639                   MVI     B,'9'           ;  AND UPPER LIMIT
02D0 CDDF02                 CALL    LIMITS
02D3 DADA02                 JC      CHKERR          ; ERROR IF OUT OF LIMITS
02D6 D630                   SUI     '0'             ; OK, CONVERT TO BINARY
02D8 C1                     POP     B               ; RESTORE AND
02D9 C9                     RET                     ; RETURN
02DA D630           CHKERR: SUI     '0'             ; CONVERT ANYWAY
02DC 37                     STC                     ;  BUT FLAG ERROR
02DD C1                     POP     B
02DE C9                     RET                     ;   AND RETURN

                    ; CHECK FOR A EQUAL TO OR GREATER THAN C
                    ;         AND A EQUAL TO OR LESS THAN B

02DF B9             LIMITS: CMP     C               ; A .GE. C?
02E0 D8                     RC                      ; NO, RETURN WITH CARRY
02E1 04                     INR     B               ; YES, INCREMENT B
02E2 B8                     CMP     B               ; A .LE. B?
02E3 3F                     CMC                     ; REVERSE "SIGN" OF CARRY
02E4 C9                     RET                     ; AND ALL DONE

                    ; FIND THE FIRST HEX CHARACTER IN THE INPUT BUFFER (D,E)

02E5 1A             HFIELD: LDAX    D               ; GET AN INPUT CHARACTER
02E6 FE00                   CPI     0               ; ABORT IF END OF LINE
02E8 C2ED02                 JNZ     HFIEL1          ; ELSE GO AHEAD
```

```
02EB 37                STC                      ; CARRY = END OF LINE
02EC C9                RET
02ED CDB102  HFIEL1:   CALL    CHKHEX           ; HEX CHARACTER?
02F0 D0                RNC                      ; RETURN IF
02F1 13                INX     D                ; ELSE POINT AHEAD ONE
02F2 C3E502            JMP     HFIELD           ;   AND TRY AGAIN

             ; FIND THE FIRST DECIMAL CHARACTER IN THE INPUT BUFFER (D,E)

02F5 1A      DFIELD:   LDAX    D                ; GET AN INPUT CHARACTER
02F6 FE00              CPI     0                ; ABORT IF END OF LINE
02F8 C2FD02            JNZ     DFIEL1           ; ELSE GO AHEAD
02FB 37                STC                      ; CARRY = END OF LINE
02FC C9                RET
02FD CDC902  DFIEL1:   CALL    CHKDEC           ; DECIMAL CHARACTER?
0300 D0                RNC                      ; RETURN IF
0301 13                INX     D                ; ELSE POINT AHEAD ONE
0302 C3F502            JMP     DFIELD           ;   AND TRY AGAIN
```

Along the way they call another useful subroutine, LIMITS:, which tests for A greater than or equal to C and less than or equal to B. This could be useful in a number of places in programs, which only have to initialize A, B, and C; call LIMITS:; and test the carry bit (cleared if within limits, set if out of limits) on the return.

The functions of HFIELD: and DFIELD: have already been discussed. Note that they use the DE register pair to point into a string of ASCII characters, which they will scan for the first hex or decimal character. Programs or subroutines that call them have only to remember to first set up the DE register to point to the string and can then expect it to be updated at the return. The carry will indicate a successful find if cleared, or end of line if set.

Parsing Input

Scanning through an input line, identifying the various fields, and interpreting each field is a process known as "parsing" the input line. If an assembler produces an assembly listing, shouldn't a parser produce a parsley listing?

HEXADD TESTS HEXADECIMAL INPUT

After you have keyed in HEXNUMBI.LIB and NICOMMON.LIB, you will be ready to enter HEXADD.LIB and link *everything* together into our biggest test program yet. The listings for these three new modules, as well as Listing 6.2 back in Chapter 6, were derived from the complete listing of HEXADD.PRN. Examination of their assembled addresses will show that HEXADD.ASM was produced by linking:

BEGIN.LIB
HEXADD.LIB
HEXNUMBI.LIB
NICOMMON.LIB
CONBUFFI.LIB
SHOWNUMB.LIB

in that exact order into one big test program.

Since the interdependencies among all of these modules are more than a little complicated, Figure 7.3 is included to help you remember

Figure 7.3 Program module interdependencies. Modules that require support from lower-level modules are shown by the descending arrows. Routines within main programs HEXADD or DECADD call subroutines contained in module SHOWNUMB and in HEXNUMBI or DECNUMBI. A more complicated program could require both of the latter modules at the same time. All programs require the basic support of BEGIN.LIB, even though there may not be any direct calls from the main program to subroutines within BEGIN.

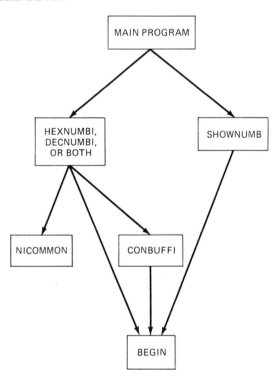

what routines are dependent on others. The downward-pointing arrows indicate that the module above requires support from those it points to directly. We have been careful in our module headers to list the support required by each module, but drawing a map like this makes the relationships a little more obvious.

HEXADD.COM will fill up almost 1,000 bytes of memory, all to add two hex numbers. That size reflects the overhead incurred by using modular programming, structuring all subroutines for general purpose use, and performing extensive error checking. But it is all worth it in the long run, when you will be using these subroutines in larger programs and can rely on them to help you produce error-free, documented, maintainable, portable software.

Once again, with all the little tasks broken up into subroutines, the main program becomes almost self-documenting. HEXADD expects to be invoked with the command line "tail" containng two valid hexadecimal character strings separated by just about any combination of punctuation.

Listing 7-7

```
; MODULE NAME:    HEXADD.LIB
; LAST UPDATE:  3 MAR 84    BY: KMB
; FUNCTION: ADD & DISPLAY 2 HEX NUMBERS FROM COMMAND LINE
; REQUIRES: HEXNUMBI.LIB, NICOMMON.LIB, CONBUFFI.LIB
;           SHOWNUMB.LIB, BEGIN.LIB
;=============================================================

0200 CD6902   HEXADD: CALL   LI6HEX           ; GET A NUMBER
0203 DA2602           JC     HEXERR           ; ABORT IF NO GOOD
0206 CD5701           CALL   CCRLF            ; SHOW THE FIRST
0209 CD3D04           CALL   CO6BHD           ;   IN BIN, HEX, & DEC
020C EB               XCHG                    ; SAVE THE FIRST IN D,E
020D CD7802           CALL   BI6HEX           ; GET THE SECOND
0210 DA2602           JC     HEXERR           ; ABORT IF NO GOOD
0213 CD5701           CALL   CCRLF            ; SHOW THE SECOND
0216 CD3D04           CALL   CO6BHD
0219 19               DAD    D                ; ADD THE TWO
021A CD5401           CALL   TWOCR            ; SHOW THE TOTAL
021D CD3D04           CALL   CO6BHD
0220 CD5701           CALL   CCRLF            ; AND ALL DONE
0223 C38B01           JMP    DONE

0226 CD5401   HEXERR: CALL   TWOCR            ; SHOW ERROR
0229 CD4801           CALL   SPMSG
022C 494E505554       DB     'INPUT FORMAT ERROR',0
023F CD5701           CALL   CCRLF
0242 C38B01           JMP    DONE
```

Free Format Input

We allow this free format input to save the computer operator from the burden of having to remember whether this program wants a comma or space as delimiter between fields. Let the operator throw in half a dozen spaces and "#$%&' (#", for all we care. HEXADD will find the proper character strings, add them and display the results, or slap our wrists if the inputs are in error or out of our 16-bit unsigned integer range.

INPUT IN DECIMAL

DECNUMBI.LIB (Listing 7.8) is virtually identical to HEX-NUMBI.LIB, and in fact was produced from it by extensive use of the global search and replace commands available in your text editor or word processor. The only differences are in the designation of a new buffer pointer, DIBPNT, which replaces IBPNT, and in the shift and add sequence as the new characters are added into the previous value in HL.

A new pointer would not be required unless DECNUMBI.LIB is included in the same program along with HEXNUMBI.LIB. Having the label "IBPNT" appearing in two modules within the same program is a no-no, as far as the assembler is concerned. With two different labels, there is no reason you can't use both modules in a program at the same time. Both will derive support from the same NICOMMON.LIB module, of course.

Shifting in Decimal

To accumulate a 16-bit binary value from a string of decimal digits, the previous value has to be multiplied by 10 as each new digit is input and converted to binary. The new digit can then be added to the 16-bit accumulator HL. Along with the error checking for overflow, this multiplication by 10 is a little more complex than the times-16 shifting in HEXNUMBI.LIB. But not too much.

To multiply the previous value by 10, we add it to itself once (times 2) and save the result. Then we add it to itself two more times (times 4, times 8) and add in the previously saved times-2, which produces the original number times 10. Only a few lines of code differ from the hex subroutine. There should be a way to combine the two. You can tackle that project, if you want.

Listing 7-8

```
                ; MODULE NAME: DECNUMBI.LIB
                ; LAST UPDATE:  7 MAR 84    BY: KMB
                ; FUNCTION: INPUT DECIMAL NUMBERS
                ; REQUIRES: CONBUFFI.LIB, NICOMMON.LIB, BEGIN.LIB
                ;===========================================================

                ; INPUT 1-3 DEC CHARACTERS FROM COMMAND LINE AS 8 BITS IN A

0245 218100     LI8DEC: LXI     H,TBUFF+1       ; POINT TO TRANSIENT BUFFER
0248 C35102             JMP     CI8DE1          ; USE THAT FOR INPUT

                ; INPUT 1-3 DEC CHARACTERS FROM CONSOLE AS 8 BITS IN A

024B CD0F03     CI8DEC: CALL    CIMSG           ; GET AN INPUT LINE
024E 215303             LXI     H,INBUF+2       ; POINT INTO IT
0251 22B902     CI8DE1: SHLD    DIBPNT          ; INITIALIZE BUFFER POINTER

                ; FALL THROUGH INTO BI8DEC:

                ; INPUT 1-3 DECIMAL DIGITS POINTED TO BY DIBPNT INTO A
                ;   RETURNS WITH NO CARRY IF INPUT IS LEGAL
                ;   RETURNS WITH CARRY AND A = 0 IF NO DIGITS BEFORE E.O.L.
                ;   RETURNS WITH CARRY AND A = FF IF OVERFLOW

0254 E5         BI8DEC: PUSH    H               ; SAVE TEMPORARY REGISTER
0255 CD7802             CALL    BI6DEC          ; USE 16 BIT INPUT
0258 DA6502             JC      DE8ERR          ; IMMEDIATE ERROR
025B 7C                 MOV     A,H             ; ELSE CHECK 8 BIT OVERFLOW
025C B7                 ORA     A
025D C26502             JNZ     DE8ERR          ; IS H NOT ZERO
0260 37                 STC                     ; NO ERROR, CLEAR CARRY
0261 3F                 CMC
0262 7D         BI8DE1: MOV     A,L             ; GET 8 INPUT BITS TO A
0263 E1                 POP     H               ; RESTORE TEMPORARY
0264 C9                 RET                     ; AND ALL DONE

0265 37         DE8ERR: STC                     ; FLAG ERROR
0266 C36202             JMP     BI8DE1          ; RESTORE AND RETURN

                ; INPUT UP TO 5 DEC CHARACTERS FROM COMMAND LINE
                ;   AS 16 BITS IN H,L

0269 218100     LI6DEC: LXI     H,TBUFF+1       ; POINT TO TRANSIENT BUFFER
026C C37502             JMP     CI6DE1          ; USE THAT FOR INPUT

                ; INPUT UP TO 5 DEC CHARACTERS FROM CONSOLE AS 16 BITS IN H,L

026F CD0F03     CI6DEC: CALL    CIMSG           ; GET AN INPUT LINE
0272 215303             LXI     H,INBUF+2       ; POINT INTO IT
0275 22B902     CI6DE1: SHLD    DIBPNT          ; INITIALIZE BUFFER POINTER

                ; FALL THROUGH INTO BI6DEC:
```

Listing 7-8 (continued)

```
              ; INPUT UP TO 5 DECIMAL DIGITS POINTED TO BY DIBPNT INTO H,L
              ; RETURNS WITH NO CARRY IF INPUT IS LEGAL
              ; RETURNS WITH CARRY AND H,L = 0 IF NO DIGITS BEFORE E.O.L.
              ; RETURNS WITH CARRY AND H,L = FFFF IF OVERFLOW

0278 C5       BI6DEC: PUSH    B          ; SAVE WORKING REGISTERS
0279 D5               PUSH    D
027A 2AB902           LHLD    DIBPNT     ; GET INPUT BUFFER POINTER
027D EB               XCHG               ;  INTO D,E
027E 210000           LXI     H,0        ; START WITH ZERO
0281 CDFF02           CALL    DFIELD     ; FIND DECIMAL FIELD
0284 DAAA02           JC      BI6DE4     ; ABORT IF NONE IN BUFFER
0287 1A       BI6DE1: LDAX    D          ; GET AN INPUT DIGIT
0288 CDD302           CALL    CHKDEC     ; VALIDATE AND CONVERT
028B DAA802           JC      BI6DE3     ; DONE IF NOT 0-9
028E 13               INX     D          ;  NOT DONE, POINT AHEAD
028F 29               DAD     H          ; DOUBLE THE PREVIOUS VALUE
0290 DAB202           JC      DE6ERR     ; ABORT IF OVERFLOW
0293 44               MOV     B,H        ; SAVE TWO TIMES PREVIOUS
0294 4D               MOV     C,L
0295 29               DAD     H          ; NOW TIMES FOUR
0296 DAB202           JC      DE6ERR
0299 29               DAD     H          ; NOW TIMES EIGHT
029A DAB202           JC      DE6ERR
029D 09               DAD     B          ; PLUS TIMES TWO = TIMES TEN
029E 0600             MVI     B,0        ; ADD IN NEW DIGIT
02A0 4F               MOV     C,A
02A1 09               DAD     B
02A2 DAB202           JC      DE6ERR     ; ABORT IF OVERFLOW
02A5 C38702           JMP     BI6DE1     ; ELSE GET ANOTHER DIGIT

02A8 37       BI6DE3: STC                ; NORMAL EXIT,
02A9 3F               CMC                ;  CLEAR CARRY
02AA EB       BI6DE4: XCHG               ; UPDATE BUFFER POINTER
02AB 22B902           SHLD    DIBPNT
02AE EB               XCHG
02AF D1               POP     D          ; RESTORE AND
02B0 C1               POP     B
02B1 C9               RET                ;  RETURN

02B2 21FFFF   DE6ERR: LXI     H,-1       ; OVERFLOW ERROR EXIT
02B5 37               STC
02B6 C3AA02           JMP     BI6DE4

              ; SET DIBPNT TO THE INPUT BUFFER TO BE PARSED

02B9          DIBPNT  DS      2          ; INPUT BUFFER POINTER
```

DECADD IS YOUR PROJECT

With only a minor change from hex to decimal inputting, it would be
overkill to include the listing of a decimal addition test program here.
Feel free to write your own. You shouldn't find that very difficult, after

all the nice structured assembly language programming tools you have just been handed.

I really wanted to say "CP/M assembly language . . ." in that last sentence, but since we have used only four BDOS I/O functions (three in BEGIN.LIB, one in CONBUFFI.LIB), it would be easy to adapt all of these software tools to any other operating system. If anyone would ever want any other OS, that is.

While you are writing and testing your own DECADD, try fixing the lack of overflow checking following the DAD instruction in both of the main programs: 65534 + 2 is not zero! You should also be able to dream up other, more practical uses for these I/O techniques. Just in case you can't, we will give you more ways to use them in the next two sections. We didn't do all this groundwork just for drill!

part 2

Disk mass storage

chapter 8

Floppy disks

The computer operator works with named files somehow magically stored automatically on disks. At the other extreme, the disk controller works with the physical disk address: DRIVE n HEAD p TRACK x SECTOR y. Separating the two stand CP/M, BDOS, and the CBIOS disk drivers working together to translate physical disk addresses into logical named files.

Some ancient disk operating systems required the operator to keep track of the the physical characteristics of disk mass storage. CP/M does this for us, fortunately, and it is a good thing, because modern floppy disks have a confusing proliferation of sizes and formats. Some even have format changes from track to track. Keeping track of these variations is not fit work for a human.

In this chapter we will look at the differences in floppy disk formats, how CP/M handles the differences, and how the operating system allocates and keeps track of disk space. We will develop some investigative subroutines and combine them into a test program that will illustrate these lessons. This programming can be the basis for future expansion into a more complete disk diagnostic program.

IN THE BEGINNING

When CP/M came into being, there was only one size and density of floppy disk, the 8-inch disk with 77 tracks containng 26 sectors each, with 128 bytes of data stored in each sector. As a result of this original format, the smallest unit of disk storage that CP/M is concerned with is the 128-byte logical record. Records are assembled into allocation blocks by the operating system, and it is not possible under CP/M to allocate disk storage space in increments of sectors or records. The minimum disk space that can be allocated to any file is the block, which contains multiples of eight records.

This is just as well, because the basic physical disk sector is no longer always the same size (128 bytes) as the logical record. Before we accuse anyone of foresight, that is not the reason that CP/M allocates disk space in blocks. After setting aside the first two tracks on the original 8-inch floppy for system storage, the remainder of the disk provides 243 K bytes of storage. By allocating that in 1 K byte blocks, a single 8-bit value can be used to address any one of those 243 blocks. That was the original CP/M scheme: disk space was allocated in 1 K byte blocks addressed by an 8-bit block number. The first two blocks (numbers 0 and 1) were reserved for disk directory storage, and the user could access blocks 2 up through 241.

MINIFLOPPY
AND MULTIDENSITY

Things were too simple. The advent of minifloppy disks with other physical format arrangements, and the appearance of multiple sides and densities on both sizes of floppy disks, soon overwhelmed the 8-bit block addressing scheme found in CP/M V1. Now, with versions 2 and up, disk space can be allocated in blocks of 1, 2, 4, 8 or 16 K bytes per block. For the larger capacities of disks, the blocks can be addressed by 16-bit numbers, so there can be lots of them.

Our experiences with different number bases in the previous chapter pointed up the desirability of keeping calculations simple when working with the 8080 instruction set, and CP/M V1 carried that to an extreme when performing the disk space allocations. The desirability of making the operating system easily adaptable to the proliferation of disk sizes and formats was the driving force behind the creation of version 2, and to accomplish this some tables of values that define the various disk formats were moved from BDOS in version one to the user-modifiable CBIOS in later versions. We will look at these disk parameter tables later in this chapter and in other chapters in this book. Meanwhile, we have to look at some of the other consequences of having many different disk formats and capacities available.

SECTORS, RECORDS,
AND BLOCKS

CP/M transfers data to and from the user in 128-byte records that are moved between the disk and the DMA buffer, which can appear anywhere in the computer's memory address space under user program control. These records are slices out of an allocation block that may consist of 8, 16 . . . 128 records (1 to 16 K bytes), depending on values set into the disk parameter table. Those values are determined when CP/M is installed in the computer system and can't be changed because they control the logical to physical mapping of the data stored on the disk.

These records and blocks are logical entities. Storage on disk is in physical sectors. Figure 8.1 illustrates the relationship between them and introduces a further complication resulting from those cases where the physical sector is greater than 128 bytes. To get from the disk sector to the user's record-sized DMA buffer, an intermediate sector-sized host buffer is introduced, and software must handle the record blocking and deblocking.

Figure 8.1 Record blocking and deblocking. This simplified diagram illustrates how a single disk sector containing four logical records must be buffered in a sector-sized host buffer in RAM. Individual records are then transferred to or from the destination DMA buffer elsewhere in the computer memory space. The disk shown in this example has 18 sectors per track, a sector skew of two, and a 2 K byte allocation block size.

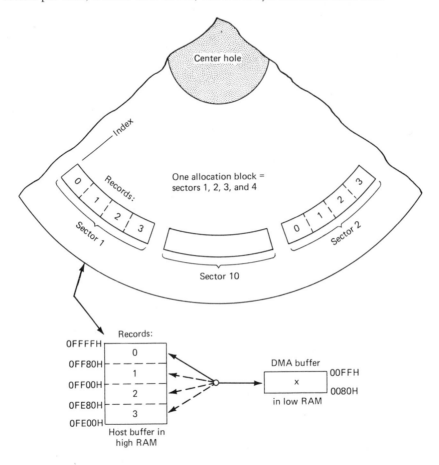

The example shown is for a disk that stores data in 512-byte sectors, 18 sectors per track, and incorporates an interleave, or skew factor, of two. This skew factor is used to speed up disk transfers, because it gives the computer time to work with sector 1 before sector 2 comes under the read-write head. Skews can range from zero up to one-half the number of sectors per track, with a skew factor of six being standard for our old 8-inch floppies. Once the skew has been established it will not be changed, because it affects the physical format of the disk.

Skew, sector size, sectors per track, tracks per disk side, and number of sides are physical attributes that don't often change once a computer system has been integrated, and now that we have seen examples, we won't have to be concerned with them very much in the future. What we as systems programmers must become expert in are the logical, programming aspects of disk storage that are affected by the physical attributes.

When the computer operator calls for a named program to be executed, or a user program performs a BDOS call requesting disk data to be read, CP/M in the person of BDOS and the CBIOS disk drivers will translate the request into information that the disk controller hardware can understand: "Give me track x sector y on the currently selected disk." The controller will then let the CBIOS driver know when the address field of the desired sector has been detected. The driver must then read the entire sector, one byte at a time, into the host buffer as the data passes under the disk drive read/write head, because the disk can't stop in the middle of a sector.

Record Deblocking

CP/M will request only one record at a time, and the disk can not deliver less than one sector, so the driver software has to buffer the sector, figure out which record to extract, and pass that record on to the DMA buffer. Once the sector has been buffered, subsequent CP/M requests for additional records contained in that sector can be supplied from the host buffer, with no need to read more disk data.

This process is known as record deblocking. In our example, one 512-byte sector is deblocked into four records. It is easy to see that if records are requested in sequence (the usual case), this operation can provide data faster than the case in which each sector contained only one record. But the cost is increased software complexity and the need to dedicate memory space for the host buffer.

Record Blocking

The picture is a little more complicated when writing to the disk. To provide a similar speed advantage, the DMA buffer is written into the appropriate record space in the host buffer with each call to the CBIOS WRITE entry point. To prevent data from being lost in case fewer than four records are written into the host buffer, the host buffer will have to be flushed (written to the disk) any time calls are received by the CBIOS SELDSK, SETTRK, or SETSEC entry points with an inappropriate selection. This is illustrated in the simplified flowchart of the record blocking/deblocking process, Figure 8.2.

Figure 8.2 Record blocking/deblocking flowchart. This flowchart illustrates the record blocking and deblocking problem in general terms. Disk access subroutines READ and WRITE can share much of the logic of the blocking/deblocking programming, with the particular original entry recorded in the read flag. Any host buffer contents that have been "dirtied" by a logical record write must be "flushed" (written to disk) before another sector can be read into the host buffer. The write flag controls this function.

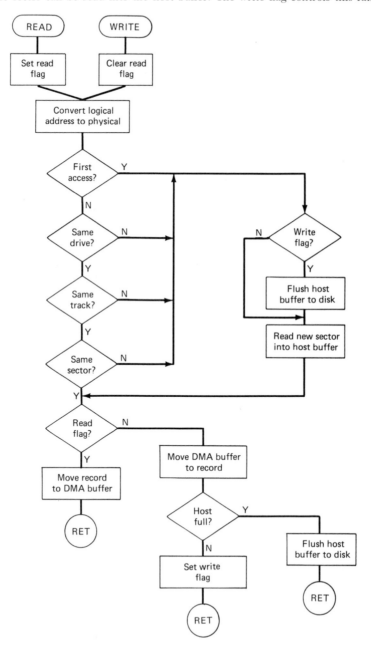

Since a lot of the code is identical for BDOS calls to the CBIOS READ and WRITE entries, either entry will begin with the setting of a flag that will keep track of whether this is a record read or a record write. Then the common code is entered at the section where the conversion is made from the logical record address to the appropriate physical sector address.

In the simplest case for which the flowchart applies, CP/M requests a record to be read from a sector that has been previously accessed. Since the new request is to the same drive, track, and sector as before, the flow is straight down through the five decision diamonds in the left column, and the appropriate record will be found in the host buffer.

If no previous access to this disk drive had been performed, or if a new drive, track, or sector was selected since the previous disk access, a new read into the host buffer will be required before the correct record can be found. If a write from the DMA buffer into the host buffer has been accomplished since the last disk access, and a new sector is addressed for either read or write, the existing host buffer will have to be written to the disk before the next sector can be moved from the disk into the host buffer for dissection.

All of these possibilities can be traced through the flowchart. Good old Digital Research has provided us with complete software algorithms for performing this sector blocking and deblocking, and we can incorporate their source code into our own CBIOS when it comes time to adapt new disk sizes and formats. This flowchart will give you a feel for what those algorithms have to accomplish. As you can imagine from examining this flowchart, the paths through those routines are not straightforward. However, we won't have to look at these procedures in more detail, now that we know the basic principles.

Meanwhile, don't forget that the "block" in "record blocking/ deblocking" does not refer to the allocation blocks themselves, but to the blocking of records into sectors. Someone else invented this conflicting nomenclature. Don't blame me! Let's take a closer look at allocation blocks right now, to clear up any confusion.

ALLOCATION BLOCKS

Getting away from the record blocking/deblocking that was forced upon us by the physical characteristics of our disks, we return to the subject of allocation blocks, which are an intrinsic part of the way CP/M handles disk storage.

Looking back at Figure 8.1, we can see that sectors 1 through 4 are combined into one allocation block, so we know that this example is a case of the 2 K byte-sized allocation block. Except for version 1, which we will ignore here since it is totally inflexible, CP/M permits just about any combination of disk formats and allocation block sizes within the wide limits specified in the *Alteration Guide*. The physical disk characteristics forced on us by the disk drive/controller combination and our selections of allocation block size and number of directory entries are all specified in the disk parameter tables in our CBIOS.

Since we have specified 2 K byte blocks in our example, let's see what that means in terms of disk allocation. When a named file is created by CP/M, one allocation block is initially assigned to the file and the lowest available block number is inserted into the first position in the allocation block address portion of the file control block (FCB). When we have written the sixteenth 128-byte record into the file, the first block is filled, and another block must be allocated to receive subsequent write data. This will continue until the file is closed, or all of the allocation block address positions in the FCB are filled.

Disk Directory FCB

As each FCB is filled, most of it will be written into the disk directory. The FCB in memory contains a disk selection byte (the first byte) and three optional random record number bytes tacked onto the end. The first byte will have a different function in the FCB image in the disk directory than it does in the FCB in memory, and the last three bytes in memory are not written into the directory. There are 32 bytes of data in each directory image of the FCB, so there will be four directory entries in each 128-byte directory record.

If a file requires more space than can be addressed by the block numbers in one directory entry, additional extensions to the directory FCB image will be created to hold subsequent block numbers. The extension will be flagged by a number greater than zero in the extent number byte in the FCB.

If our disk holds no more than 255 blocks (510 K bytes in our 2 K byte block example) we can address each block with an 8-bit block number. An example of just such a directory record is shown in Figure 8.3(a), where the blocks assigned to PIP.COM are numbered 01, 02, 03, and 04 (block zero is the directory). The first directory entry is a special case, a zero-length "file" used for disk cataloging. Its file name exists in the directory, but it has no blocks assigned to it because the record count byte (the last byte in the first row) is zero.

Figure 8.3 Disk directory entries. The file control blocks as recorded in the disk directory have been dumped in hexadecimal, with ASCII equivalents shown in the right-hand column. Each directory record contains four file entries. The dump of the first directory record (a) shows 8-bit allocation block addresses, while a different CP/M installation produces 16-bit block addresses (b). The second system could not read the directory of a disk written by the first, and vice versa.

```
                DRIVE A:     TRACK 3    SECTOR 1

0000 00 2D 31 30 2D 32 39 2D  31 30 35 37 00 00 00 00  .-10-29- 1057....
0010 00 00 00 00 00 00 00 00  00 00 00 00 00 00 00 00  ........ ........
0020 00 50 49 50 20 20 20 20  20 43 4F 4D 00 00 00 34  .PIP     COM...:
0030 01 02 03 04 00 00 00 00  00 00 00 00 00 00 00 00  ........ ........
0040 00 42 49 47 46 49 4C 45  20 43 4F 4D 01 00 00 80  .BIGFILE COM....
0050 05 06 07 08 09 0A 0B 0C  0D 0E 0F 10 11 12 13 14  ........ ........
0060 00 42 49 47 46 49 4C 45  20 43 4F 4D 02 00 00 20  .BIGFILE COM...
0070 15 16 00 00 00 00 00 00  00 00 00 00 00 00 00 00  ........ ........
```

(a)

```
                DRIVE A:     TRACK 3    SECTOR 1

0000 00 2D 31 30 2D 32 39 2D  32 30 35 38 00 00 00 00  .-10-29- 2058....
0010 00 00 00 00 00 00 00 00  00 00 00 00 00 00 00 00  ........ ........
0020 00 50 49 50 20 20 20 20  20 43 4F 4D 00 00 00 3A  .PIP     COM...:
0030 01 00 02 00 03 00 04 00  00 00 00 00 00 00 00 00  ........ ........
0040 00 42 49 47 46 49 4C 45  20 43 4F 4D 00 00 00 80  .BIGFILE COM....
0050 05 00 06 00 07 00 08 00  09 00 0A 00 0B 00 0C 00  ........ ........
0060 00 42 49 47 46 49 4C 45  20 43 4F 4D 01 00 00 80  .BIGFILE COM....
0070 0D 00 0E 00 0F 00 10 00  11 00 12 00 13 00 14 00  ........ ........
```

(b)

The third directory entry is an example of a file that was larger than would fit into a single extent, so it has two FCBs recorded in the directory with the extent byte of the first entry flagged with a one, and the final, unfilled extent is numbered two. More extents can be opened if the file grows even larger. Because there is room in each directory entry FCB for 16 block addresses using 8-bit block numbers, extents zero and one both fit into the first BIGFILE.COM directory entry. Note that PIP.COM has its extent byte equal to zero because it fills less than the first extent.

If the disk can hold more data than can be addressed by 8-bit block numbers, CP/M will automatically use 16-bit block numbers, as is shown in Figure 8.3(b). Note for the future that there is no explicit Disk Parameter Table entry that you can use to tell CP/M that you want 16-bit block numbers. It will make up its mind on the basis of the size of the blocks and the number of blocks that the disk can hold. In Figure 8.3(b) each directory entry has room for only eight 16-block numbers, so each entry contains only one extent, and we will need more entries to hold all the block addresses for BIGFILE.COM.

Given a particular track and sector format on the disk, as we have here, a given numbered block will occupy the same place on the disk in either case. Since the directories in Figure 8.3(a) and (b) look different in the areas devoted to block numbers, even though the block numbers are the same and will exist at the same places on both disks, the disks are not interchangeable between the two slightly different CP/M installations that produced them. The CP/M installed in case (a) would get lost trying to find the blocks addressed by the 16-bit entries shown in case (b), and vice versa. Just one little incompatibility that can trip up the unwary program pirate!

Whenever a file is erased, the first byte in its directory FCB (all zeros in Figure 8.3) will be set to 0E5H, which is the bit pattern written throughout a new disk when it is first formatted. By recognizing 0E5H as an erased file, a new disk will appear to CP/M as a disk with all files erased, and no initializing will be necessary. When a file has been erased, the next time CP/M needs a disk block to allocate, it will use the block numbers in the erased FCB(s). When a new directory FCB entry is needed, the old one will be overwritten.

DISK PARAMETER TABLES

Using the previous examples of disk formats, we have just seen that CP/M can be adapted to different sizes and formats of floppy disks. Mention has been made of the disk parameter tables that were fixed in CP/M V1 but have been made user-modifiable in versions 2 and up. A detailed discussion of the tables and how to set them up would be out of place in this chapter, but we will take a quick look at the table that contains the specifications for the disk drives and then write a program that accesses that table and displays the allocation vector that stores a map of the blocks in use on each disk.

A Simple Little System

The Digital Research manuals contain lots of examples using the old 8-inch, single-density floppy disk, so we should pick a different example for this discussion. Our last example that included record blocking might complicate the following discussion, so we will abandon that example for now and use a real-life computer that has been around for a while: the computer that was used to prepare the text of this book.

This will be a good example because the system has two unequal minifloppy disk drives: one 80-track drive and one 40-track. The record blocking and deblocking routines are holdovers from CP/M 1.4 days and are not integrated into CBIOS in the usual 2.2 manner, so while the disks actually record ten 256-byte sectors per track, to CP/M their track format looks like 20 sectors of 128 bytes each.

To provide enough disk space for recording the CP/M disk bootstrap loader and the operating system image, it was necessary to reserve three system tracks, so the 80-track drive provides 77 tracks × 20 sectors × 128 bytes or 192.5 K bytes of usable storage, and the 40-track drive holds 37 × 20 × 128 = 92.5 K bytes. (Remember that one K byte equals 1024.)

We already know that CP/M cannot allocate disk space in less than 1 K byte blocks, so 0.5 K bytes of disk space way out on the last track on each disk is wasted. This is often the case; it was so on the original 8-inch floppy. Figure that one out yourself.

Disk Parameter Block

The part of the disk parameter tables that holds the disk format information is the DPB, and there will be one for each different disk drive. Table 8.1(a) is the source code for the 80-track disk as found in the CP/M 2.2 CBIOS, and (b) is the table for the 40-track. Right at the top a simple-to-understand entry is made for the Sectors Per Track (SPT), but following this are three values (BSH, BLM, EXM) that can only be understood by BDOS. We determine the values required for them from tables in the DRI manuals. The three numbers define the block size and tell CP/M whether there will be more than 255 blocks on the disk.

Since assembly language programmers like to count up from zero, instead of one like real people do, we next enter a value for the maximum block number, DSM (192 − 1), and the maximum directory entry, DRM (64 − 1). Depending on the size of most of your files, it might be better to have 128 directory entries on a floppy disk. If DRM were set to 127, CP/M would then allocate twice as many blocks for the directory. Since each directory FCB takes 32 bytes, a 64-entry directory fills up 2 K bytes, and 128 entries would require 4 K bytes.

Our simple little example system uses 1 K byte blocks, so the directory will have to reserve two of them (blocks 0 and 1), and our named files will begin with block number 2. The next two table entries are the 2-byte directory **AL**location vector (AL0 and AL1), which maps the blocks dedicated to the directory. We set up the allocation vector by entering two 1-byte values, 0C0H and 0. In binary this would look like:

11000000 00000000

telling BDOS that the first two blocks are dedicated for directory use.

```
DPB1:
  SPT:    DW     20        ; SECTORS/TRACK
  BSH:    DB      3        ; BLOCK SHIFT FACTOR
  BLM:    DB      7        ; BLOCK MASK
  EXM:    DB      0        ; EXTENT MASK
  DSM:    DW    191        ; DISK SIZE MAXIMUM
  DRM:    DW     63        ; DIRECTORY MAXIMUM
  AL0:    DB   0C0H        ; DIRECTORY ALLOCATION BYTE 0
  AL1:    DB      0        ; DIRECTORY ALLOCATION BYTE 1
  CKS:    DW     16        ; DIRECTORY CHECK VECTOR SIZE
  OFF:    DW      3        ; OFFSET FOR SYSTEM TRACKS
```

(a)

```
DPB2:
  SPT:    DW     20        ; SECTORS/TRACK
  BSH:    DB      3        ; BLOCK SHIFT FACTOR
  BLM:    DB      7        ; BLOCK MASK
  EXM:    DB      0        ; EXTENT MASK
  DSM:    DW     91        ; DISK SIZE MAXIMUM
  DRM:    DW     63        ; DIRECTORY MAXIMUM
  AL0:    DB   0C0H        ; DIRECTORY ALLOCATION BYTE 0
  AL1:    DB      0        ; DIRECTORY ALLOCATION BYTE 1
  CKS:    DW     16        ; DIRECTORY CHECK VECTOR SIZE
  OFF:    DW      3        ; OFFSET FOR SYSTEM TRACKS
```

(b)

```
DPB1:
  SPT:    DW     20        ; SECTORS/TRACK
  BSH:    DB      4        ; BLOCK SHIFT FACTOR
  BLM:    DB     15        ; BLOCK MASK
  EXM:    DB      1        ; EXTENT MASK
  DSM:    DW     95        ; DISK SIZE MAXIMUM
  DRM:    DW     63        ; DIRECTORY MAXIMUM
  AL0:    DB   0C0H        ; DIRECTORY ALLOCATION BYTE 0
  AL1:    DB      0        ; DIRECTORY ALLOCATION BYTE 1
  CKS:    DW     16        ; DIRECTORY CHECK VECTOR SIZE
  OFF:    DW      3        ; OFFSET FOR SYSTEM TRACKS
```

(c)

Table 8.1 Example Disk Parameter Blocks. DPBs are for an 80-track minifloppy disk (a) and a 40-track minifloppy (b), both using 1 K byte allocation blocks. The DPB shown in (c) is for the same disk as (a) but with allocation blocks changed to 2 K bytes. CP/M versions 2 and greater permit mixing different sizes and configurations of disks within a single computer installation.

Note that there can never be more than 16 blocks dedicated for directory space, no matter how large the disk.

For floppy disks, we will seldom need more than two blocks for the directory. Double-side, double-density disks will have to use larger allocation block sizes anyway, and with 32 directory entries per K byte, a couple of 2 K byte blocks would provide 128 entries. Four would permit 512, which is a lot of files to stick on one floppy disk!

Removable Directories

Since floppy disks can be removed from their drives, CP/M will want to check the disk before writing onto it to make sure it hasn't been swapped inadvertently. You are probably familiar with the error message you get if you try to write to a changed disk:

    Bdos Err On A: R/O

telling you that is a no-no. The CKS table entry is another coded value determined by the system integration programmer from an equation in the DRI manuals, and it is used by BDOS to decide how much of the directory to check to determine if some dummy has changed the disk since the last warm boot.

ALLOCATION VECTORS

The reason CP/M is so finicky about writing on a changed disk is that the first time any disk is accessed following system cold or warm bootup, the disk directory is searched by BDOS and a map of all the allocation blocks is built up in the computer's RAM in another table, the disk **AL**location **V**ector (ALV). There is one ALV for each disk drive. Its contents look just like that for the directory allocation vector, but of course it is much bigger: one bit for each block on the disk.

When BDOS reads the directory that first time, each block that has been assigned to a file will have its corresponding bit in the ALV set to a one. Erasing a file will return the bit to a zero. When BDOS needs to assign more disk space, it does not have to reread the whole directory; it uses the ALV disk block map to pick out the lowest-numbered block to assign next. This is why you can't change disks at random. The disk map must agree with the directory entries, or BDOS would try to write over a block that contains valuable data, and you wouldn't want it to do that!

Although the directory allocation vector is fixed once the DPB has been set up, the disk ALV is constantly changing as files are written and deleted. To take a peek at what the ALV looks like, we will have to write a program to do that in real time, so you can run it on your own computer. After all this theoretical background, you are probably ready to get started writing. Before we can do that, however, let's take a quick look at some maps and see how they relate to what STAT tells us about our disk formats.

THE DISK MAP

Figure 8.4 shows displays that result from running the test program for this chapter on the simple little computer system described above. There are three subroutines you will be constructing. One selects the disk named in the command line, the next displays the block and disk size, and the last displays a map of the allocation vector for that disk.

The first map shown is for the 80-track drive A:, and the second is for the 40-track drive B:. Blocks that are currently assigned to files are marked with "1" and unallocated blocks are marked "0." These quick snapshots of the ALVs show where disk space is available. The zeros surrounded by ones indicate where files have been erased.

To provide you with flexible subroutines that can be used in other diagnostic programs, these displays have been broken down into the three components mentioned above. To further illustrate how to parse a command input line, the commands to invoke the test program require that you specify the drive to map ("A:" or "B:" in these examples), and you also have to include a command number: 0, 1, or 2.

A command of "0" only selects the disk. A command of "1" selects the disk and shows the sizes. A command of "2" gives the complete display as shown in Figure 8.4. We will discuss the program itself and how it parses the input line later on.

Maps, DPBs, and STAT

Figure 8.4(a) and (b) map the disks as defined in the DPBs shown in Table 8.1(a) and (b). The STAT DSK: command produces the corresponding displays shown in Figure 8.5(a) and (b). Studying all of these together will help you integrate your understanding of the use of the DPBs and ALVs. You might notice that our own disk size displays are easier to interpret than those provided by STAT DSK:.

Figure 8.4 Console disk map displays. These are displays that result from running the Chapter 8 test program on the disk configurations shown in Table 8.1. The displays (a), (b), and (c) correspond to the table DPBs (a), (b), and (c). The command line parameter "2" produces the complete displays shown, including the bit map of the disk allocation vectors.

```
A TESTC8 A: 2

Show disk sizes      15 Mar 84

SELECTED:    A:
EACH BLOCK:     1 K BYTES
DISK SIZE:    192 K BYTES

                  DISK MAP:

      11111111 11111111 11111111 11111111
      11111111 11111111 11111111 11111111
      11111111 11100011 11000001 11101111
      10010000 01100000 00000000 11110111
      10100011 11110000 00001110 00000000
      00000000 00000000 00000000 00000000

                     (a)

A TESTC8 B: 2

Show disk sizes      15 Mar 84

SELECTED:    B:
EACH BLOCK:     1 K BYTES
DISK SIZE:     92 K BYTES

                  DISK MAP:

      11111111 11111111 11111111 11111111
      11111111 11111111 11011111 11111100
      00111111 11111111 11111110 0000

                     (b)

A TESTC8 A: 2

Show disk sizes      15 Mar 84

SELECTED:    A:
EACH BLOCK:     2 K BYTES
DISK SIZE:    192 K BYTES

                  DISK MAP:

      11111111 11111111 11111111 11111111
      11111101 10011111 11001100 00001111
      11011100 00110000 00000000 00000000

                     (c)
```

Figure 8.5 Console STAT DSK: displays. These three displays correspond to the three disk configurations shown in Figure 8.4 and Table 8.1. The STAT program provides more information than TESTC8, but the test program includes a direct display of allocation block size.

```
A STAT DSK:

      A: Drive Characteristics
   1536: 128 Byte Record Capacity
    192: Kilobyte Drive Capacity
     64: 32  Byte Directory Entries
     64: Checked  Directory Entries
    128: Records/ Extent
      8: Records/ Block
     20: Sectors/ Track
      3: Reserved Tracks

                 (a)


A STAT B:DSK:

      B: Drive Characteristics
    736: 128 Byte Record Capacity
     92: Kilobyte Drive Capacity
     64: 32  Byte Directory Entries
     64: Checked  Directory Entries
    128: Records/ Extent
      8: Records/ Block
     20: Sectors/ Track
      3: Reserved Tracks

                 (b)


A STAT DSK:

      A: Drive Characteristics
   1536: 128 Byte Record Capacity
    192: Kilobyte Drive Capacity
     64: 32  Byte Directory Entries
     64: Checked  Directory Entries
    256: Records/ Extent
     16: Records/ Block
     20: Sectors/ Track
      3: Reserved Tracks

                 (c)
```

To illustrate how flexible the disk parameter tables used in CP/M versions 2 and up are, we have temporarily changed the 80-track drive A: from 1 K byte blocks to 2 K byte blocks by incorporating the DPB shown in Table 8.1(c), while leaving drive B: unchanged. Now you can see from the map (Figure 8.4(c)) and the STAT display (Figure 8.5(c)) that CP/M will allow you to mix disk sizes and formats any way you can imagine. All you need to know is how. These lessons should provide you with the ability to take advantage of all of the power of CP/M.

DISPLAYING THE DISK MAP

When we input the command line shown at the top of Figure 8.4, CCP knows that we want to invoke the program named TESTC8.COM from the current drive. CCP will also check the rest of the input line (the command line "tail") and will provide us with an image of it in the default transient buffer at location 80H. CCP will also assume that, if any entries follow the program name, they will probably be the names of other disk files.

Selecting a Disk

Since the first entry in the command line tail is a valid disk designator of "A" through "P" followed by a colon, CCP will set the appropriate disk drive code into the first byte of the default transient file control block (TFCB), because it knows we want to reference that disk. If we follow the disk designator immediately with a file name, as in "A:BIGFILE.COM," CCP would fill in the rest of the top line of the TFCB (first 16 bytes) with the file name in the proper FCB format.

We didn't include a file name, but we did add a space and another entry to the command line tail. This is not a valid drive designator (no colon), so CCP will stuff that entry into the second byte of the second half of the TFCB, and it is up to us to move it to another complete FCB image if it is the name of another file.

Decoding a Command

In this case, the second entry is a command number, not a file name, and our program knows that the first entry will be only a disk drive designator. This means that we will not be making any use of the TFCB as a file control block, so we don't have to move the second entry out of the way of block numbers that BDOS would insert in that space if we opened a file for read or write.

What CCP has provided for us, then, is the TFCB set up with the decoded drive designator in the first byte, and the command character in the second byte of the second line of the TFCB, at TFCB + 17. After

all this is set up for us by CCP, our program, TESTC8.COM, will be
loaded into the TPA and executed.

A Tiny Main Program

TESTC8.ASM will, of course, start with a properly edited version of
BEGIN.LIB. Next will come TESTC8.LIB, Listing 8.1. All we will do
here is extract the command number, in ASCII, from the TFCB second
line. We then subtract the ASCII for zero to convert the command to an
8-bit integer: 0, 1, or 2 in the A register.

Listing 8-1

```
; MODULE NAME: TESTC8.LIB
; LAST UPDATE: 15 MAR 84    BY: KMB
; FUNCTION: TEST SHOWDISK SUBROUTINES
; REQUIRES: SHOWDISK.LIB, SHOWNUMB.LIB, BEGIN.LIB
;===============================================================

0200 3A6D00          LDA     TFCB+17    ; GET COMMAND NUMBER
0203 D630            SUI     '0'        ; NORMALIZE TO ZERO
0205 CD0B02          CALL    DSHOW      ; EXECUTE THE COMMAND
0208 C38B01          JMP     DONE       ; AND ALL DONE
```

The actual decoding of the command number will be accomplished
in our first subroutine, DSHOW:. Usually, the main program would
perform this function, but it was decided to move the decoding into a
subroutine in order to make that subroutine and the ones that do the
actual displaying more usable in other diagnostic programs.

An Executive Subroutine

DSHOW: (Listing 8.2) actually executes the command by calling
DLOGI: (A = 0), or DLOGI: followed by DSIZE: (A = 1), or DLOGI:,
DSIZE:, and DMAP: if the A register contains 2 or more. All of the
other registers are saved and restored at the subroutine entry and exit.
This is not necessary within TESTC8, but might be if any of these
subroutines are used in other programs. This is consistent with our
established practice.

Listing 8-2

```
              ; MODULE NAME: SHOWDISK.LIB
              ; LAST UPDATE: 13 MAR 84      BY: KMB
              ; FUNCTION: SHOW SELECTED DISK, SIZE, AND MAP
              ; REQUIRES: SHOWNUMB.LIB, BEGIN.LIB
              ;============================================================
              ;
              ; ENTER DSHOW: WITH THE DRIVE TO BE SELECTED IN TFCB
              ;                        (0= CURRENT, 1=A:,....16=P:)
              ;                  WITH A = 0 TO SELECT DISK
              ;                         = 1 TO SELECT AND SHOW SIZE
              ;                         = 2 TO SELECT, SHOW SIZE, AND MAP

000C =        VERSF    EQU      12            ; TEST CP/M VERSION
000E =        DSELF    EQU      14            ; SELECT DISK FUNCTION
0019 =        GCURF    EQU      25            ; GET CURRENT DRIVE
001B =        GALVF    EQU      27            ; GET ALLOC. VECTOR ADRS
001F =        GDPBF    EQU      31            ; GET DPB ADDRESS

005C =        TFCB     EQU      5CH           ; TRANSIENT FCB

020B C5       DSHOW:   PUSH     B             ; SAVE ALL
020C D5                PUSH     D
020D E5                PUSH     H
020E F5                PUSH     PSW           ; SAVE COMMAND
020F CD2702            CALL     DLOGI         ; SELECT AND LOG IN
0212 F1                POP      PSW           ; MORE TO DO?
0213 3D                DCR      A
0214 FA2302            JM       DEXIT         ; QUIT HERE OR
0217 F5                PUSH     PSW
0218 CD5E02            CALL     DSIZE         ;   SHOW BLOCK & DISK SIZE
021B F1                POP      PSW           ; MORE TO DO?
021C 3D                DCR      A
021D FA2302            JM       DEXIT         ; QUIT HERE OR
0220 CD1803            CALL     DMAP          ;   SHOW DISK MAP
0223 E1       DEXIT:   POP      H             ; RESTORE ALL
0224 D1                POP      D
0225 C1                POP      B
0226 C9                RET
```

Disk Log-in

CCP leaves the byte at TFCB set to zero for the "current" disk drive, or
1 for A:, 2 for B:, etc. Our program has no way of knowing what drive it
was invoked from. We may have been working with B: or any other
drive as the current drive. So DLOGI: tests for zero in TFCB and
fetches the current drive number by a call to BDOS (GCURF function)
if necessary. Otherwise, the drive specified is selected (DSELF function).

Listing 8-3

```
                      ; SELECT (LOG IN) DISK AND SHOW IT
                      ; DISK TO BE SELECTED IS DEFINED IN THE TRANSIENT FCB

0227 3A5C00   DLOGI:  LDA    TFCB            ; GET DISK TO SELECT
022A 3D               DCR    A               ; NORMALIZE TO A: = 0
022B F23302           JP     DLOG1           ;   AND -1 = CURRENT DISK
022E 0E19             MVI    C,GCURF         ; GET CURRENT DRIVE
0230 CD0500           CALL   BDOS            ;   INTO A
0233 F5       DLOG1:  PUSH   PSW             ; SAVE DRIVE TO SELECT
0234 5F               MOV    E,A             ;   AND SELECT IT
0235 0E0E             MVI    C,DSELF
0237 CD0500           CALL   BDOS
023A CD5701           CALL   CCRLF
023D CD4801           CALL   SPMSG           ; SHOW SELECTION
0240 53454C4543       DB     'SELECTED:   ',0
024D F1               POP    PSW             ; GET THE SELECTION
024E C641             ADI    'A'             ; CONVERT TO ASCII
0250 E67F             ANI    7FH             ;   LIMIT 7 BITS
0252 CD5E01           CALL   CO              ; SHOW THE DRIVE
0255 3E3A             MVI    A,':'           ;   AND A COLON
0257 CD5E01           CALL   CO
025A CD5701           CALL   CCRLF           ; START A NEW LINE
025D C9               RET
```

When a disk is selected by this BDOS call, it is logged into the list of active disks maintained by BDOS, its directory is read, and its ALV is updated to show the current status of all of its allocation blocks. This, obviously, is necessary before we can display the map.

Since DLOGI: is a diagnostic subroutine, we display a line showing that the selection has been made. Disk selections made within the normal course of program execution are not displayed, because this would make for a very cluttered CON: screen. You have to keep looking at the little lights on the drives if you want to see what drives are being selected, normally.

Showing Disk Sizes

DSIZE: will look into the Disk Parameter Block, figure out how big each disk allocation block is, and how many bytes of usable storage the disk provides. You will note from Table 8.1 that neither of these values is explicitly stated in the DPB. So we have to do some decoding and calculating in this subroutine.

Before we can begin, we have to test for CP/M version number. Since CP/M V1 did not provide DPBs in the CBIOS, we have to cheat here and find the corresponding values embedded within BDOS. DSIZ1: finds the start address of V1.4 BDOS by looking at the address

Listing 8-4

```
                 ; SHOW DISK BLOCK SIZE AND TOTAL CAPACITY
                 ;    FOR THE LAST SELECTED DISK

025E 0E0C        DSIZE:  MVI     C,VERSF      ; CHECK CP/M VERSION
0260 CD0500              CALL    BDOS
0263 7C                  MOV     A,H          ; FILTER OUT MP/M
0264 B7                  ORA     A
0265 C2F702              JNZ     SIZERR       ; SHOW UNABLE TO SHOW
0268 7D                  MOV     A,L
0269 B7                  ORA     A            ; CHECK FOR VERSION 1
026A C28202              JNZ     DSIZ2        ;   ELSE GET 2.2 SIZE

                 ; GET VERSION 1 BLOCK AND DISK SIZE

026D 2A0600      DSIZ1:  LHLD    BDOS+1       ; GET BDOS ENTRY ADDRESS
0270 7D                  MOV     A,L          ; CHECK FOR POSSIBLE RSX
0271 FE06                CPI     6
0273 C2F702              JNZ     SIZERR       ; COULD BE DDT, QUIT
0276 C636                ADI     36H          ; ADD OFFSET TO VERSION 1
0278 6F                  MOV     L,A          ;   DPB BLOCK SHIFT FACTOR
0279 4E                  MOV     C,M          ; GET BSH INTO C
027A 23                  INX     H            ; POINT AHEAD TO DISK SIZE
027B 23                  INX     H
027C 5E                  MOV     E,M          ; GET DSM INTO D,E
027D 1600                MVI     D,0          ;   ONLY 8 BITS IN VERSION 1
027F C39002              JMP     DSIZ3        ; NOW SHOW SIZES

                 ; GET VERSION 2 OR 3 BLOCK AND DISK SIZE

0282 0E1F        DSIZ2:  MVI     C,GDPBF      ; GET DISK PARAMETER
0284 CD0500              CALL    BDOS         ;   BLOCK ADDRESS
0287 23                  INX     H
0288 23                  INX     H            ; POINT TO BSH
0289 4E                  MOV     C,M          ;   AND GET IT
028A 23                  INX     H
028B 23                  INX     H
028C 23                  INX     H            ; POINT TO DSM
028D 5E                  MOV     E,M          ;   WHICH CAN BE 16 BITS
028E 23                  INX     H            ;    IN THESE VERSIONS
028F 56                  MOV     D,M

                 ; SHOW THE BLOCK SIZE

0290 79          DSIZ3:  MOV     A,C          ; GET BSH = 3 THROUGH 7
0291 D603                SUI     3            ;   MAKE IT 0 THROUGH 4
0293 4F                  MOV     C,A          ;    PUT IT BACK
0294 AF                  XRA     A            ; START AT ONE
0295 37                  STC                  ;   (IN CARRY BIT)
0296 17          DSIZ4:  RAL                  ; SHIFT A LEFT THRU CARRY
0297 0D                  DCR     C            ;   BSH-3 TIMES
0298 F29602              JP      DSIZ4        ; FOR 1, 2, 4, 8, 16 K/BLOCK
029B 4F                  MOV     C,A          ; SAVE RESULT
029C CD4801              CALL    SPMSG        ; SHOW THE MESSAGE
029F 4541434820          DB      'EACH BLOCK: ',0
02AC 79                  MOV     A,C          ; BLOCK SIZE IS IN C
02AD CDAB03              CALL    CO8DEC       ; SHOW THE BLOCK SIZE
02B0 CD4801              CALL    SPMSG
02B3 204B204259          DB      ' K BYTES',0
02BC CD5701              CALL    CCRLF
```

field of the BDOS call vector always found at location 5. If an RSX, such as DDT, is in operation, we can't find BDOS, and have to abort to SIZERR: (Listing 8.5). Otherwise, we get the address of BDOS and fetch BSH into register C, and DSM into register pair DE. Since V1.4 is limited to 255 blocks per disk, register D will always be set to zero.

Since the Digital Research manuals for CP/M version 1 didn't document the disk parameter tables, investigators have had to poke into BDOS and discover where to find the values that we need here. Such poking can discover valuable trade secrets, and we couldn't disclose these addresses here if DRI hadn't later made them public domain knowledge by virtue of the documentation for version 2.

Show the Block Size

CP/M version 2 provides a BDOS call (GDPBF) that returns the start address of the DPB for the last selected disk, and DSIZ2: fetches BSH and DSM into C and DE, so that the actual block size and disk size calculations will be the same for 1.4 or 2.2 when DSIZ3: is finally entered. A look at the DRI manuals discloses that BSH encodes the block size options:

BSH	BLOCK SIZE
3	1 K bytes
4	2 K "
5	4 K "
6	8 K "
7	16 K "

so all we have to do is normalize C by subtracting 3, then shift a one bit in A left one bit for each remaining count in C. Then a call to our 8-bit decimal display subroutine CO8DEC: (remember?) will show the block size that could have been included in the DPB in a more understandable format in the first place.

Show the Disk Capacity

We fall right out of the bottom of Listing 8.4 into Listing 8.5 (the pair constitutes subroutine DSIZE:) to display the total capacity of the disk, after the reserved system tracks are subtracted. We know that this number is stored in the DPB in **D**isk **S**ize **M**aximum (DSM) in units of the allocation block size, so we had to compute the block size first anyway.

Listing 8-5

```
                     ; SHOW THE DISK SIZE (D,E = SIZE IN BLOCKS-1)
                     ;                    (  C = BLOCK SIZE IN K BYTES)
02BF 210000              LXI    H,0             ; CLEAR 16-BIT ACCUMULATOR
02C2 0600                MVI    B,0             ;  AND BLOCK SIZE MS BYTE
02C4 13                  INX    D               ; START AT 1, NOT ZERO
02C5 EB                  XCHG                   ;; STORE DISK SIZE IN BLOCKS
02C6 227003              SHLD   BLOKS           ;  FOR FUTURE USE
02C9 EB                  XCHG                   ;  PUT IT BACK IN D,E
02CA 09        DSIZ5:    DAD    B               ; ADD BLOCK SIZE TO H,L
02CB DAF702              JC     SIZERR          ;  ABORT IF .GT. 65 M BYTES
02CE 1B                  DCX    D               ;  DECREMENT "MULTIPLIER"
02CF 7B                  MOV    A,E             ;   AND TEST IT FOR ZERO
02D0 B2                  ORA    D
02D1 C2CA02              JNZ    DSIZ5           ; COUNTING IN H,L UNTIL DONE
02D4 CD4801              CALL   SPMSG           ; SHOW THE MESSAGE
02D7 4449534B20          DB     'DISK SIZE:  ',0
02E4 CDB203              CALL   CO6DEC          ; SHOW THE DISK SIZE
02E7 CD4801              CALL   SPMSG
02EA 204B204259          DB     ' K BYTES',0
02F3 CD5701              CALL   CCRLF
02F6 C9                  RET

02F7 CD5701    SIZERR:   CALL   CCRLF
02FA CD4801              CALL   SPMSG           ; SHOW UNABLE TO SHOW
02FD 554E41424C          DB     'UNABLE TO COMPUTE SIZE',0
0314 CD5701              CALL   CCRLF
0317 C9                  RET
```

With the block size in register C and the number of blocks in DE, all we have to do is multiply to figure out the total capacity of the disk. We multiply in 8080 assembly language by successive adds into the 16-bit accumulator (HL) while counting down the multiplier in C. Our 16-bit limit is 65,535, so if the disk provides more than 65 M bytes we can't show it, or even figure out where you got one that big!

Obviously, these subroutines can be used with large capacity hard disks as well as the floppies we are working with in these examples. But you may not want to display the whole disk map of a large hard disk. That would be a lot of ones and zeros.

Show the Map

Subroutine DMAP: in Listing 8.6 is all that is needed to make the pretty picture of the allocation vector. After displaying a centered header, it calls BDOS to get the address of the ALV for the last selected disk (GALVF function). There is no flag at the end of ALV to let us know when we are done, so we have to count the total number of blocks as we display each "1" or "0" in the map.

Listing 8-6

```
            ; SHOW THE ALLOCATION VECTOR DISK MAP
            ;   FOR THE LAST SELECTED DISK
            ; EXPECTS TO FIND # OF BLOCKS AS 2 BYTES IN "BLOKS"

0318 CD5701    DMAP:   CALL    CCRLF       ; DROP DOWN A LINE
031B 3E16              MVI     A,22        ; CENTER HEADER
031D CD6B01            CALL    SPACES
0320 CD4801            CALL    SPMSG       ; SHOW MAPPING DISK
0323 4449534B20        DB      'DISK MAP:',0
032D CD5401            CALL    TWOCR
0330 0E1B              MVI     C,GALVF     ; GET ALLOC VECTOR ADRS
0332 CD0500            CALL    BDOS        ;   INTO H,L
0335 EB                XCHG                ; TO D,E TEMPORARILY
0336 2A7003            LHLD    BLOKS       ; GET TOTAL NUMBER OF
0339 EB                XCHG                ;   BLOCKS ON DISK INTO D,E
033A 0604      LINE:   MVI     B,4         ; COUNT BLOCKS OF BLOCKS
033C 3E0A              MVI     A,10        ;   ON EACH LINE
033E CD6B01            CALL    SPACES      ; SPACE OVER
0341 0E08      BYTE:   MVI     C,8         ; COUNT BITS PER BYTE
0343 7E                MOV     A,M         ; GET AN ALLOCATION BYTE
0344 23                INX     H           ;   UP INDEX TO NEXT
0345 17       BYTE1:   RAL                 ; SHIFT BIT INTO CARRY
0346 F5                PUSH    PSW         ; SAVE THE REST
0347 3E30              MVI     A,'0'       ; SHOW A ZERO OR
0349 D24E03            JNC     BIT         ;   IF NOT ZERO
034C 3E31              MVI     A,'1'       ;     SHOW A ONE
034E CD5E01    BIT:    CALL    CO
0351 1B                DCX     D           ; COUNT THE ALLOCATION BLOCK
0352 7B                MOV     A,E
0353 B2                ORA     D           ;   UNTIL ZERO,
0354 CA6B03            JZ      DMAPX       ;     THEN EXIT
0357 F1                POP     PSW         ; RESTORE THE BYTE
0358 0D                DCR     C           ; COUNT THE BIT
0359 C24503            JNZ     BYTE1       ; AND SHOW MORE, OR
035C 3E20              MVI     A,' '       ;   SPACE OVER
035E CD5E01            CALL    CO
0361 05                DCR     B           ; COUNT THE BLOCKS OF BLOCKS
0362 C24103            JNZ     BYTE        ;   TIL THE END OF LINE
0365 CD5701            CALL    CCRLF       ; START A NEW LINE
0368 C33A03            JMP     LINE
036B F1       DMAPX:   POP     PSW         ; KILL LAST PUSH
036C CD5701            CALL    CCRLF       ;   AND ALL DONE
036F C9                RET

0370 0000      BLOKS   DW      0           ; STORE BLOCKS PER DISK
```

We couldn't pass the total number of blocks from DSIZE: to DMAP: in a register because we ran out of registers again. So we stored the number in BLOKS immediately before DSIZ5:, and now we have to fetch this 16-bit value out again and place it in the DE register pair. Our register usages in this subroutine will be:

HL   Index into ALV

DE   Number of blocks counter

    B   Number of groups of blocks per line

    C   Number of bits per ALV byte

    A   ALV byte bit pattern

    A   Indent SPACES count

    A   Output characters

and it is obvious that we have run out of registers again. Fortunately, by carefully planning their use throughout the subroutine, it is only necessary to save the bit pattern by PUSHing and POPping the A register at appropriate places. The accumulator is then free to perform its two other functions. With one more 16-bit register, we could have kept a running total of the number of available blocks remaining on the disk by counting the number of times we display "0."

After your previous exposures to flowcharts, you should be able to draw your own for this subroutine. An inner loop beginning at BYTE1: displays each map bit as C is counted down from 8 to 0. The next outer loop starts at BYTE: and counts B down from 4 to 0 as the groups of bits are displayed on each line. The outermost loop starts at LINE: and includes the 10-space indenting of the display. An exit is made from within the innermost loop when DE counts down to zero, signaling the end of the map. Maybe you won't need a flowchart after all. They are pretty old-fashioned.

EXERCISES

Listings 8.2 through 8.6 all have to be combined into the one library module SHOWDISK.LIB. Then TESTC8.ASM is put together by linking BEGIN.LIB, TESTC8.LIB, SHOWDISK.LIB, and SHOW-NUMB.LIB. If you find the display suitable as is for your own use, you might want to rename the whole thing as something other than a test program.

However, with SHOWDISK.LIB as a starting point, you might want to add some features of your own. Other values from the DPB could be fetched and displayed within DSIZE:, replacing the need for STAT DSK: entirely, since it misses some values we want to see and includes others we never need. By saving and restoring the HL pair at the proper places within DMAP:, you could count the blocks left on each disk and display the space remaining on the disk in decimal K bytes using the code in DSIZE: as a guide.

We have covered a lot of ground in this chapter on the way to understanding how CP/M handles disk space allocation dynamically.

There are other details to learn before you can begin integrating new disk hardware into your own customized CP/M system, but the hard part, the overall picture, has now been covered. Getting the big picture meant looking at a lot of aspects of disk storage all at once, but now you should be well prepared to learn the little details you have to know to write your own CBIOS. If you don't feel prepared and don't understand all we have covered here, go back to Chapter 1; go directly to Chapter 1; do not pass GO; do not collect $200.

chapter 9

More massive
storage

While everyone knows that it was the microprocessor that brought about the personal computer (PC) revolution, it is easy to lose sight of the fact that when the first PC hit the marketplace, 1 K bytes of RAM was a lot. In fact, the first PC, the Altair 8800, offered two main memory options: a 1 K byte static RAM board or a 4 K byte dynamic RAM board. It was said that the difference between the two was that the static RAM worked. Remember, the Altair executed the same 8080 instruction set we are still working with today.

Obviously, the world was not screaming for floppy disk drives in those early days, much less for hard disks. Of course there were hard disks in existence then, some giant ones storing as much as 20 million bytes, but the controller boards for them used more integrated circuits (ICs) than you would find in some microcomputers today. No one wanted a $20,000 mass storage device to hang onto a $2,000 personal computer.

Times have changed. PCs come with a minimum of 64 K bytes of RAM, which costs less than $100 for the ICs, and floppy disks are hard pressed to supply enough storage for all our exotic programs. We still could not afford hard disks for our little computers, however, if the same technology that brought us 64 K RAM ICs hadn't also brought about affordable hard disk controllers.

WINCHESTER HARD DISKS

Another advance that brought us the affordable hard disk is the "Winchester" technology, named after an IBM project originally designated "30-30," which should make sense to gun nuts and Western movie buffs. "Winch" disks employ a media-protecting hardware design that permits them to be installed in the typical home or office environment without needing special air filtering and air conditioning. The same combination of hardware design features permits high-density recording, so a 10, 20, or even 50 M byte disk drive can fit into the same physical form factor as a 5¼-inch floppy disk. And 100 to 400 M byte drives are beginning to appear, first in advertisements, next in spec sheets, and some even in real hardware!

Before we get into the nitty-gritty details of writing a floppy disk CBIOS, we are going to look at the differences between the programming requirements for CBIOS drivers for floppies and for more massive storage devices. We will see that CP/M provides the tools to enable you to easily integrate hard disks with floppies just by setting up the proper values in the disk parameter tables and providing the proper interfacing software.

Hard Disk Organization

Unlike most floppies, hard disks always include more than one read-/write head, and all but the smallest have more than one platter. The platters are stacked on the central axle, and each platter has two heads, one reading and writing from the top surface, the other working on the bottom surface. However, only one head is active at any one time.

Consider for example a two platter, four head, 5¼-inch Winchester hard disk. The first track that will be read or written is the outside track on the top of the first platter. Unlike on a floppy disk, the next track is not accessed by stepping the head in one notch. It is accessed by switching to another head: the bottom head on the first platter. In this way access is speeded up because there was no physical movement of the read/write (R/W) heads needed to get from the first track to the second.

Similarly, the third track is on the top surface of the second platter, and track four would be on its bottom surface. So four tracks can be accessed before there is any need to move the heads. This greatly speeds up disk data transfers, because it takes only microseconds to switch the read/write electronics from one head to another, but it takes milliseconds to move the heads.

Since four tracks are accessed at each position of the head stepper, each of those positions is referred to as a cylinder. Each cylinder will contain a number of tracks equal to the number of R/W heads, which is twice the number of platters. And that is all you need to know about what is inside that sealed Winchester disk/head assembly. Just as well, since those clear plastic disk covers only exist for demonstrations. Real disks are delivered in opaque metal cans, and you can't see what is going on inside.

A Real Example

We are going to look at an example hard disk taken from real life to illustrate the programming considerations necessary in working with massive storage. Our hard disk is variously rated at anywhere from 12 to 14 M bytes of "unformatted storage" by different manufacturers, in their efforts to out-specify the competition. You will see that specifying unformatted storage is meaningless, and all of these plug-compatible drives will provide you with the same amount of storage regardless of their seller's claims.

The reason for the various claims is that some vendors use strange and exotic recording techniques to pack more sectors per track onto their hard disks. These techniques do the end user no good if the off-the-shelf disk controller will not support the funny recording formats. And they never do. What you get in this 12 to 14 MB capacity range is (almost always) two platters, four heads, and 306 usable cylinders.

Disk Capacity

Just as was true for floppy disks, there are various recording formats on hard disk tracks. One of the most common is also one that provides about the maximum possible storage. This format writes 512 bytes per sector and 18 sectors per track, or 72 CP/M records per track. Since our example is a standard 306 cylinder drive with four R/W heads, the drive contains 1,224 tracks. Multiplying that out shows you that the end user is provided with 11,016 K bytes of formatted, usable storage on each of these little drives.

As we saw previously, CP/M version 1.4 had no provisions for being upgraded to use storage of this capacity. Version 2 provides the user with disk parameter tables that can be set up to use this level of disk capacity, except that it has one built-in limitation: a maximum disk capacity of 8 MB. While this limit is documented in the DRI manuals, no reason is given for it. It would appear that some internal computation is responsible, because a maximum value expressible by 16 bits is 65,536 and that times a 128-byte record size just happens to be 8,192 K bytes, or 8 MB in round bytes.

Dividing a Disk

Since V2 can't address all of our 11 MB of formatted storage, and we don't want to waste any, we will have to divide our single, physical hard disk drive up into two equally sized logical drives. As we will see from a real-world example, this is not a real hardship, because it turns out that not only do we want to have two logical drives, but we want them to have unequal numbers of directory entries. Our good old disk parameter tables make it easy for us to accomplish this.

Since we are using an example with lots of storage, compared to any floppy disk system, we don't want to be selfish and hog all of that disk space, so our example is from a multiuser computer system. In brief, the disk is set up so that all of the users have their own private files stored on logical drive A:, and all of the common stuff, like system files and application programs, are stored on logical drive B:. With five or ten users sharing space on A:, it is obvious that we will need more directory entries available on the private file drive A: than we need on the shared system drive B:. We will split up the hard disk into two logical drives and provide the maximum number of directory entries for drive A:.

Allotting Tracks

The first thing we have to do is reserve tracks for storing the CP/M operating system. When we add a hard disk to our computer, we won't want to boot the system from a floppy disk any more. Our Winch disk stores 72 records per track, or 9 K bytes per track, so we need to set aside two system tracks for the boot loader and the CP/M operating system.

This leaves us with 1,222 tracks to split between two logical drives. Although there is no real need to make them the same size, it proves to be a reasonable decision in practice, so each logical drive will have 611 tracks, and with 9 K bytes per track, we have two logical 5,499 K byte drives. Hmmmm. That was not an even number.

Block Size?

How big should our block sizes be? One K byte per block is illegal on a drive this size. We can choose 2, 4, 8, or 16 K bytes per block. The largest block size would waste too much storage if we had lots of little files, so although it might be reasonable for a computer that crunches numbers for a bank or the Census Bureau, 16 K bytes per block would waste too much of our disk space if we wrote lots of little programs like the exercises so far in this book.

If efficient disk space utilization were the only criterion, we would obviously choose 2 K bytes per block. But two other factors enter into the decision: how many directory entries we want, and how much memory space we can dedicate to the allocation vectors. We know from our disk map program that each block requires one bit in memory to flag its status, so the larger the blocks, the smaller the allocation vector. But if the blocks are as small as possible, and our directory allocation vector contains only 16 bits, we may not be able to have enough directory entries to keep all of those users happy.

So you see that the decision must be based on intended use, and is going to be influenced by experience. For our example we are using a real computer system, and the decisions made for it were well thought out: 4 K byte blocks for reasonable disk space efficiency and the maximum possible directory entries for the user's private drive. The disk parameter table entries that define this disk division are shown in Table 9.1.

Since our disk division provides for two drives of 5,499 K bytes each, and our block size is 4 K bytes, each drive will have 1,374 blocks and 3 K bytes left over that can't be accessed. But that is only a .055% waste, so who cares? Our maximum directory size will be sixteen 4 K byte blocks divided by 32 bytes per entry, or 2,048 directory entries. Five users would each have access to over a megabyte of disk space each and could name about 400 files, given equal opportunities for each. That is a reasonable division, as has proved to be the case in practice.

After the discussion of disk parameter blocks in the last chapter, you should have no trouble deciphering the examples in Table 9.1. The

```
DPB1:
SPT:    DW      72      ; SECTORS/TRACK
BSH:    DB       5      ; BLOCK SHIFT FACTOR
BLM:    DB      31      ; BLOCK MASK
EXM:    DB       1      ; EXTENT MASK
DSM:    DW    1373      ; DISK SIZE MAXIMUM
DRM:    DW    2047      ; DIRECTORY MAXIMUM
ALO:    DB    0FFH      ; DIRECTORY ALLOCATION BYTE 0
AL1:    DB    0FFH      ; DIRECTORY ALLOCATION BYTE 1
CKS:    DW       0      ; DIRECTORY CHECK VECTOR SIZE
OFF:    DW       2      ; OFFSET FOR SYSTEM TRACKS
```

(a)

```
DPB2:
SPT:    DW      72      ; SECTORS/TRACK
BSH:    DB       5      ; BLOCK SHIFT FACTOR
BLM:    DB      31      ; BLOCK MASK
EXM:    DB       1      ; EXTENT MASK
DSM:    DW    1373      ; DISK SIZE MAXIMUM
DRM:    DW     511      ; DIRECTORY MAXIMUM
ALO:    DB    0F0H      ; DIRECTORY ALLOCATION BYTE 0
AL1:    DB       0      ; DIRECTORY ALLOCATION BYTE 1
CKS:    DW       0      ; DIRECTORY CHECK VECTOR SIZE
OFF:    DW     613      ; OFFSET FOR SYSTEM TRACKS
```

(b)

Table 9.1 Winchester hard disk DPBs. A single physical disk drive has been subdivided into two logical drives by the use of two Disk Parameter Blocks. Each drive can record the same amount of data, but the directory of logical drive A: can contain more file names than that for drive B: as defined by the different table entries for DRM:. This configuration was established for a multiuser microcomputer with private files on A: and system files on B:.

first logical drive is offset from the start of the disk by the two system tracks, and the second is offset from the start of the disk by those two tracks plus the 611 tracks assigned to the first logical drive. The other values are self-explanatory, and BSH, BLM, and EXM were derived from the guidelines in the *Alteration Guide*.

Figure 9.1 shows that STAT:DSK: and TESTC8 displays for this divided hard disk. The disk map display would have filled up a bunch of pages with ones and zeros, so it isn't included here, now that you know what it represents. That is about all you need to know about how hard disks are integrated into a CP/M system. The only question remaining is how in the world did we ever get along without them in the past? They sure spoil you! Until it comes time to back up all of those files.

Figure 9.1 Winchester disk characteristics. The STAT DSK: and TESTC8 displays correspond to the hard disk configuration defined in Table 9.1. A single hard disk drive has been divided into two equal-size logical drives.

```
A STAT DSK:

    A: Drive Characteristics
43968: 128 Byte Record Capacity
 5496: Kilobyte Drive Capacity
 2048: 32  Byte Directory Entries
    0: Checked  Directory Entries
  256: Records/ Extent
   32: Records/ Block
   72: Sectors/ Track
    2: Reserved Tracks

A STAT B:DSK:

    B: Drive Characteristics
43968: 128 Byte Record Capacity
 5496: Kilobyte Drive Capacity
  512: 32  Byte Directory Entries
    0: Checked  Directory Entries
  256: Records/ Extent
   32: Records/ Block
   72: Sectors/ Track
  613: Reserved Tracks

A TESTC8 A: 1

Show disk sizes     15 Mar 84

SELECTED:    A:
EACH BLOCK:     4 K BYTES
DISK SIZE:   5496 K BYTES

A TESTC8 B: 1

Show disk sizes     15 Mar 84

SELECTED:    B:
EACH BLOCK:     4 K BYTES
DISK SIZE:   5496 K BYTES
```

BACKING UP
MASSIVE STORAGE

Although little Winchester hard disks have recently become almost indispensable to the serious microcomputerist, a practical, standard means for backing up all those megabytes of data has not yet been invented, so there is not much hard information on the subject that can be included here. Some of the methods for backup are listed below, along with comments on their failings.

Streaming Tape

Invented specifically for backing up hard disks, streaming tape drives range from those giant 10½-inch reels of ½-inch computer tape, through smaller cartridge tapes, down to the familiar cassette tape of often doubtful reliability. They all have one major failing: the lack of random access.

The "streaming" refers to the fact that, in order to record as fast as possible, the tape is allowed to run past the read/write heads at full speed, and it is up to the computer/controller combination to provide the tape with data as fast as it needs it. To provide streaming speeds, the drives themselves are not built to work in the more common start-stop mode, so it is not easy to skip down the tape for x files and y records. Finding a named file on such a tape is virtually impossible without tons of software that you won't find in any standard CP/M installation.

Whatever size, streamers are meant to store the complete image of a hard disk, from the first track to the end, thereby providing a complete disk image in case the hard disk drive fails or is inadvertently erased. Obviously, then, if a bunch of users have updated files on the disk at random intervals, and the entire disk image has been backed up onto a streamer once a week or so, it is possible for any one user to lose up to a week's worth of data if the disk needs to be regenerated from the tape made last Monday morning.

Therefore, individual users should also back up their files on floppies as well, on an hour to hour basis, and in that case who needs the streamer? Add to this the high cost of such drives, their required controllers, and the software to run them, and streaming tape does not appear to be the ideal solution to hard disk backup for the average small microcomputer user like you and me.

Floppy Backup

At first glance the familiar floppy disk does not look like a reasonable medium for backing up a massive hard disk because of the great difference in their storage capacities. However, a floppy disk looks more acceptable if you think in terms of each user backing up his or her own files as they are updated. This requires some discipline, in addition to a handful of blank diskettes, because each user will be responsible for providing his or her own backup.

This is made easier by features in CP/M Plus that provide for automatic time and date stamping of files, and the flagging of files that are in need of backup. In the next chapter, when we look at the format of the disk directory entries in more detail, we will see how this is done. Without CP/M Plus, however, or some program you write to emulate its extra features, it is up to the individual user to ensure that no disk data would be lost in the unlikely event of a hard disk crash.

Optical Disks

Digital data stored optically by using a laser to burn tiny holes in a thin disk coating has passed the research, announcement, and advertisement stages and has become a readily available comsumer item. Unfortunately for microcomputer users, as this book is written, the only optical disk drives available are read-only devices for playing back music recordings. However, the technology is easily expandable to read/write, and all of the factors of cost, capacity, and random access point to the optical disk as the archival data storage standard for the very near future.

Optical disks prerecorded with track and sector address fields, as are floppies, can simplify the head positioning requirements for a digital Write-Once-Read-Mostly (WORM) optical disk drive. All that is needed in addition to the existing hardware is an increase in the laser power output capability over that used in the read-only music disk to provide for writing data bit patterns to the disk. The fact that the disk cannot be erased is not critical, because one disk can store tens of gigabits (billions of bits) of data, and the application is for backup anyway. What better backup medium than one that can never be erased?

A LITTLE BREATHER

There hasn't been a lot of hard information covered in this chapter, and no programming exercises. The author was ready for a little break here in the middle of the book, and you probably were, too. So we looked at some topics that are certainly of interest even if not in the direct path toward the ultimate goal of learning enough about CP/M to permit the construction of your own CBIOS. There is more ground yet to cover before you are ready to tackle a complete CBIOS project, in Part III. Since there are no exercises to insert here, let's get back to work.

chapter 10

The disk directory

One purpose of an operating system like CP/M is to isolate the computer user from the chores involved in dynamically allocating disk space. We have seen how the physical disk space is broken up into logical blocks and how CP/M allocates those blocks. In this chapter we will look at the disk directory entries in more detail and will see how they can be used to help us keep track of our disks and what is on them.

DIRECTORY ENTRY FORMATS

Back in Chapter 8 we took a peek at a hexadecimal dump of one record from a disk directory (Figure 8.3), and saw how the allocation blocks were addressed by block numbers recorded in each file's directory entries. That dump also shows us how the file name/file type is recorded in the directory. In addition to the block addresses and the file name, the directory entries contain other information, some of it accessible to the user through CP/M BDOS functions, some of it accessible through the application of ESP (Extra Sneaky Programming), and some of it is information that only the operating system knows how to use.

Control Bytes

A look at Figure 10.1 will show that we have put some Digital Research standard labels on the bytes that are recorded in each directory entry. In addition to the 16 bytes shown here, which correspond to the top line of the dumped data in Figure 8.3, there are another 16 bytes associated with each entry, and they hold the block numbers.

We don't need to look at the block addresses here, but we want to take a close look at some of the control bytes, as shown in Figure 10.1. The first byte in each directory entry originally held only one of two values: zero, signifying that a valid directory entry exists, or 0E5H, indicating an erased file. This last value was inherited from the original IBM diskette standard, which uses that bit pattern in every data byte when a disk is first formatted. With an 0E5H in each directory entry first byte, a newly formatted disk looks like it has had all of its files erased.

Since 8 bits can represent more than two states, it was easy to start using that first byte for other purposes. One of the first tricks discovered by experimenters working with CP/M, but otherwise not mentioned in the Digital Research documentation, was the use of the value 80H (one bit in the most significant position in the first byte). When a file is tagged with this value, CP/M 1.4 will not be able to find the file, but it will not reuse the blocks allocated to it, as it would if that first byte

Figure 10.1 Disk directory FCB. The first 16 bytes of the file control block recorded in the disk directory contain a number of one-byte and one-bit controls. The first byte at FCB+0 has grown in use from the original two-valued control of CP/M V1.4 to the multiple uses found in CP/M Plus. Individual most significant bits of the file name (f1' through f8') bytes and file type (t1' through t3') bytes are now dedicated to flagging file attributes as defined by CP/M or by user programs.

FCB+	0	1	2	3	4	5	6	7	8	9	10	11	12	13	14	15
		f1'	f2'	f3'	f4'	f5'	f6'	f7'	f8'	t1'	t2'	t3'				
		f1	f2	f3	f4	f5	f6	f7	f8	t1	t2	t3	ex	s1	s2	rc

Value(s)	Function	Version(s)
0	Existing file	1.4
0 – 15	User number	2.2, 3.0
16 – 31	Extended FCB AND user number	3.0
21H	Special FCB	3.0
80H	Hidden file (undocumented)	1.4
0E5H	Erased file	ALL

Bytes/Bits	Function	Version(s)
f1 – f8	File name	ALL
t1 – t3	File type	ALL
f1' – f4'	User defined attributes	3.0
f5' – f6'	Interface attributes	3.0
f6' – f7'	Reserved for system use	ALL
t1'	Read-only (R/O) file	2.2, 3.0
t2'	System (SYS) file	2.2, 3.0
t3'	Archive attribute	3.0
ex	File extent number	ALL
s1	Reserved for system use	ALL
s2	Reserved for system use	ALL
rc	File/extent record count	ALL

contained the "erased" value 0E5H. This was useful for "hiding" bad disk tracks or sectors from the operating system.

CP/M version 2 introduced the use of USER numbers ranging from 0 through 15 so that up to 16 different directories could be generated on one disk, with each invisible to all of the others. This is especially valuable on large-capacity hard disks, because scanning through one giant directory can cause considerable eyestrain. Although the use of USER numbers does not change the total number of directory entries that can be stored on any one disk, given a large disk with lots of blocks dedicated to the directory, it can provide the appearance of many smaller private disk drives.

Figure 10.1 shows that CP/M Plus shares the version 2 use of USER numbers, but adds the capability of setting one more bit in the first byte and using it to flag another state: an eXtended directory **FCB** entry. Do not confuse this extension with the directory entry extent value recorded in the byte at FCB + 12. The version 3 XFCB is used to record the secret password that can be used to protect files under CP/M Plus running in a banked memory (more than 64 K bytes of RAM) computer. Since there was no room in the original directory entry for passwords, extra entries that have been flagged by this bit are created for each protected file, taking up even more directory space.

Another CP/M Plus innovation that takes up more directory space is flagged by writing the value 21H into that first byte. This signifies a Special **FCB** (SFCB) entry that contains date and time information for three files. We saw in Figure 8.3 that each 128-byte record can contain four 32-byte directory entries. On disks properly initialized for CP/M Plus, each directory record contains three normal entries and one SFCB that contains values recording when each of the other three entries was first accessed for creation or last accessed for read or write.

The use of these CP/M Plus functions is discussed in detail in the *Programmer's Guide*, so we won't have to mention them further here. If you have access to or want to write a program that can dump the disk directory in a format like that in Figure 8.3, you might someday run across some or all of the first-byte values listed in Figure 10.1.

Note once again that the contents and use of the first byte in the directory FCB differ from the first (drive selection) byte in the memory FCB.

In addition to the control bytes at FCB + 0 and FCB + 12, there are two more that are used exclusively by BDOS (S1 and S2), and that final one, the record count (rc), at FCB + 15. For files that will fit within one extent, this last byte will contain a value equal to the total number of 128-byte records in the file. For multiextent files it will contain the maximum number of records per extent for each filled extent, and what is left over in the final unfilled extent. Our investigative or diagnostic programs can look at these "rc" bytes to determine file size, as does STAT.

Control Bits

Even before CP/M Plus came along and began cluttering up the directory with XFCBs and SFCBs, DRI began confusing the directory entries by making use of the most significant bit of each byte in the file name and type fields. Since these bytes contain ASCII characters, and each character needs only 7 bits, 1 bit per byte was going unused in CP/M version 1, so version 2 was able to add functions without adding new directory entries and taking up valuable directory space.

CP/M version 2 used the most significant bits (t1' and t2') of the first two file type characters (t1 and t2) to flag files as R/O for write protection and as SYStem files so they would not show up in directory listings. This was some help in reducing DIR: display clutter as large capacity disks became common.

CP/M Plus is even more hard disk-oriented and uses more of the bits. The last bit in the file type, t3, is used by version 3 to flag a file that has been updated but not yet copied (archived) to another disk. PIP has been enhanced to search out files with t3' set, copy them to another specified disk, and clear the t3' bits as each file is successfully copied. Unfortunately, you still have to tell the version 3 PIP that you want to do this, and when. Maybe someday a background task will be written to do this automatically.

Since use of these bits is so handy, DRI decided to let us mess with some of them ourselves, and CP/M Plus has set aside four bits (f1' through f4') for us to use as we wish. We can set, clear, and test them through BDOS calls. Bits f5' and f6' are used by the CP/M Plus BDOS during the time files are open, and their exact use is determined by the particular BDOS function that was called. The version 3 *Programmer's Guide* has pages full of details on the subject, so we won't cover it in more detail here. That guide also specifies that the last two bits, f7' and f8', are reserved for future system use, so don't try to use them yourself.

Do-It-Yourself Controls

Since version 1 used none of these available control bits, and version 2 used only a couple, some adventuresome programmers over the years have implemented special functions using them and have gotten into trouble because of conflicts with later versions of CP/M. Well, now that CP/M Plus has arrived, we have been given a license to use four of these bits however we want, and even if you are still working with version 2, you can implement special functions using them. If you can figure out how to get access to them. It takes ESP.

ESP Techniques

The sector dumps in Figure 8.3 indicate that there is a way to access these disk sectors directly. There is such a way: the not-recommended technique known as direct BIOS calls. This involves using techniques such as the system mapping program in Chapter 7 that was used to find out where the BIOS jump table is in memory. Entries into those jumps are then used to set drive, track, and sector selections, and read or write physical disk addresses. Since this violates our "all access through BDOS calls" principle, it is possible to write programs that will prove inoperable on later versions of CP/M.

In spite of this, and the danger that your programs can really garbage the disk, many useful programs have been written using direct BIOS calls, and many will be written in the future. So if you must, go ahead. You are an experienced programmer and should be able to verify that your sneaky programs work properly. But don't test your programs on the boss's favorite data base. Or mine, either.

There is another ESP technique that can be used to at least read all of these control bytes and bits, if not write them, and our next investigative program will show you how, even if it has no other useful purpose.

FINDING FILES IN THE DIRECTORY

We have seen how CP/M will set up one or two FCBs for us if the name(s) of one or two desired files are entered into the command line tail by the computer operator when a program is invoked. This permits our programs to access files named by the computer operator. However, if we want to work with particular files that are unnamed at the time our program begins execution, we will need to prompt the operator for a file name or search the directory for an ambiguous or unambiguous file name.

To illustrate how a program can do this, FINDASMS was written to search the directory of the disk specified in the command line tail for

all files with the ambiguous file name of ???????? and the unambiguous
file type of .ASM. Since we can do the same thing with a command of:

DIR d:*.ASM

the program has no useful purpose except to show how your programs
can not only find files in the directory, but can also read the actual
directory records, including all control bytes and bits, in the process.

AFIND: (Listing 10.1) is our main program, and it is supported by
subroutines TSHOW: and FSHOW: (Listing 10.2), with the two listings
constituting one file, FINDASMS.LIB. This file should be merged with
BEGIN.LIB to form FINDASMS.ASM.

Listing 10-1

```
                ; MODULE NAME: FINDASMS.LIB
                ; LAST UPDATE: 22 MAR 84    BY: KMB
                ; FUNCTION: FIND AND DISPLAY ALL .ASM FILES ON DISK d:
                ; REQUIRES: BEGIN.LIB
                ;============================================================
                ;
005C =          TFCB    EQU    5CH           ; TRANSIENT FCB
0080 =          TBUFF   EQU    80H           ; TRANSIENT (DEFAULT) BUFFER
0011 =          SFRSF   EQU    17            ; SEARCH FOR FIRST FILE
0012 =          SNXTF   EQU    18            ; SEARCH FOR NEXT FILE

0200 213102     AFIND:  LXI    H,FNSTR       ; "Asm file FIND"
0203 115D00             LXI    D,TFCB+1      ; MOVE SEARCH STRING TO
0206 7E         AFIN1:  MOV    A,M           ;  TRANSIENT FILE CONTROL
0207 B7                 ORA    A             ;   BLOCK, UP TO THE ZERO
0208 CA1102             JZ     AFIN2
020B 12                 STAX   D
020C 23                 INX    H
020D 13                 INX    D
020E C30602             JMP    AFIN1
0211 CD3D02     AFIN2:  CALL   TSHOW         ; SHOW THE SEARCH STRING
0214 0E11               MVI    C,SFRSF       ; SEARCH FOR FIRST ENTRY
0216 115C00     AFIN3:  LXI    D,TFCB        ;  OF FILE NAMED IN TFCB
0219 CD0500             CALL   BDOS
021C B7                 ORA    A             ; NO MORE FILES?
021D FA8B01             JM     DONE          ;  THEN QUIT
0220 218000             LXI    H,TBUFF       ;  ELSE POINT INTO RECORD
0223 0F                 RRC                  ; MULTIPLY OFFSET * 32
0224 0F                 RRC                  ;  (3 RIGHT = 5 LEFT SHIFTS
0225 0F                 RRC                  ;   = * 32)
0226 85                 ADD    L             ; ADD OFFSET * 32 TO POINTER
0227 6F                 MOV    L,A           ; (CAN'T OVERFLOW FROM 80H
0228 23                 INX    H             ; POINT TO FILE NAME
0229 CD4002             CALL   FSHOW         ; SHOW THE FILE NAME AT (H,L)
022C 0E12               MVI    C,SNXTF       ; SEARCH FOR NEXT FILE
022E C31602             JMP    AFIN3         ;  AND SHOW IT TOO

0231 3F3F3F3F3FFNSTR    DB     '????????ASM',0 ; FIND FILES STRING
```

Listing 10-2

```
                    ; SHOW THE FILENAME IN THE TFCB

023D 215D00         TSHOW:  LXI     H,TFCB+1            ; "Transient file name SHOW"

                    ; FALL RIGHT THROUGH INTO:

                    ; SHOW THE FILENAME POINTED TO BY H,L

0240 C5             FSHOW:  PUSH    B                   ; "File name SHOW"
0241 E5                     PUSH    H
0242 0E08                   MVI     C,8                 ; FILE NAME CHARACTERS
0244 7E             FSHO1:  MOV     A,M
0245 23                     INX     H
0246 CD5E01                 CALL    CO
0249 0D                     DCR     C
024A C24402                 JNZ     FSHO1
024D 3E2E                   MVI     A,'.'               ; AND A SEPARATOR
024F CD5E01                 CALL    CO
0252 0E03                   MVI     C,3                 ; FILE TYPE CHARACTERS
0254 7E             FSHO2:  MOV     A,M
0255 23                     INX     H
0256 CD5E01                 CALL    CO
0259 0D                     DCR     C
025A C25402                 JNZ     FSHO2
025D CD5701                 CALL    CCRLF               ; START A NEW LINE
0260 E1                     POP     H
0261 C1                     POP     B
0262 C9                     RET
```

When you assemble and run FINDASMS, you will see that it does about the same thing as the CCP command shown above, but without the fancy formatting. Since this is not a practical program in itself, we skipped all the niceties.

AFIND:

The main program uses the default transient FCB and 128-byte buffer at 5CH and 80H respectively. Two new BDOS functions are used, Search for FiRSt File (SFRSF) and Search for NeXT File (SNXTF). The program begins by moving the ambiguous file name FiNd STRing (FNSTR) into the TFCB, and it then displays it by the call to TFCB SHOW (TSHOW:). Next, the function that requests a search for the first matching file is passed to BDOS.

Since we have not specified a DMA address, CP/M automatically uses the default transient buffer at location 80H to return the directory record containing the entry for the first matching file. If you extract any of the code in this program to use in other programs (that's what it's for!), make sure that you restore the DMA address to TBUFF if you have previously changed it within a program. CP/M will automatically restore the DMA address to TBUFF at any cold or warm start, so this program doesn't bother to set it up.

Both of the BDOS search calls will deliver the complete directory record containing the directory FCB of the found file. Since there are four directory entries in each record, BDOS returns with the contents of the accumulator equal to 0, 1, 2, or 3, depending on which quarter of the record is the correct directory FCB.

To display that file name, we have taken the contents of A and multiplied by 32 to point to the first byte of the proper FCB image in the record. The file name field in that image begins at the next byte, so HL is incremented before **File** name **SHOW** (FSHOW:) is called to display the name.

If you are more interested in examining all of those control bytes and bits instead of just showing the file name, your program will stop here to work with whatever subfield you are interested in. When done with the first file, successive calls to BDOS with the search for next file function code in C will produce another directory record in TBUFF and another offset value in A.

It is easy to see that if our find string, FNSTR, was set to all "?"s, we would step through the whole disk directory one record at a time. Or, actually, one record four times followed by the next record four times, etc. This technique is used by STAT and other programs that analyze the directory and provide statistics about the files.

Since we can see all of the records of the disk directory by looping through the search-for-next loop beginning at AFIN3:, we have access to the complete disk directory from beginning to end and don't have to know how big it is or what physical disk sectors contain it. But, of course, all we can do is read it.

So the BDOS search functions have provided us with an ESP technique for directly accessing disk directory records one at a time. To change things in the directory, we will have to use the even sneakier direct BIOS call techniques discussed in Part III.

TSHOW: and FSHOW:

These simple subroutines can be used in other programs, so they are written in conformity without "save all of the registers" convention. You should have no trouble figuring them out, even with the sparse commenting that they deserved.

That is the whole story of finding files in the directory. All you got was the basic techniques. You will have to fill in the details for any programs you want to write to use these techniques. One possible investigative program would analyze and display the first-byte options, so you could detect the presence of a CP/M Plus formatted diskette in a 2.2 system or find out if anyone has been using the hidden file technique that worked for version 1.

HIDING FILES

If you should run across a diskette that has a bad track or sector, but is otherwise usable, the block number(s) covering the defect can be written into the directory FCB of a file that can then be made read-only and invisible during directory displays.

Hiding in Version 1

We have already seen how the undocumented first-byte value 80H worked to hide files on computers running CP/M V1.4, but experiments have shown that this won't work with newer versions.

USER, SYS, and R/O

In CP/M versions 2 and up, a file can be hidden from user access by making it a read-only (R/O) SYStem file, and it can be further protected by PIPing it over to USER 15 or some other obscure, unused user number. CP/M Plus also provides for password protection on a file-by-file basis, so the USER 15, R/O, SYStem file can have a secret password as well.

These, of course, are file-hiding techniques that make use of the disk directory and its options to make sure a particular file is not accessible to most users. This will work most of the time to provide secrecy or a place to stuff those media defect block numbers.

Hard Disk Hiding

Most hard disk systems have another technique for "covering up" media defects. The disk controller itself provides for sparing a complete track, or a number of them. That way, if one track is known to contain a defect, a track beyond the last normally accessed track on the inside of the disk is readdressed with the track and sector address fields of the bad track. Then the bad track is written throughout with a special code that tells the controller where to find the spare.

Since all of that requires special controller functions, and the defective track contains no data areas after the sparing operation, it is of no help to anyone wanting to hide files for security or other sneaky purposes. However, it does point to one opening left for the knowledgeable systems programmer. Since the disk parameter tables tell CP/M how many tracks there are on a disk, but we know from the disk sparing techniques that the drive can actually find and use tracks beyond the "last" track on almost all hard disks, a good programmer can change the disk tables from within a program and get access to extra tracks that no other users can find.

The reason that this is possible is that virtually all small Winchester hard disks, when first initialized, are formatted with a larger last cylinder parameter than is used when specifying the disk capacity for CP/M. This is done to provide unused disk space between the usually accessed last track and a "landing zone" for the read/write heads to be parked on before the drive or the whole computer is moved. These extra tracks can be accessed, but any techniques that sneaky will require the use of direct BIOS calls to select the invisible tracks, because CP/M can't be forced to use high-numbered blocks selectively.

Obviously, then the programmer with an intimate knowledge of CP/M and the computer's BIOS can perform all kinds of sneaky tricks. So we have many reasons for our continued study of CP/M techniques.

CATALOGING DISKS

Anyone who has used more than a few floppy disks knows that keeping track of all of them and the files they contain can be a real chore. Fortunately, there are several really good disk cataloging programs available at moderate prices, and one nice program is free from the CP/M User's Group.

What all of these programs do for the user is keep track of all of the files on all of your disks. They do this by reading the directory of each disk in turn, creating a data base containing a list of each program and the disk on which it is found. The smarter catalog programs keep track of each file both by name and by size in blocks, and the smartest programs can detect size differences as small as one 128-byte record. This is done by reading the "rc" byte in the directory entry for each file. Files with the same name on two different disks can then be separated by size, and it is usually safe to assume that the larger file is the most recent update, since programs very seldom get smaller with time. But, then, neither do programmers.

Since CP/M provides few clues to which file is the most recent update, except for CP/M Plus, it is still up to the programmer to maintain the date information in the program and module headers. So far no supersmart catalog program has appeared that will automatically catalog all disks and programs and include the version 3 date stamping. There is an opportunity for you.

Disk Numbers

Each of your floppy disks, and each removable hard disk cartridge if you are so fortunate, should be assigned a disk number. One method is illustrated in the directory record dump in Figure 8.3. Here the first directory entry is a zero-length file that was created by entering:

SAVE 0 -10-29-1.057

immediately after the diskette was formatted and the system tracks written, so this is the first entry in the directory. The disk ID need not be the first entry, but it is convenient to have it always in that place.

Almost all of the disk catalog programs want to see such a disk number entry beginning with a "-" and ending with a disk number from 1 up to 255 in the file type field. Eight-bit arithmetic again! The rest of the file name after the "-" can be whatever you like. In the example in Figure 8.3, the file name indicates that it is 10-sector diskette number 29 side 1, in the author's minifloppy disk collection. In this case the minifloppies can be turned over and written on the back side, using a single-sided drive. This technique is usually referred to as a "flippy-disk." Since each side looks like a different disk to the cataloger, disk 29 side 1 ends up as disk 57, and side 2 is disk 58.

Whatever method you use, it is recommended that you start by assigning a disk number to each removable disk and use the format shown even if you do not yet have an automatic disk catalog program. What those programs will do for you, once you have let them scan each of your disks, is provide a means for searching their data base for files using the CP/M ambiguous file name conventions. You can, therefore, enter a command like: *.ASM and have the catalog program list all of the .ASM files on all of your disks. Similarly, *.* would show you the entire data base, and FIND*.COM would list all object programs that you have written with names that begin with the string "FIND" and have any numbers of other characters in the file name field.

Manual Cataloging

You can also keep track of all of your disks and their contents without a fancy program if you start by numbering each disk and then make a hard copy of the directory contents for each disk, one to a page. It is best to use STAT to record each file size, because the command **STAT *.*** will produce an alphabetic listing that includes file sizes. Make up a bundle of such printouts, one for each disk, keep them updated, and you will be able to find most files by a simple manual search. But if you have more than a few disks, a cataloging program is almost indispensable.

CATALOGING PROGRAM MODULES

Since we have gone one step farther in structuring our programs in this book and have broken up each program into modules, some method is needed for keeping track of which modules, and which update of each module, are used in each of your programs. One reason behind the use of the standard module header (Listing 5.1) is to permit a program to be created that can scan each .ASM file and extract the information contained in each module header within the program.

Since you have been exhorted to keep these headers up to date, it wouldn't be nice to leave you with no means for keeping track of all of them automatically. So now all you have to do is key in, debug, and run PGMCAT, and your disk cataloging can be extended to include keeping track of modules within programs.

A PROGRAM CATALOGER

While a disk catalog program is indispensable to the serious programmer, especially when working with piles of floppy disks, (and the kind that can differentiate programs on the basis of size is a great help), we need to go one step further and keep track of what is inside each version of each program and module. Our standard headers were designed to encourage the programmer to flag each program modification in the date field, and adhering to that practice can prevent much grief in the future.

Since it is often desirable to upgrade a preexisting module by either modifying its subroutines or adding new ones, it is inevitable that some programs will exist with "outdated" modules, even though those modules work properly within the older program. We should not be forced to always relink the old programs, and neither is it a good idea to restrict the upgrading of modules. Some method for keeping track of program revisions as well as module updates is necessary. Card files could be used, but the computer is a better tool for this job, and **Pro**-**GraM CAT**alog (PGMCAT) is designed to work with our standard headers.

Figure 10.2 illustrates how PGMCAT extracted the program and module header information from DECADD.ASM (Chapter 7), and it does the same job just as well working with DECADD.PRN. The techniques used, and even PGMCAT itself, will work with source programs written in any language provided that the headers are in comment lines flagged with the initial characters appropriate to the language used, as in "REM * PROGRAM NAME:" for BASIC source programs in their ASCII format.

Figure 10.2 PGMCAT display. The program module cataloger PGMCAT is invoked to search and display the individual modules contained in the source file DECADD.ASM. The main program and each supporting module are identified by name, date of last update, and function as derived automatically by PGMCAT from the standard module headers embedded within the source file.

```
A PGMCAT B:DECADD.ASM

Program Catalog      27 Mar 84

*   PROGRAM NAME:    DECADD.ASM                                *
*   LAST UPDATE:    8 MAR 84    BY: KMB                        *
*   FUNCTION: ADD 2 DECIMAL NUMBERS FROM CCP LINE BUFFER       *

;  MODULE NAME:    DECADD.LIB
;  LAST UPDATE:   8 MAR 84      BY: KMB
;  FUNCTION: ADD & DISPLAY 2 DEC NUMBERS FROM COMMAND LINE

;  MODULE NAME: DECNUMBI.LIB
;  LAST UPDATE:   7 MAR 84      BY: KMB
;  FUNCTION: INPUT DECIMAL NUMBERS

;  MODULE NAME: NICOMMON.LIB
;  LAST UPDATE:   1 MAR 84      BY: KMB
;  FUNCTION: NUMBERS BUFFERED INPUT COMMON SUBROUTINES

;  MODULE NAME: CONBUFFI.LIB
;  LAST UPDATE: 19 FEB 84      BY: KMB
;  FUNCTION: BUFFERED CONSOLE INPUT SUBROUTINES

;  MODULE NAME: SHOWNUMB.LIB
;  LAST UPDATE: 19 FEB 84      BY: KMB
;  FUNCTION: DISPLAY IN BINARY, HEXADECIMAL, OR DECIMAL
```

More Subroutines

In addition to standing on its own merits, PGMCAT includes string search subroutines that might come in handy in other programs. Since the figure shows instantly what PGMCAT does, let's jump right into a discussion of how it does it.

You will note that the program does not extract the entire image of the program or module headers from the source code. What we have done is define the following strings to be searched for:

```
PROGRAM HEADER:  '* PROGRAM NAME:'
                 ' LAST UPDATE:'
                 ' FUNCTION:'
MODULE HEADER:   ' MODULE NAME:'
                 ' LAST UPDATE:'
                 ' FUNCTION:'
```

and the entire line containing each string is listed.

Since two strings are common to both program and module headers, there are only four actually defined in the program. It is important to note that they are searched for in a particular order and that the program listings cannot contain exact duplicates of those strings in any places other than the headers, or simple-minded PGMCAT will get lost in its searching. Well, the whole program assembles down to less than one K byte. What do you want?

Searching for Strings

PGMCAT's search technique is best understood by looking at the main program, Listing 10.3. At the bottom you can see the search strings, which include "SPACE" to define ASCII 20H, because defining the strings exactly as shown above would result in their being found outside of headers when PGMCAT.COM is used to scan PGMCAT.ASM! Since the program searches for three strings from the program header in the normal order, and then three strings from any number of module headers in their normal order, any find of a nonheader string will upset the sequence and can easily result in a futile search through the remainder of the program.

The main program, as all of our programs have been, is exquisitely simple. The subroutine to find a String **IN** a FiLe (SINFL:, pronounced "sinful" if you like) will open the file defined in the transient file control

Listing 10-3

```
                ; MODULE NAME:   PGMCAT.LIB
                ; LAST UPDATE: 27 MAR 84     BY: KMB
                ; FUNCTION: PROGRAM CATALOGER MAIN PROGRAM
                ; REQUIRES: FINDSTRN.LIB, MISC-SU.LIB, BEGIN.LIB
                ;================================================================

0200 213002     PGMCAT: LXI     H,HEAD1         ; "ProGraM CATaloger"
0203 CD6802             CALL    SINFL           ; FIND THE FIRST HEADER LINE
0206 DA8B01     PGMCA1: JC      DONE
0209 CD3904             CALL    SHOLN           ; DISPLAY IT
020C 214102             LXI     H,HEAD2         ;  AND NEXT LINE
020F CDB502             CALL    SINXT           ;   AND SO ON....
0212 DA8B01             JC      DONE
0215 CD3904             CALL    SHOLN
0218 214F02             LXI     H,HEAD3
021B CDB502             CALL    SINXT
021E DA8B01             JC      DONE
0221 CD3904             CALL    SHOLN
0224 CD5701             CALL    CCRLF           ; SPACE DOWN
0227 215A02             LXI     H,MODU1         ; FIND MODULE HEADER
022A CDB502             CALL    SINXT
022D C30602             JMP     PGMCA1

                ; "SPACE" PREVENTS THE STRING IMAGES BELOW FROM BEING
                ;   IDENTICAL TO THE ASSEMBLED SEARCH STRINGS, ELSE
                ;   THEY WOULD BE FOUND ERRONEOUSLY BY PGMCAT ITSELF

0020 =           SPACE    EQU     ' '

0230 2A20205052HEAD1:   DB      '*',SPACE,SPACE,'PROGRAM NAME:',0
0241 204C415354HEAD2:   DB      SPACE,'LAST UPDATE:',0
024F 2046554E43HEAD3:   DB      SPACE,'FUNCTION:',0
025A 204D4F4455MODU1:   DB      SPACE,'MODULE NAME:',0
```

block and search it for the first occurrence of the string pointed to by the HL register pair. Once the first string is found, subsequent searches do not want to reopen and rewind the file, so SINXT:, an alternate entry into the same subroutine, searches for the next string following any previous finds by SINFL: or by SINXT: itself.

As each string is found, the entire line containing it is displayed on the CON: by subroutine **SHOw LiNe** (SHOLN:). If you want a hard copy printout, as would most often be the case, CTRL P should get it for you. The program as presented here does not send the display to the list device or store it in a disk data base, but feel free to add those features yourself as soon as you get it up and running.

Once the three header lines are found and displayed, the program searches for the first line of the first module header. When this is found, the program loops back to PGMCA1:, displaying module headers in turn until an end of file is reached. That is all there is to PGMCAT, except for a few details in the subroutines that you might find interesting and useful in the future. These include the search technique that can

. handle any size source file, yet the whole object program will still fit into less than one K byte, even with the buffer that is used to contain the program being searched. The read and search subroutines may prove just as valuable to your programming efforts as PGMCAT itself, especially if you make PGMCAT less valuable by forgetting to keep those header lines updated. PGMCAT won't be able to help lazy programmers, but who can?

PGMCAT SUBROUTINES

The main program calls SINFL: and SINXT: to find the search strings, and they in turn call **NEW BuFfer** (NEWBF:) and String **IN LiNe** (SINLN:) to access the file being searched and to find the search strings within it, line by line. These subroutines are part of module FIND-STRN.LIB, and some other miscellaneous subroutines are found in MISC-SU.LIB as well.

SINFL: To find the first string in the target file, SINFL: is called. It opens the named file if it can be found, aborting through SINER: if the file does not exist. Following a successful open, SINFL: "rewinds" the file by clearing the current record byte (FCBCR) in the TFCB and then calls **READ Record** (READR:) to read the first two 128-byte records into LOBUF and HIBUF. Subroutine READR: includes a call to OPINT: down in BEGIN.LIB to allow an operator abort of the search any time the file is being accessed.

   With data loaded into the two-record buffer, a loop is entered at SINF1: that will search for the string pointed to by the HL register pair by calling SINLN: to search each line in the target file, one line at a time. A line is defined as being all the characters between one carriage return (CR) and the next carriage return.

   Programs that have been written to our established specs will not have any source lines longer than 64 characters (see Chapter 5), so we know that our 256-byte buffer will hold at least four text lines. When we have searched to the end of a line, and that end (the CR) falls in the top quarter of the buffer (HIBUF + 64) as determined by **COM**pare **H**1 to **D**e (COMHD: in MISC-SU.LIB), a call to NEWBF: will cause the top half of the buffer (HIBUF) to be moved into LOBUF and the next sequential target file record to be read into HIBUF. The **BuFfer PoiNTer** (BFPNT) is then "rewound" by subtracting 128 so that it points to the same place in the text, now down in LOBUF, with fresh data in the top of the buffer. SINFL: is now ready to call SINXT: to continue the search.

Listing 10-4

```
                    ; MODULE NAME: FINDSTRN.LIB
                    ; LAST UPDATE: 25 MAR 84    BY: KMB
                    ; FUNCTION: FIND STRINGS IN BUFFERS OR FILES
                    ; REQUIRES: MISC-SU.LIB, BEGIN.LIB
                    ;============================================================

                    ; FIND A STRING IN A FILE POINTED TO BY TFCB
                    ;   ENTER WITH H,L POINTING TO A STRING TERMINATED BY ZERO
                    ;   EXITS WITH BFPNT POINTING TO LINE WITH MATCHING STRING
                    ;        WITH CARRY SET IF END OF FILE WITH NO MATCH

000F =              OPENF   EQU     15            ; OPEN FILE FUNCTION
005C =              TFCB    EQU     05CH          ; TRANSIENT FILE CONTROL BLOCK
007C =              FCBCR   EQU     TFCB+32       ; CURRENT RECORD IN TFCB

0268 C5             SINFL:  PUSH    B             ; "String IN a FiLe"
0269 D5                     PUSH    D             ; SAVE REGISTERS
026A E5                     PUSH    H
026B 115C00                 LXI     D,TFCB        ; USE DEFAULT FCB
026E 0E0F                    MVI     C,OPENF       ; OPEN FILE FOR READ
0270 CD0500                 CALL    BDOS
0273 B7                     ORA     A             ; TEST RETURN CODE
0274 FABB02                 JM      SINER         ; ERROR IF NO SUCH FILE
0277 AF                     XRA     A             ; REWIND READ FILE
0278 327C00                 STA     FCBCR
027B 213503                 LXI     H,LOBUF       ; FILL DOUBLE BUFFER WITH
027E 223504                 SHLD    BFPNT
0281 CD4B04                 CALL    READR         ;   TWO CP/M RECORDS
0284 DABB02                 JC      SINER         ; ERROR IF NOT EVEN ONE
0287 21B503                 LXI     H,HIBUF
028A CD4B04                 CALL    READR
028D E1             SINF1:  POP     H             ; SEARCH TIL NC OR EOF
028E E5                     PUSH    H             ; RE-SAVE STRING POINTER
028F CDD502                 CALL    SINLN         ; SEE IF STRING IN LINE
0292 D2B102                 JNC     SINF2         ; GOT IT, EXIT
0295 11F503                 LXI     D,HIBUF+64    ; NEED MORE DATA?
0298 2A3504                 LHLD    BFPNT         ;   POINTER IN TOP QUARTER
029B CD6904                 CALL    COMHD         ;   OF DOUBLE BUFFER?
029E DA8D02                 JC      SINF1         ; NO, CONTINUE SEARCH
02A1 CD1903                 CALL    NEWBF         ; YES, FILL NEW BUFFER
02A4 DAB102                 JC      SINF2         ;   TIL END OF FILE
02A7 1180FF                 LXI     D,0-128       ; REWIND BUFFER POINTER
02AA 19                     DAD     D             ;   TO CORRECT PLACE
02AB 223504                 SHLD    BFPNT         ;   IN LOW BUFFER
02AE C38D02                 JMP     SINF1         ;   AND SEARCH NEW BUFFER
02B1 E1             SINF2:  POP     H             ; RESTORE AND RETURN
02B2 D1                     POP     D
02B3 C1                     POP     B
02B4 C9                     RET

02B5 C5             SINXT:  PUSH    B             ; "NeXT String In file"
02B6 D5                     PUSH    D
02B7 E5                     PUSH    H
02B8 C38D02                 JMP     SINF1         ; ALTERNATE ENTRY TO SINFL

02BB CD5401         SINER:  CALL    TWOCR         ; "String IN file ERror"
02BE CD4801                 CALL    SPMSG
02C1 4E4F20494E             DB      'NO INPUT FILE',0
02CF CD5701                 CALL    CCRLF
02D2 C38B01                 JMP     DONE
```

The carry flag is used throughout to signal search success or failure from SINLN:, or end-of-file found by READR: and echoed back through NEWBF:. With only one simple loop, the logic of SINFL: is easy to follow.

Searching Techniques

Imagine that you have the first search string, "* PROGRAM NAME:", printed on a card stuck to the top of your desk. Then imagine the text of a source file like PGMCAT.ASM printed on a long piece of ticker tape. Our search procedure will be:

1. Align the first character on the tape with the first character on the card, and align a pointer to this pair of characters. This was done initially in SINFL:. The following is done in SINLN:.
2. Slide the ticker tape along the edge of the card until a tape character matches the first character on the card.
3. Now, without moving the card or the tape, move the pointer along the tape from those matching characters, one character pair to the right.
4. a. If the two characters now pointed to match, go to 3.
   b. If the pointer points to a CR on the tape, the string is not in this line, so return with carry set to signal failure.
   c. If the pointer points to the zero on the card, the string has been found, so return with no carry to signal success.
   d. If the character pair do not match, pick up the pointer and the tape together and move them back to the first character on the card. Go to 2.

SINLN: Steps 2 through 4 are performed in the line-oriented search subroutine SINLN:, which also handles the updating of the buffer pointer, depending on the outcome. If the string was not found in the line, BFPNT is updated to the end of that line, ready for another line to be searched. If the string was found, BFPNT is not updated so that the line containing the string can be printed by SHOLN:, which is called way back in the main program.

This segregation of duties, with SINLN: only testing for the presence of a particular string in one line, and SINFL: handling the spooling of the file through the buffer, and the main program deciding what to do with the string when found, makes these subroutines more adaptable to other similar spool and search tasks.

NEWBF: This subroutine is written to be completely compatible with any programs you may want to write in the future, because it blindly saves all registers before performing its simple task. The subroutine moves the top half of the buffer, HIBUF, down to the low half, LOBUF, and then calls READR: to fill up the high half. By not messing around with BFPNT, this subroutine makes no assumptions about how it will be used, so it is adaptable to functions that do not use a buffer pointer or that want to handle a pointer differently.

SHOLN: This subroutine does use BFPNT, but only to get an initial address from which to begin the display of whatever text it finds between that initial address and the following CR. HL is saved so that only the accumulator will be changed by a call to this general purpose subroutine.

READR: One of the two subroutines in MISC-SU.LIB, READR: is so general purpose that it doesn't belong in FINDSTRN.LIB. All of the above subroutines do belong there, because even though they are easy to use in other programs, they all refer to other routines within the .LIB file or to the four named memory addresses at the bottom of Listing 10.6.

To read one record from a named file, READR: assumes that a file has been previously opened for read, and it simply calls BDOS to fill the 128 bytes of memory pointed to by HL with the next sequential record from the opened file pointed to by the default TFCB. All of the registers are saved and restored here in case BDOS wants to change them. And BDOS does.

Along the way, READR: checks OPINT: in case the operator wants to abort the read in the middle of the file. Our OPINT: tests for CTRL Z from CON: to cause an abort, which differentiates this function from the CTRL C convention that is common to the CP/M operating system.

COMHD: Our final subroutine simply subtracts DE from HL and tests for a "borrow," indicating that DE was greater than HL. For compatibility with other tests, the sense of the carry bit is inverted before the subroutine restores the original contents of both registers and returns.

Listing 10-5

```
                ; FIND A STRING IN A BUFFERED LINE
                ; ENTER WITH H,L POINTING TO A STRING TERMINATED BY ZERO &
                ; BFPNT (BUFFER POINTER) CONTAINING CURRENT BUFFER ADDRESS

02D5 D5         SINLN:  PUSH    D           ; "String IN a LiNe"
02D6 E5                 PUSH    H           ; SAVE REGISTERS
02D7 223704             SHLD    STPNT       ; SAVE STRING POINTER
02DA EB                 XCHG                ;  AND PUT IT IN D,E
02DB 2A3504             LHLD    BFPNT       ; GET LINE BUFFER POINTER
02DE 7E                 MOV     A,M         ; MAKE SURE WE ARE PAST
02DF FE0D               CPI     CR          ;  THE INITIAL CR
02E1 C2E502             JNZ     SINL1
02E4 23                 INX     H
02E5 7E         SINL1:  MOV     A,M         ; FIND THE FIRST MATCH
02E6 FE0D               CPI     CR          ;  OR END OF LINE
02E8 CA1203             JZ      SINL7
02EB 1A                 LDAX    D           ; CHECK FOR STRING CHAR
02EC BE                 CMP     M           ;  SAME AS LINE CHARACTER
02ED CAF402             JZ      SINL2       ; GO OR
02F0 23                 INX     H           ;  NO-GO, SO TRY ANOTHER
02F1 C3E502             JMP     SINL1
02F4 13         SINL2:  INX     D           ; FIRST MATCH, POINT AHEAD
02F5 23                 INX     H           ;  IN STRING AND BUFFER
02F6 7E         SINL3:  MOV     A,M         ; END OF LINE?
02F7 FE0D               CPI     CR
02F9 CA1203             JZ      SINL7       ;  (E.O.L. IS FAILURE)
02FC 1A                 LDAX    D           ; NO, END OF STRING?
02FD B7                 ORA     A           ;  (E.O.S. IS SUCCESS)
02FE CA0D03             JZ      SINL5
0301 BE                 CMP     M           ; NEITHER, STILL MATCH?
0302 CAF402             JZ      SINL2       ; YES, DO ANOTHER
0305 EB         SINL4:  XCHG                ; NO, REWIND STRING
0306 2A3704             LHLD    STPNT       ;  POINTER AND RETRY
0309 EB                 XCHG                ;   THE COMPARE
030A C3E502             JMP     SINL1
030D 37         SINL5:  STC                 ; FOUND THE STRING, LEAVE
030E 3F                 CMC                 ; BFPNT, FLAG WITH NO CARRY
030F E1         SINL6:  POP     H           ; RESTORE REGISTERS
0310 D1                 POP     D
0311 C9                 RET                 ;  AND RETURN
0312 223504     SINL7:  SHLD    BFPNT       ; STORE START OF NEXT LINE,
0315 37                 STC                 ;  FLAG STRING NOT IN THIS
0316 C30F03             JMP     SINL6       ;   LINE, SO GIVE UP
```

Listing 10-6

```
          ; NEW BUFFER: MOVE HIGH BUFFER TO LOW BUFFER,
          ;   READ 1 RECORD INTO HI BUFFER, RETURN WITH
          ;      CARRY IF END OF FILE

0319 C5       NEWBF:  PUSH    B           ; "NEW BuFfer"
031A D5               PUSH    D           ; SAVE ALL
031B E5               PUSH    H
031C 0E80             MVI     C,128       ; SIZE OF BUFFER TO MOVE
031E 21B503           LXI     H,HIBUF     ; SOURCE ADDRESS
0321 E5               PUSH    H           ;  SAVED
0322 113503           LXI     D,LOBUF     ; DESTINATION ADDRESS
0325 7E       NEWB1:  MOV     A,M         ; FROM HERE
0326 12               STAX    D           ;  TO HERE
0327 23               INX     H
0328 13               INX     D
0329 0D               DCR     C           ; TIL DONE
032A C22503           JNZ     NEWB1
032D E1               POP     H           ; RESTORE SOURCE START
032E CD4B04           CALL    READR       ;  READ A RECORD INTO THERE
0331 E1               POP     H           ; AND ALL DONE
0332 D1               POP     D
0333 C1               POP     B
0334 C9               RET

0335          LOBUF:  DS      128         ; LOW HALF OF BUFFER
03B5          HIBUF:  DS      128         ; HIGH HALF OF BUFFER
0435 0000     BFPNT:  DW      0           ; BUFFER POINTER
0437 0000     STPNT:  DW      0           ; STRING POINTER
```

Listing 10-7

```
          ; SHOW ONE ASCII LINE FROM (BFPNT) TO TERMINATING CR
          ;   (WILL OUTPUT LEADING CR, IF ANY)
          ; LEAVES BFPNT UNCHANGED

0439 E5       SHOLN:  PUSH    H           ; "SHOw one LiNe"
043A 2A3504           LHLD    BFPNT       ;  SAVE ONE POINTER
043D 7E               MOV     A,M         ; GET ONE CHARACTER
043E 23               INX     H           ;  POINT AHEAD
043F CD5E01   SHOL1:  CALL    CO          ; OUTPUT ONE CHARACTER
0442 7E               MOV     A,M         ; GET THE NEXT
0443 23               INX     H           ;  AND POINT AHEAD
0444 FE0D             CPI     CR          ; END OF LINE?
0446 C23F04           JNZ     SHOL1       ;  NO, LOOP
0449 E1               POP     H           ;  YES, ALL DONE
044A C9               RET
```

146

Listing 10-8

```
                    ; MODULE NAME:   MISC-SU.LIB
                    ; LAST UPDATE: 26 MAR 84     BY: KMB
                    ; FUNCTION: MISCELLANEOUS SUBROUTINES
                    ; REQUIRES: BEGIN.LIB
                    ;=========================================================

                    ; READ ONE RECORD INTO (H,L)
                    ;   RETURN WITH CARRY SET IF END OF FILE

0014 =              READF   EQU     20              ; READ ONE RECORD FUNCTION
001A =              SDMAF   EQU     26              ; SET DMA ADDRESS FUNCTION

044B C5             READR:  PUSH    B               ; "READ one Record"
044C D5                     PUSH    D               ; SAVE ALL
044D E5                     PUSH    H
044E EB                     XCHG                    ; ADDRESS TO D,E
044F 0E1A                   MVI     C,SDMAF         ;   WILL BE DMA ADDRESS
0451 CD0500                 CALL    BDOS            ;    SET IT
0454 CD7C01                 CALL    OPINT           ; PERMIT OPERATOR ABORT
0457 115C00                 LXI     D,TFCB          ; USING DEFAULT FCB,
045A 0E14                   MVI     C,READF         ;   FOR RECORD READ,
045C CD0500                 CALL    BDOS            ;    FILL MEMORY FROM DISK
045F B7                     ORA     A               ; TEST RETURN FOR ZERO = OK
0460 37                     STC                     ; PUT RETURN INTO CARRY
0461 C26504                 JNZ     READ1
0464 3F                     CMC
0465 E1             READ1:  POP     H               ; RESTORE AND RETURN
0466 D1                     POP     D
0467 C1                     POP     B
0468 C9                     RET

                    ; COMPARE H,L TO D,E
                    ;   RETURNS WITH CARRY SET IF H,L GREATER THAN D,E

0469 D5             COMHD:  PUSH    D               ; "COMpare H,1 to D,e"
046A E5                     PUSH    H               ; SAVE REGISTERS
046B 7B                     MOV     A,E             ; COMPLEMENT D,E
046C 2F                     CMA
046D 5F                     MOV     E,A
046E 7A                     MOV     A,D
046F 2F                     CMA
0470 57                     MOV     D,A
0471 19                     DAD     D               ; NOW "SUBTRACT"
0472 3F                     CMC                     ; CORRECT THE CARRY
0473 E1                     POP     H               ; RESTORE AND RETURN
0474 D1                     POP     D
0475 C9                     RET
```

147

PUT IT ALL TOGETHER

All of the components of PGMCAT.ASM are listed in order, with FINDSTRN.LIB being dissected into Listings 10.4, 10.5, 10.6, and 10.7. Merge BEGIN.LIB, PGMCAT.LIB, FINDSTRN.LIB, and MISC-SU.LIB into PGMCAT.ASM, and assemble it. Since there are no simple-minded individual tests for each subroutine possible in such a program, you will have to debug the program in one piece. Given the .PRN listings here to compare with your own object code, it should not be too hard to get PGMCAT running.

EXPERIMENTS

The normal use for PGMCAT consists of making a hard copy listing of the components of each of your programs as they are created and updated. Then, if any question ever arises as to which version of program X that is you just found on a particular disk, PGMCAT can produce a screen display of the program in question to be matched against the PGMCAT printouts of known configurations.

It should not be too difficult for you to go one step further and create one big disk file with all of the output from PGMCAT, as it scans all of your source programs. Then you can write another program, FINDPGM, to search that file for a particular version of a program or module. A quick analysis of PGMCAT and Figure 10.2 will show you that most of FINDPGM already exists in PGMCAT. The new program will need two input parameters: the file name of your data base and the name of the program to search for. Techniques for parsing command line parameters were covered in Chapter 8, so you should have lots of tools to work with now.

This is the end of the general purpose programming presented in this book. Part III contains bits and pieces of CBIOS writing techniques that are largely hardware-specific, so no complete do-it-yourself programs are possible for inclusion in that section. You had better key in and check out PGMCAT right now. It is the last program present you are going to get. You have to write your own from here on.

part 3

Your own customized BIOS

chapter 11

The structure of a CBIOS

There are a number of reasons that you might want to write, or even need to write, your own Customized Basic Input/Output System. The most obvious, and most complicated, is to adapt CP/M to an entirely new computer. Much simpler is adapting some new hardware item to an existing computer. You can even benefit from modifying the CBIOS of a computer that has no new hardware, because you can add more operator-friendly features to an existing configuration.

Some CBIOS additions that the computer operator can notice instantly are the addition of a single-key pause control to replace the CTRL S - CTRL S sequence or the provision for a remote console that can let you operate your computer from two different locations, even both at the same time.

In addition to enhancing console operation, we will see how you can implement a program autoloader that will skip over the usual initial CP/M prompt and start executing some named program at every cold and/or warm start. These are only a few of the features that an assembly language programmer can add to a CP/M system, once familiarity with the CBIOS has been acquired.

GETTING STARTED

You don't need new hardware to work with to get started writing your own super CBIOS. The easiest task to undertake initially is to add some feature to an existing computer. To do that you will need the source code for the CBIOS that has been installed on your computer. Most manufacturers of single-board computers, computer component boards, and industrial development systems supply this with their machines in the form of printouts and, if you are lucky, the source code on disk. In addition, the schematics of the hardware are useful if you know how to read them, and the data sheets on any programmable components used for the serial ports, parallel ports, and disk controllers contain information for the programmer as well as the hardware designer.

If you are working with a computer that does not include all that documentation, try to get it from the manufacturer. If it is a very popular model, some ambitious investigator might have psyched out the BIOS and may have published the results. If the source program is not available from any source, scream loudly to the seller of the system. All CP/M-based computer systems should come with full documentation, just as CP/M purchased directly from Digital Research does.

Even if you have absolutely no CBIOS source code documentation for your computer, there are ways for you to add some features to your system, provided that you know the characteristics and hardware port addresses of your I/O device interfaces. We will be looking at how to do this, using Extra Sneaky Programming, in the next chapter.

In addition to the documentation, you will need a copy of the original CP/M distribution diskette that includes MOVCPM.COM and SYSGEN.COM. Some system integrators have renamed those programs to reflect the fact that they have already customized the operating system to run on their hardware. It doesn't matter what the programs are named as long as they provide you with the ability to generate a new-sized version of CP/M and to write the resulting CP/M system image from memory out onto the system tracks on your disk.

Easy to Do

Writing a CBIOS, or a small part to add to an existing CBIOS, is really easy once you learn the basics. Also, the structure of the CP/M BIOS provides you with a handy outline to follow in creating a CBIOS from scratch. That outline is the jump table that must exist at the very start of every CP/M BIOS. The table itself is a list of subroutines that you must write, one at a time, to create a new system from scratch. Of course, you can pick a line or two out of the table as a guide to making small enhancements to your system. After looking at the table as a whole, we will see how easy it is to add that first new feature to your own version of CP/M.

THE JUMP TABLE

Memory locations 6 and 7 contain the address of the entry into the Basic Disk Operating System, and along with the JMP opcode at location 5, forms the three-byte jump instruction into BDOS. When our programs pass a function code to BDOS through that JMP, the function is decoded. BDOS will set proper values into the CPU registers and perform a CALL operation to one of the CBIOS jump table entries as listed in Table 11.1.

The table shows the complete list of 33 three-byte JMP instructions that constitute the CBIOS jump table for a full implementation of a banked memory CP/M Plus installation. In such a system, all of these jumps must exist at the beginning of CBIOS in exactly the order shown so that BDOS will be able to access each of the subroutines that the JMP instructions point to.

Table 11.1

JMP BOOT	; ARRIVE HERE FROM COLD START LOAD
JMP WBOOT	; ARRIVE HERE FOR WARM START
	(a)
JMP CONST	; CHECK FOR CONSOLE CHARACTER READY
JMP CONIN	; READ CONSOLE CHARACTER IN
JMP CONOUT	; WRITE CONSOLE CHARACTER OUT
JMP LIST	; WRITE LIST DEVICE CHARACTER OUT
JMP PUNCH	; WRITE PUNCH DEVICE CHARACTER OUT
JMP READER	; READ READER DEVICE CHARACTER IN
	(b)
JMP HOME	; MOVE TO TRACK 0 ON SELECTED DISK
JMP SELDSK	; SELECT DISK DRIVE
JMP SETTRK	; SET TRACK NUMBER
JMP SETSEC	; SET SECTOR NUMBER
JMP SETDMA	; SET DMA ADDRESS
JMP READ	; READ SELECTED SECTOR
JMP WRITE	; WRITE SELECTED SECTOR
	(c)
JMP LISTST	; CHECK FOR LIST DEVICE NOT BUSY
JMP SECTRAN	; TRANSLATE LOGICAL TO PHYSICAL SECTOR
	(d)
JMP CONOST	; CHECK OUTPUT STATUS OF CONSOLE
JMP AUXIST	; CHECK INPUT STATUS OF AUX DEVICE
JMP AUXOST	; CHECK OUTPUT STATUS OF AUX DEVICE
JMP DEVTBL	; GET ADDRESS OF CHARACTER I/O TABLE
JMP DEVINI	; INITIALIZE CHARACTER I/O DEVICES
JMP DRVTBL	; GET ADDRESS OF DISK DRIVE TABLE
JMP MULTIO	; SET NUMBER OF MULTI-R/W SECTORS
JMP FLUSH	; FLUSH HOST BUFFER (USER SUPPLIED BLOCKING)
JMP MOVE	; MEMORY-TO-MEMORY BLOCK MOVE
JMP TIME	; GET OR SET TIME CLOCK
JMP SELMEM	; SET MEMORY BANK—ABSOLUTE
JMP SETBNK	; SET MEMORY BANK FOR NEXT DMA MOVE
JMP XMOVE	; SET MEMORY BANK NUMBERS FOR NEXT MOVE CALL
JMP USERF	; RESERVED FOR SYSTEM INTEGRATOR
JMP RESERV1	; RESERVED FOR FUTURE USE
JMP RESERV2	; RESERVED FOR FUTURE USE
	(e)

Table 11.1 The BIOS jump table. Table entries provide access to routines for system cold and warm start (a), input/output device access (b), and mass storage access (c). CP/M version 2 enhancements added two more entries (d), and the greatly expanded capability of CP/M Plus (version 3) requires at least some of the entries in (e), depending on the features incorporated.

Version 1 Jumps

A subset of Table 11.1, groups (a), (b), and (c), forms the BIOS jump table that existed in CP/M version 1. Later versions duplicate this basic table, which consists of the bootup entries (a), the I/O entries (b), and the disk access entries (c). Anything the operating system or a user program needed to do with any I/O devices or the disk drives could be done through these basic entry points. Later versions of CP/M duplicate these entries and add to them.

Version 2 Adds Two

As we have seen, CP/M 2.2 permits the user more flexibility in defining the disk subsystem and also introduces Despool, which implements overlapped printing and system operation. To facilitate these new features, two new jumps (Table 11.1 (d)) are added to the table, but it is not absolutely necessary for the system integrator to include them. Most of the changes from version 1 to 2 were buried within the disk access subroutines in group (c).

CP/M Plus Doubles the Jumps

As we have seen, CP/M Plus in a banked memory computer adds many new features to the operating system, and its jump table is about twice the size of the earlier versions. A quick look at the functions shown in Table 11.1 (e) will disclose that there are enhancements to the basic I/O and disk functions as well as new functions required to support the operating system in a banked memory environment.

In spite of all these new jumps, the basic list of 17 subroutine entries is the same for CP/M Plus as it was for earlier systems. We will be concerned only with these first, common jumps in this section. There is not enough space available to cover the new CP/M Plus functions in detail, and they are adequately documented in the *System Guide* for the new operating system. Once you have become familiar with how to write a CBIOS using the version 2 subset of functions, you should have no trouble tackling CP/M Plus on your own.

Direct BIOS Calls

We know that a pointer to the BIOS jump table exists at memory location zero, because programs return to CP/M through the warm start entry (JMP WBOOT) into the BIOS. This jump is set up initially by the code at BOOT, which is executed immediately after CP/M is read in from the system tracks on the disk. BOOT is part of CBIOS and knows the start address of CBIOS, and so writes that address plus three into memory locations 1 and 2, following the JMP opcode at zero.

Since any program can read the address field at locations 1 and 2, programmers found out that they could find where the BIOS entries were by reading that address and adding six to get a CONST, nine to access CONIN, etc. Obviously, the same I/O functions are available through BDOS calls (Table 5.1), but by moving up to BIOS + 24 through BIOS + 42, a program can directly access the subroutines that handle disk selection, head positioning, and data transfers at the most primitive level.

The program that produced the disk sector dumps in Figure 8.3 used such direct BIOS calls to select drive A:, step the R/W head to track 3, and read sector 0. For such a program to work, the address at locations 2 and 3 must point to the JMP WBOOT instruction at BIOS + 3 and *not* to WBOOT itself, which is located further on within the CBIOS. If you try to run such a program on MP/M, or on a banked memory CP/M Plus, SELDSK (for example) may not actually exist where you expect to find it at BIOS + 27.

Digital Research states, in the manuals for CP/M 2.2 and Plus, that direct BIOS calls are not recommended because of possible incompatibilities with future versions of the operating system. However, they do acknowledge that direct BIOS calls are indispensable for programs like SYSGEN and disk formatting routines like the one that sets up the special directory format for CP/M Plus time and date stamping. The programmer is warned to have all programs make sure they are running in a version that should have a standard BIOS jump table directly accessible in main RAM. Also, it wouldn't hurt for the program to check for the existence of the correct number (15, 17, or 33) of three-byte JMP instructions beginning at the address believed to be the base of BIOS. Only then should a program try to execute direct BIOS calls.

The Programmer's Outline

The CBIOS jump table can be used as an outline for the programmer adapting CP/M to a completely new hardware environment. Simply write code to execute the startup functions accessed by group (a) and write one subroutine to perform each of the functions required for each table entry in group (b) and up, and you have a CBIOS. We will have to postpone coverage of group (a) until Chapter 13, but we can start right in by looking at the requirements for accessing the computer console, adding fancy features to make the computer operator's life easier, and providing for multiple consoles through use of the IOBYT.

REAL-LIFE EXAMPLES

Since no two computer systems have identical I/O hardware, we will not be able to include many key-in-and-run program examples in this section of the book. The examples included here are not hypothetical, however. They are all drawn from computer systems that have CBIOS installations written by the author of this book. They have been chosen because most of the device drivers are common types in the real world: Intel 8251 USARTs (Universal Synchronous/Asynchronous Receiver/Transmitters) for serial ports, common latch ICs for parallel ports, and Western Digital floppy disk controllers.

The hardware you will be working with may differ in minor details, but experience shows that most serial communication, programmable parallel port, and disk controller ICs all show familial similarities, as would be expected from the tasks they perform. Learning a new hardware environment still takes some study, but the examples shown in this section should provide a framework on which you can hang your own programming efforts.

A Simple Sample System

We will be looking at an example computer system running CP/M version 2.2 that has two serial ports, one parallel port, and two floppy disk drives. One serial port will normally be used for the CON:, one for the AUX: (PUN: and RDR:) device, and the parallel port will connect to a Centronics compatible printer, so it will be the LST: device. Those are the default uses for all of the ports, but later on we will want to implement the IOBYT function to permit them to be used for other purposes.

Since we now have to work with absolute hardware addresses in these CBIOS examples, real port addresses from the author's little computer system will be used. These are defined in Listing 11.1, which also defines the address of the 2-bit latch that selects the disk drives. At the bottom of the listing the default setting of the IOBYT is defined, with comments displaying the binary bit pattern of the IOBYT and what it means.

Listing 11-1

```
0001 =          TXRDY   EQU     1       ; 8251 TX BUFFER EMPTY
0002 =          RXRDY   EQU     2       ; 8251 RX CHAR READY
0008 =          P1RDY   EQU     80H     ; PRINTER BUSY BIT
0001 =          KBRDY   EQU     1       ; KEYBOARD PAUSE KEY

00E8 =          S1DAT   EQU     0E8H    ; SERIAL 1 DATA (I/O)
00E9 =          S1STA   EQU     0E9H    ; SERIAL 1 STATUS (I)
00E9 =          S1CMD   EQU     0E9H    ; SERIAL 1 COMMAND (O)

00F8 =          S2DAT   EQU     0F8H    ; SERIAL 2 DATA (I/O)
00F9 =          S2STA   EQU     0F9H    ; SERIAL 2 STATUS (I)
00F9 =          S2CMD   EQU     0F9H    ; SERIAL 2 COMMAND (O)

00C2 =          P1O     EQU     0C2H    ; PARALLEL 1 OUTPUT
00C2 =          P1I     EQU     0C2H    ; PARALLEL 1 INPUT

00C0 =          DSEL    EQU     0C0H    ; DISK DRIVE SELECT (O)

0003 =          IOBYT   EQU     3       ; I/O ASSIGNMENT BYTE
0004 =          CDISK   EQU     4       ; CURRENT DISK DRIVE
0080 =          STAK    EQU     80H     ; CP/M STACK

0000 =          DDISK   EQU     0       ; DEFAULT CURRENT DRIVE

0094 =          DIOBYT  EQU     94H     ; DEFAULT I/O BYTE:
                ;                 MSB 76    54      32     10 LSB
                ;                     10    01      01     00 BIN
                ;                      2     1       1      0 DEC
                ;                 LST:  PUN:    RDR:   CON:
                ;                 P 1:  S 2:    S 2:   S 1:
```

IOBYT Fundamentals

This 8-bit memory location is divided up into four 2-bit fields for the four logical devices shown in the listing. Two bits can express up to four values, or in this case up to four different hardware devices that can be assigned to each logical device. We won't need to select that many for each logical device, so the parts of our CBIOS that have to decode the appropriate fields within the IOBYT can be somewhat simplified. Each of our four logical devices will have three possible physical device assignments.

Any time you enter the command **STAT VAL:** you will be presented with a list of four possible I/O devices that can be assigned to each logical device, but the names that are embedded within the STAT.COM program are archaic, so we will be changing them to reflect the possible assignments within our example computer. Our new **STAT VAL:** will look like this:

```
CON: = S 1: S 2: S12:    :
RDR: = S 1: S 2: P1I:    :
PUN: = S 1: S 2: P10:    :
SLT: = S 1: S 2: P10:    :
```

showing the three possible options for each logical device, with the fourth option field blank except for the necessary ":" terminator.

After booting up our example computer, with BOOT setting up the default IOBYT shown in Listing 11.1, a command of STAT DEV: will display:

```
CON: is S 1:
RDR: is S 2:
PUN: is S 2:
LST: is P10:
```

once we have written our own CBIOS and "corrected" STAT.COM as will be discussed in the next chapter.

You should relate these names to the I/O port and IOBYT bit pattern data shown in Listing 11.1. That should make our I/O scheme obvious, except for the CON: configuration "S12:" that would result from an IOBYT of xxxxx10. For that bit pattern we will write a CON: device driver subroutine that will permit two consoles to be operated in parallel. That is an unusual configuration, but might prove handy for a computer that is controlling some large machine where you would want access to the application program from either of two locations without having to reassign the CON: device.

It is also a good technique for illustrating the flexibility provided by the use of the IOBYT. Before we get that far, we will examine some more simple CBIOS implementation examples where IOBYT has not yet been implemented.

CBIOS STRUCTURE DEFINED

From all this we can see that the structure of a CP/M V2.2 CBIOS is defined by the hardware elements of the computer that have to be serviced and by the software elements: the IOBYT and the jump table. All that is left to do is to fill in the details.

For CP/M Plus, all of this will still apply, except that a somewhat different implementation of IOBYT is incorporated in that operating system. Most of our examples will still apply when you are ready to move up to the big Plus.

chapter 12

Input/output
implementations

In this chapter we will start by assuming that you have never written any assembly language routines that directly access I/O devices through absolute hardware port addresses. The very simple basics of doing that will be quickly covered using the CON: device, because that is the first task to be tackled in writing a CBIOS. Once we have the CON: working in both input and output directions, we will see how easy it is to add the other I/O devices and then implement the IOBYT, as described in the preceding chapter. Finally, we will get around to some of those niceties you have been teased with.

IMPLEMENTING CON:

The first three jumps in Table 11.1(b) access subroutines to check the console status to see if the operator has pressed a key (CONST), to read that character when it is ready (CONIN), and to output a character to the CON: screen (CONOUT). All of these operations are trivial in a system that has not implemented the IOBYT or any fancy bells and whistles.

Typical Serial Port

Virtually all microcomputers connect the CON: through one of the popular USART devices, which convert an incoming serial bit stream into a parallel 8-bit data byte and set a received character ready (RXRDY) bit when each character has been completely shifted in. It is the duty of the operating system and applications programs to make sure that they are ready to read each character as soon as it is typed by the operator.

The simplest implementation is polled I/O, where the programs constantly check to see if a character has been received. The USART contains a status register, read by inputting data from the S1STA port (Listing 11.1). The status byte thus read includes bits other than the received data ready bit, so our CONST: subroutine will mask off all the bits except RX ready and return with the contents of the A register set to zero if no character is ready, or set to the flag value 0FFH if a character has been received. CONST: does not read-in the character, it only checks to see if one is ready to be read. Our CONST: subroutine looks like this:

```
CONST:    IN      S1STA       ; CHAR READY?
          ANI     RXRDY       ; MASK RX READY
          RZ                  ; RETURN ZERO IF NO
          MVI     A,0FFH      ; RETURN FLAG IF YES
          RET
```

for those hardware implementations where the RXRDY bit is low (zero) for no character ready, or high (one) for character ready.

If the sense of the bit is reversed, CONST: will look like this:

```
CONST:    IN      S1STA     ; CHAR READY?
          ANI     RXRDY     ; MASK RX READY
          MVI     A,0       ; SET A = ZERO
          RNZ               ; RETURN ZERO IF NO
          CMA               ; SET A = 0FFH
          RET               ; RETURN FLAG IF YES
```

which has inverted the sense of the value returned in the A register, relative to the sense of the RXRDY bit, without adding much code. This is made possible because the 8080 **Mo**Ve **I**mmediate (MVI) opcode does not disturb the condition code bits between the **AN**d Immediate (ANI) operation, which sets them and the conditional **R**eturn on **N**ot **Z**ero (RNZ) opcode that tests the zero flag. Once you know which bit to test and what its sense is, I/O device programming is simple.

The operating system can call CONST:, and if no character is ready, go on about its business. You might have noticed that mode of operation during PIP, when disk data transfers can be interrupted by pressing the carriage return key while PIP is doing things with the drives. Periodically, PIP calls BDOS and requests a check of the console status, and goes on about its business if no key has been pressed.

Our own OPINT: subroutine (Listing 6.1) does the same thing. OPINT: calls BDOS, and BDOS calls CONST:, and we write CONST: to reflect the hardware characteristics of the computer that is executing CP/M. This is typical for all CBIOS programming.

Reading the Character

When OPINT: saw that a CON: character had been received, it called BDOS to read it in, and BDOS calls CONIN: to do that. In order to service programs that do not call CONST: first, CONIN: will call CONST: itself and will wait for the character ready flag, even if it takes forever, before reading the USART data buffer.

```
CONIN:    CALL    CONST     ; CHAR READY?
          ORA     A
          JZ      CONIN     ; NO, WAIT FOR ONE
          IN      S1DAT     ; YES, GET IT
          ANI     7FH       ; MASK TO 7 BITS
          RET               ; AND ALL DONE
```

Notice here that all of the hardware-specific details of which particular bit within the status byte detects character ready, and what its sense is, are handled in CONST:, so the code for CONIN: will probably never have to be changed to enable it to run on any computer. So even here, deep within CBIOS, we have isolated ourselves from hardware specifics, at least in one subroutine.

Output to the Console

When the operating system wants to send a character out to the console, the ASCII character code is placed in the C register, and CONOUT: is called. This frees the A register for use to check that the transmit (TX) side of the USART is ready to accept data:

```
CONOUT:   IN      S1STA       ; TRANSMIT BUFFER EMPTY?
          ANI     TXRDY
          JZ      CONOUT      ; NO, WAIT FOR IT
          MOV     A,C         ; YES, GET THE CHARACTER
          OUT     S1DAT       ; AND OUTPUT IT
          RET
```

Note that the status and data port addresses are the same for transmit and receive, but the status bit for TX buffer empty is different from that for RX data ready. If the sense of the status bit is the opposite, only the JZ CONOUT opcode will have to be changed to JNZ CONOT. Also note that all absolute values, like port addresses and status bits, are defined in one place (Listing 11.1, which would be placed at the beginning of the CBIOS source program), so that hardware reconfigurations can be accommodated by simple changes in defined constants at the very beginning of the program.

IMPLEMENTING AUX:

Since our default assignments for the auxiliary device (PUN: and RDR:) are to serial port two, and it uses the same type of USART as serial port one, the PUN: driver will be virtually identical to CONOUT:, but RDR: will look like a merger of CONST: and CONIN:, as in:

```
READER:   IN      S2STA       ; CHAR READY?
          ANI     RXRDY
          JZ      READER      ; NO, WAIT FOR ONE
```

```
          IN          S2DAT          ; YES, GET THE CHAR
          RET
```

Note that there is no eighth-bit mask because RDR: can read binary data, but CON: always gets ASCII.

For CP/M versions before 3, there is no equivalent to CONST: for the PUN: and RDR: devices, which together constitute AUX:, but you can see that writing one would mean simply copying the code for CONST: and plugging in the proper port address.

IMPLEMENTING LST:

Our default list device will be an 8-bit parallel output port that is implemented in the computer hardware using a single 8-bit-wide octal latch IC that connects to the Centronics compatible printer data input pins. The strobe that is generated by the OUT P10 instruction and that latches the contents of the accumulator into the octal latch will be buffered and sent along to the printer as the signal that tells the printer to read the data.

If the printer is busy when it is time for us to send it another ASCII character, as will most often be the case since printers are very slow compared to microprocessors, we will have to read in and test the printer's BUSY signal before we output the character. If we hook that BUSY signal to the parallel input port and define the bit that it is connected to by the label P1RDY, the LIST output subroutine looks like:

```
LIST:     IN          P1I            ; GET PRINTER STATUS
          ANI         P1RDY          ; MASK THE BUSY BIT
          JZ          LIST           ; WAIT FOR NOT BUSY
          MOV         A,C            ; GET THE CHARACTER AND
          OUT         P10            ; SENT IT TO THE PRINTER
          RET
```

and we see once again that we haven't done anything new in writing this peripheral driver subroutine either, even though it is for a parallel port instead of a serial device. The principles are the same: test for busy, wait for not busy, and read or write the data.

Now that you see how easy it is to write CBIOS drivers for all of the I/O devices in Table 11.1(b), it is time to complicate things a little by implementing the IOBYT so that we could LIST to a serial printer on port S 2:, for instance, or run two console devices at once. Since that last is a little complicated, let's look first at the LST: device driver controlled by IOBYT.

IMPLEMENTING IOBYT

As we saw in Listing 11.1, the two **M**ost Significant **B**its (MSBs), 7 and 6, of the IOBYT contain the pattern that tells us which device is to be our LST: device. If those two bits are 00, we list to S 1:; if 01, LST: is S 2:; and if they are 10, then our output will go to parallel port P1O:, which is the default device because the top two bits of DIOBYT are 10. This default setting for the IOBYT will be written into memory location 3 by BOOT, and when we call the LIST driver in CBIOS with a character in register C, our LIST: subroutine has to read in and decode IOBYT, and then send the character to the proper output port.

We can see how this is handled from Listing 12.1, where the first action is to read IOBYT and shift the two most significant bits two positions to the left. The RLC opcode will cause a circular left shift, with bit 7 ending up in bit 0 on the first shift, and then moving into bit 1 on the second shift. Our original bits 7 and 6 are now in positions 1 and 0, so if we mask with 3 (11 in binary) we will cause all the other bit positions to be set to zero. If bits 1 and 0 are 00, the zero flag will be set as well, telling us to send the list character to serial port 1.

A complete driver subroutine for serial port 1 appears next, embedded within LIST:, beginning at S1OUT:. As you can see, there is no new code here! We fall into S1OUT: when our IOBYT bits are 00. If they are 01, we will end up in S2OUT: after the decrement at LIST2:. If those bits are either 10 or 11, we will end up in P1OUT:, and the character will be sent to the parallel port.

Punch Output

Since the PUN: device is also capable of being assigned to either S 1:, S 2:, or P1O:, depending on the setting of its own IOBYT bits, all we have to do to implement a PUNCH: subroutine is shift the PUN: bits four places to the right or four places to the left, which is the same thing in an 8-bit circular shift. So PUNCH: (Listing 12.2) begins by shifting IOBYT two places to the left and then lets the LIST1: entry (Listing 12.1) complete the shift, the decode of the bits, and the output of the PUN: character to the appropriate device driver.

Listing 12-1

```
                        ; OUTPUT REGISTER C TO LST:

BA83 3A0300    LIST:    LDA     IOBYT   ; GET LST: ASSIGNMENT
BA86 07        LIST1:   RLC             ; SHIFT LST: BITS "DOWN"
BA87 07                 RLC             ;   TO 2 LSB POSITIONS
BA88 E603               ANI     3       ; MASK LST: BITS
BA8A C298BA             JNZ     LIST2   ;   IS LST: = S 1:?
BA8D DBE9      S1OUT:   IN      S1STA   ; OUTPUT C TO S 1:
BA8F E601               ANI     TXRDY   ;   BUSY?
BA91 CA8DBA             JZ      S1OUT   ;     WAIT FOR NOT BUSY
BA94 79                 MOV     A,C     ;     THEN GET THE CHAR
BA95 D3E8               OUT     S1DAT   ;       AND SEND IT OUT
BA97 C9                 RET
BA98 3D        LIST2:   DCR     A       ; IS LST: = S 2:?
BA99 C2A7BA             JNZ     LIST3
BA9C DBF9      S2OUT:   IN      S2STA   ; OUTPUT C TO S 2:
BA9E E601               ANI     TXRDY
BAA0 CA9CBA             JZ      S2OUT
BAA3 79                 MOV     A,C
BAA4 D3F8               OUT     S2DAT
BAA6 C9                 RET
               LIST3:                   ; LST: IS PARALLEL PORT 1
BAA7 DBC2      P1OUT:   IN      P1I     ; OUTPUT C TO P1O
BAA9 E680               ANI     P1RDY   ; BUSY BIT IS ON P1I
BAAB CAA7BA             JZ      P1OUT   ;   WAIT FOR NOT BUSY
BAAE 79                 MOV     A,C     ;     THEN GET THE CHAR
BAAF D3C2               OUT     P1O     ;       AND SEND IT OUT
BAB1 C9                 RET
```

Listing 12-2

```
                        ; OUTPUT REGISTER C TO PUN:

BAB2 3A0300    PUNCH:   LDA     IOBYT   ; GET PUN: ASSIGNMENT
BAB5 07                 RLC             ; SHIFT PUN: BITS "DOWN"
BAB6 07                 RLC             ;   TWO SHIFTS HERE AND
BAB7 C386BA             JMP     LIST1   ;     TWO MORE SHIFTS THERE
```

Listing 12-3

```
                        ; OUTPUT REGISTER C TO CON:

BA71 3A0300    CONOUT:  LDA     IOBYT   ; GET CON: ASSIGNMENT
BA74 E603               ANI     3       ; MASK CON: BITS
BA76 CA8DBA             JZ      S1OUT   ; OUTPUT TO S 1:
BA79 3D                 DCR     A
BA7A CA9CBA             JZ      S2OUT   ;   OR TO S 2:
BA7D CD8DBA             CALL    S1OUT   ;     OR TO BOTH S 1:
BA80 C39CBA             JMP     S2OUT   ;       AND S 2:
```

CONOUT: This subroutine (Listing 12.3) also takes advantage of the individual driver routines that are embedded within LIST:, but with slightly different options. The CON: device can only be attached to one of the two serial ports, but we may want to operate with both a local and a remote terminal both active at the same time, as we discussed in the last chapter. Since the CON: bits are already the Least Significant Bits (LSBs) in IOBYT, all CONOUT: has to do is mask them and test the pattern, sending the console output character to S 1:, S 2:, or both.

Whenever we operate in the dual-terminal mode, we have to make sure that both terminals act like they are receiving data even if one of them is not connected or is turned off. This can be done at the RS-232 connectors on the computer's serial output ports by making sure that the "handshaking" signals are defeated, so that CONOUT: doesn't sit around forever waiting for a nonexistent remote terminal to accept the first character it tries to send. Fortunately for this mode of operation, almost all microcomputers will not hang up if data is sent to a disconnected device through a serial port, but just in case it doesn't work for you, here is where the problem occurs.

Since our LIST: subroutine includes three complete driver subroutines within itself, our PUN: and CONOUT: subroutines are very short. The same technique is applied to the input ports. The READER: subroutine (Listing 12.4) looks much like LIST: but implements inputs instead of outputs, and the handling of the parallel port is a little different. In our example computer, this port has 8 bits of output and 8 bits of input, and no separate ready bits like those that are available in the serial I/O USARTS. The parallel port will normally be used for the printer, and the most significant bit of the input port will be the printer BUSY signal. If we want to use that port for parallel input, we can only input 7 bits of data because we will have to use that same MSB for a character-ready handshake. P1IN: reflects that mode of operation, and we now have S1IN: and S2IN: subroutines to use for the console input.

Listing 12-4

```
; INPUT A CHARACTER FROM RDR:

BABA 3A0300   READER:  LDA   IOBYT   ; GET RDR: ASSIGNMENT
BABD 0F                RRC           ;  SHIFT RDR: BITS DOWN
BABE 0F                RRC
BABF E603              ANI   3       ; MASK RDR: BITS
BAC1 C2EBA             JNZ   READE1  ; IS RDR: = S 1:?
BAC4 DBE9     S1IN:    IN    S1STA   ; INPUT A CHAR FROM S 1:
BAC6 E602              ANI   RXRDY   ; MASK RX READY
BAC8 CAC4BA            JZ    S1IN    ; WAIT FOR A CHARACTER
BACB DBE8              IN    S1DAT   ; GET THE CHARACTER
```

Listing 12-4 (*continued*)

```
BACD C9                    RET
BACE 3D        READE1: DCR     A       ; IS RDR: = S 2:?
BACF C2DCBA            JNZ     READE2
BAD2 DBF9      S2IN:   IN      S2STA   ; INPUT A CHAR FROM S 2:
BAD4 E602              ANI     RXRDY
BAD6 CAD2BA            JZ      S2IN
BAD9 DBE8              IN      S1DAT
BADB C9                RET
               READE2:
BADC DBC2      P1IN:   IN      P1I     ; INPUT FROM PARALLEL 1
BADE E680              ANI     P1RDY   ; CHECK FOR INPUT READY
BAE0 CADCBA           JZ      P1IN    ; WAIT FOR INPUT
BAE3 DBC2              IN      P1I     ; READ IT IN
BAE5 C9                RET
```

Listing 12-5

; CHECK CON: STATUS FOR S 1:, S 2:, OR S12:

```
BA33 3A0300    CONST:  LDA     IOBYT   ; GET CON: ASSIGNMENT
BA36 E603              ANI     3       ; MASK CON: BITS
BA38 C243BA           JNZ     CONST2  ; IS IT S 1:?
BA3B DBE9      CON1S:  IN      S1STA   ;   CHECK S 1: STATUS
BA3D E602      CONST1: ANI     RXRDY   ;   MASK RX CHAR READY
BA3F C8               RZ              ;   RETURN ZERO IF NO
BA40 3EFF             MVI     A,0FFH  ;   RETURN FLAG IF YES
BA42 C9               RET
BA43 3D        CONST2: DCR     A       ; IS IT S 2:?
BA44 C24CBA           JNZ     CONST3
BA47 DBF9      CON2S:  IN      S2STA   ;   CHECK S 2: STATUS
BA49 C33DBA           JMP     CONST1  ;     USING COMMON CODE
BA4C CD3BBA    CONST3: CALL    CON1S   ; CHECK S 1:
BA4F B7               ORA     A       ;   AND THEN
BA50 C0               RNZ             ;   IF NOT S 1:
BA51 C347BA           JMP     CON2S   ;     CHECK S 2:
```

Listing 12-6

; WAIT FOR AND INPUT A CON: CHARACTER

```
BA54 3A0300    CONIN:  LDA     IOBYT   ; GET CON: ASSIGNMENT
BA57 E603              ANI     3       ; MASK CON: BITS
BA59 CAC4BA           JZ      S1IN    ; GET S 1: INPUT
BA5C 3D               DCR     A       ;   OR GET
BA5D CAD2BA           JZ      S2IN    ;   S 2: INPUT
BA60 CD3BBA    CONIN1: CALL    CON1S   ;   OR WAIT FOR FIRST
BA63 B7               ORA     A
BA64 C2C4BA           JNZ     S1IN    ; EITHER S 1:
BA67 CD47BA           CALL    CON2S
BA6A B7               ORA     A
BA6B C2D2BA           JNZ     S2IN    ;   OR S 2:
BA6E C360BA           JMP     CONIN1  ;   OR WAIT FOR FIRST
```

CONST: This subroutine (Listing 12.5) also includes two complete sub-subroutines for checking the status of the two serial port inputs: CON1S: and CON2S:. The first of these is identical to the first CONST: example subroutine way back at the beginning of this chapter, and the second one uses all of the first one's code except the first line, saving some CBIOS space by jumping from CON2S: back to CONST1: to keep from repeating the same program lines twice.

In our dual-terminal mode, CONST3: will check for a character ready on the first terminal, and if there is none, will check for a character ready on the second. Remember that CONST: wants to immediately return to the calling program whether a character is ready or not. So here we check to see if the first terminal has had a key pressed. If it has, there is no need to check the second terminal. If both have had keys pressed at the same time (not too likely!), the second USART won't forget the fact, and any later call to CONST: or CONIN: will detect that second character ready.

CONIN: Here again (Listing 12.6), for our first two IOBYT selections, an immediate jump is made to S1IN: or S2IN: to wait for and read a console character. In the dual-console mode, the loop beginning at CONIN1: will continuously poll the two serial input ports and respond to the first one that shows a character ready. So if you have to leave your plush office and walk out onto the factory floor, you can still continue your Star Trek game from a second terminal when no one is watching. This dual-terminal mode has been simple to implement using IOBYT, but it does have one failing. Two people typing away at the same time can cause problems because our simple CBIOS has no provisions for locking out either terminal for any length of time when the other is in use. We had to leave something for you to add to your own CBIOS.

These routines collectively constitute an implementation of the Table 11.1(b) I/O group of CBIOS subroutines for a 48 K byte CP/M V2.2. The listings have been broken out of the CBIOS.PRN file, and if you rearrange them in the order:

    CONST:
    CONIN:
    CONOUT:
    LIST:
    PUNCH:
    READER:

you will see that they occupy memory locations 0BA33H through 0BAE5H. Memory address 0BA00H is the start of a 48 K V2.2 CBIOS (Figure 7.1), and from there up through 0BA32H, we have the seventeen 3-byte JMP instructions that constitute the CBIOS jump table in our example computer. All of the I/O drivers have now been completed, including the use of the IOBYT, and with the added dual-terminal feature. Before we start looking at the disk control subroutines, let's see how to add some more bells and whistles to this I/O portion of the CBIOS.

BELLS AND WHISTLES

Getting access to the CBIOS on your computer opens up a world of opportunity for you to add all kinds of enhancements to your system. Even if you don't need to change the basic code of the CBIOS, you can make additions to it. Here are a couple of examples.

A Pause Switch

One very handy addition you can make to any computer that has one bit available on a parallel input port is a pause key, or switch, that will stop the CON: screen data from scrolling out of sight before you have a chance to read it. Our example system uses only the MSB on P1I: to sense printer BUSY, so a normally open, momentary contact, pushbutton switch was connected between the parallel port least significant bit and the system's common return. The input port IC normally tries to float each input pin up to a logic high level if not connected to any hardware, so with no one leaning on the pushbutton, the P1I: port bit 0 reads high, or logic 1. Push on the switch and it will read low. If the following is inserted at the very beginning of CONOUT: (Listing 12.2), pressing on the switch will cause the CON: display to pause:

```
CONOUT:   IN     P1I         ; INPUT FROM PARALLEL 1
          ANI    KBDRDY      ; MASK KEYBOARD READY
          JZ     CONOUT      ; WAIT TIL KEY IS RELEASED
          .      .
          .      .
```

where the dots indicate the continuation of the original code for CONOUT:.

On the author's computer, the pause switch is an unused key on a keyboard that is read through another parallel port. On systems that use a CON: terminal connected through a serial port, the extra key can be a pushbutton switch mounted on the side of the keyboard and connected to a parallel port through a length of two-conductor wire. Hi-fi speaker wire is ideal for this, because it is inexpensive, thin, and flexible.

Since this was such a simple "patch" to CBIOS, it could be implemented even if you do not have access to the source code for your CBIOS. Since you know where the jump table is found and can locate JMP CONOUT in the table, you could use DDT to patch in a jump to some unused area in RAM, then patch in the object code for the three lines above, followed by a jump back to the original CONOUT address. To do this, you can use the techniques for system generation in the next chapter, but instead of overlaying CBIOS.HEX into the system image in RAM, you would have to use the DDT move instruction to relocate the CBIOS area of the system in RAM down into the memory image of the system in low RAM, and then patch in the changes. You can make minor changes, even without the source code, and the first technique for implementing a program autoload can be done the same way.

Program Autoload

If you would like to have your computer load and execute an application program at every cold or warm start, you can fake CCP into loading AUTOSTRT.COM (for example) by overlaying the CCP command input buffer with the ASCII characters "AUTOSTRT" followed by a zero terminator, after you have set the buffer character counter to 8 to reflect the length of the command. To do this requires finding the character counter byte and the command input buffer at the beginning of CCP. They are at CCP + 7 for both CP/M V1.4 and V2.2. With the system image in memory following a MOVCPM, you can patch in:

    08   41   55   54   4F   53   54   52   54   00

in hex, beginning at CCP + 7, and then write the CP/M image to the disk system tracks in the usual manner. Then, whenever CCP is reloaded from disk at each cold and warm start, it will see a command of "AUTOSTRT" and will load and execute AUTOSTRT.COM from the boot disk, if it can find it. We will look at methods for working with the CP/M image in memory later on in the next chapter.

Another autostart technique that can be implemented entirely in CBIOS, and which is therefore adaptable to any version of CP/M or any other operating system or program that gets its initial command from

Listing 12-7

```
                    ; WAIT FOR AND INPUT A CON: CHARACTER

BA54 3A6BBA   CONIN:  LDA     AUTOCTR ; TEST THE COUNTER FOR
BA57 3D               DCR     A       ;   AUTOSTART COMPLETE
BA58 FA75BA           JM      CONIC   ;   CONTINUE IF DONE
BA5B 326BBA           STA     AUTOCTR ; STORE NEW COUNT
BA5E D5               PUSH    D       ; SAVE WORK REGISTERS
BA5F E5               PUSH    H
BA60 5F               MOV     E,A     ; STRING OFFSET TO D,E
BA61 1600             MVI     D,0
BA63 216CBA           LXI     H,AUTOSTR
BA66 19               DAD     D       ; POINT INTO STRING
BA67 7E               MOV     A,M     ; RETURN WITH ONE CHARACTER
BA68 E1               POP     H
BA69 D1               POP     D
BA6A C9               RET

BA6B 09        AUTOCTR DB     9         ; INITIAL COUNTER COUNT

BA6C 0D        AUTOSTR DB     13        ; CARRIAGE RETURN
BA6D 545254534F        DB     'TRTSOTUA'

               CONIC:                   ; CONTINUE WITH CON: IN
```

the CON: device, is illustrated by the CONIN: preprocessor shown in Listing 12.7.

This bit of programming will intercept any calls to CONIN:, and as long as the value stored in the **AUTO** start **C**oun**T**e**R** (AUTOCTR) is zero, will pass the call along to the **CON**sole **I**nput **C**ontinuation (CONIC:). Since CBIOS is assembled with AUTOCTR set to 9, the first nine times that CCP calls CONIN:, one of the characters stored in the command string AUTOSTR will be returned to CCP. This string has been entered in reverse order to simplify the indexing necessary to fetch each string character in turn, while counting AUTOCTR down to zero.

One advantage of this technique is that either BOOT: or WBOOT: can set AUTOCTR to 9 to implement the autostart at cold boot or warm boot or both. For a CBIOS implementation that requires any kind of system overlay after the termination of a transient program, or that wants to autostart a menu program, for instance, this technique is more flexible than the CCP patching, and is more transportable to other OS installations. But it does add quite a bit of code to CBIOS.

All of the techniques presented so far in this chapter require the modification of BIOS or the generation of a complete CBIOS from scratch. The next chapter will discuss how to get that CP/M image into memory and how to merge in the CBIOS. In the process we will see how to automate the CBIOS generation process. Before we continue with all of that let's take a quick look at how to modify STAT so that we can address our IOBYT selections by their proper names instead of using the archaic nomenclature supplied with CP/M.

PATCHING STAT.COM

Since our example computer has one parallel and two serial ports that can be reassigned among all of the logical devices, we want the program that does the reassignment to display and accept physical device names that are easy to relate to the physical devices themselves. In Chapter 11 we showed the names we want the command **STAT VAL:** to display, and here is how we can implement a customized STAT.COM.

Figure 12.1(a) shows a computer operator's session that involves using DDT.COM to read in and display the first few locations within STAT.COM, version 2.2. The V1.4 STAT.COM will look about the same, except the starting locations of the names we want to change will be at 0142H instead of 0159H, as in V2.2.

This first part of STAT.COM includes tables of logical device names (CON:, RDR:, etc.) followed by the physical device names (TTY:, CRT:, etc.) that we want to rename. All we have to do is patch the logical device names with any new names we choose, provided that each name is three capital letters followed by ":" and that the order of the names is not changed, because the position in the table corresponds directly with the patterns of bits in the IOBYT.

Overlay STAT.COM

With much patience and accuracy, you could type in the hex codes for new names using DDT, but it is much easier to write and assemble a STAT overlay (STATOVLY.ASM) like that shown in Listing 12.8 in the PRN file format. After this file has been edited and assembled correctly, the procedure shown in Figure 12.1(b) will use DDT to load STAT.COM, followed by a load of STATOVLY.HEX, which will overwrite the physical device names. A dump verifies that the overlay was correct, so DDT is exited by the command **G0** or by pressing CTRL C. Then all that is left is to SAVE the new version of STAT and test it by displaying the new names.

Now a command such as **STAT LST:=S 2:** will cause the list device to be reassigned to serial port 2. Using significant device names in STAT.COM makes using the implemented and customized IOBYT much more practical.

Figure 12.1 Customizing STAT.COM. DDT is used to display the first part of STAT.COM, illustrating the locations of the original device names stored in STAT (a). After STATOVLY.ASM has been generated to update the device names, DDT is used to read in STAT and overlay the new names (b). The updated STAT is saved on disk and then invoked with the request to display the device name options. The new device names correspond to the devices programmed into the customized BIOS.

```
A DDT STAT.COM
DDT VERS 2.2
NEXT  PC
-D100
0100 C3 33 04 20 20 20 43 6F 70 79 72 69 67 68 74 20 .3.   Copyright
0110 28 63 29 20 31 39 37 39 2C 20 44 69 67 69 74 61 (c) 1979, Digita
0120 6C 20 52 65 73 65 61 72 63 68 3F 3F 3F 3F 3F 3F l Research??????
0130 3F 3F 3F 3F 3F 3F 00 00 00 43 4F 4E 3A 52 44 52 ??????...CON:RDR
0140 3A 50 55 4E 3A 4C 53 54 3A 44 45 56 3A 56 41 4C :PUN:LST:DEV:VAL
0150 3A 55 53 52 3A 44 53 4B 3A 54 54 59 3A 43 52 54 :USR:DSK:TTY:CRT
0160 3A 42 41 54 3A 55 43 31 3A 54 54 59 3A 50 54 52 :BAT:UC1:TTY:PTR
0170 3A 55 52 31 3A 55 52 32 3A 54 54 59 3A 50 54 50 :UR1:UR2:TTY:PTP
0180 3A 55 50 31 3A 55 50 32 3A 54 54 59 3A 43 52 54 :UP1:UP2:TTY:CRT
0190 3A 4C 50 54 3A 55 4C 31 3A 52 2F 4F 00 52 2F 57 :LPT:UL1:R/O.R/W
01A0 00 53 59 53 00 44 49 52 00 52 2F 4F 20 52 2F 57 .SYS.DIR.R/O R/W
01B0 20 53 59 53 20 44 49 52 20 2A 2A 20 41 62 6F 72  SYS DIR ** Abor
```

(a)

```
A DDT STAT.COM
DDT VERS 2.2
NEXT  PC
1580 0100
-ISTATOVLY.HEX
-R
NEXT  PC
1580 0000
-D100
0100 C3 33 04 20 20 20 43 6F 70 79 72 69 67 68 74 20 .3.   Copyright
0110 28 63 29 20 31 39 37 39 2C 20 44 69 67 69 74 61 (c) 1979, Digita
0120 6C 20 52 65 73 65 61 72 63 68 3F 3F 3F 3F 3F 3F l Research??????
0130 3F 3F 3F 3F 3F 3F 00 00 00 43 4F 4E 3A 52 44 52 ??????...CON:RDR
0140 3A 50 55 4E 3A 4C 53 54 3A 44 45 56 3A 56 41 4C :PUN:LST:DEV:VAL
0150 3A 55 53 52 3A 44 53 4B 3A 53 20 31 3A 53 20 32 :USR:DSK:S 1:S 2
0160 3A 53 31 32 3A 20 20 20 3A 53 20 31 3A 53 20 32 :S12:   :S 1:S 2
0170 3A 50 31 49 3A 20 20 20 3A 53 20 31 3A 53 20 32 :P1I:   :S 1:S 2
0180 3A 50 31 4F 3A 20 20 20 3A 53 20 31 3A 53 20 32 :P1O:   :S 1:S 2
0190 3A 50 31 4F 3A 20 20 20 3A 52 2F 4F 00 52 2F 57 :P1O:   :R/O.R/W
01A0 00 53 59 53 00 44 49 52 00 52 2F 4F 20 52 2F 57 .SYS.DIR.R/O R/W
01B0 20 53 59 53 20 44 49 52 20 2A 2A 20 41 62 6F 72  SYS DIR ** Abor
-GO
A SAVE 21 STAT.COM
A STAT VAL:

Temp R/O Disk: d:=R/O
Set Indicator: d:filename.typ $R/O $R/W $SYS $DIR
Disk Status  : DSK: d:DSK:
User Status  : USR:
Iobyte Assign:
CON: = S 1: S 2: S12:   :
RDR: = S 1: S 2: P1I:   :
PUN: = S 1: S 2: P1O:   :
LST: = S 1: S 2: P1O:   :
```

(b)

Listing 12-8

```
                              ; STAT V2.2 DEVICE NAME OVERLAY

      0159                            ORG     0159H
                          ; CON:
 .    0159 5320313A               DB      'S 1:'
      015D 5320323A               DB      'S 2:'
      0161 5331323A               DB      'S12:'
      0165 2020203A               DB      '   :'
                          ; RDR:
      0169 5320313A               DB      'S 1:'
      016D 5320323A               DB      'S 2:'
      0171 5031493A               DB      'P1I:'
      0175 2020203A               DB      '   :'
                          ; PUN:
      0179 5320313A               DB      'S 1:'
      017D 5320323A               DB      'S 2:'
      0181 50314F3A               DB      'P1O:'
      0185 2020203A               DB      '   :'
                          ; LST:
      0189 5320313A               DB      'S 1:'
      018D 5320323A               DB      'S 2:'
      0191 50314F3A               DB      'P1O:'
      0195 2020203A               DB      '   :'

      0199                            END
```

OTHER CUSTOMIZING IDEAS

These are, of course, only a few things you can do to improve a CP/M system. Other enhancements that have proved valuable in many different computer systems include adding intercharacter and end-of-line delay loops in the LST: device driver subroutines to accommodate printers that can't operate at full computer I/O transfer speeds; implementing a CONIN: type ahead buffer to prevent lost characters; and setting up a CON: input translation table that can be used to convert a single incoming terminal function key code into a whole string of CCP or application program commands. This last uses a technique similar to AUTOSTRT. This and the other ideas require knowledge of your computer's hardware and the characteristics of your terminal device, so specific programs could not be included here.

Adding too many bells and whistles to a CBIOS can cause it to expand out of the limits of available memory. This can be overcome at the cost of TPA space by generating a smaller version of CP/M in the same RAM space and using the extra RAM to provide for more CBIOS features. How to move CP/M, and how to install and test a customized CBIOS without having to write it onto your disk system tracks until it is fully debugged, will be discussed next.

chapter 13

System generation

Wouldn't it be nice if each of us had $1 for every hour that has been spent puzzling over the numbers in the first few pages of the Digital Research *CP/M 2.2 Alteration Guide*? If you don't understand how rich that would make us all, you haven't yet tried to generate a new-sized version of CP/M with a customized CBIOS. Since that is the goal of the lessons to be learned in this section, and the path to that goal is smooth in spots (like the last chapter), but mighty rough in others (like the *Alteration Guide*), we will have to try to smooth out some rough spots on our way to customized versions of CP/M.

Since it is unlikely that anyone is doing much upgrading of V1.4 these days, we can ignore details specific to that version in this chapter. That does not mean that the following discussion is not applicable to 1.4, however. It is, but the absolute memory addresses and sizes won't apply to the older version. We can also ignore CP/M Plus for a while, because a lot of the detailed procedures that follow in this chapter have been very nicely automated for us in the version three system generation process. So let's look at why V2.2 system generation causes so many gray hairs.

HOW BIG IS CP/M V2.2?

The "Diskette Organization" map in the DRI *Alteration Guide* for CP/M 2.2 is based on the standard distribution disk, an 8-inch, single-density IBM format with 26 sectors of 128 bytes per track. The first sector of the first track is dedicated to a bootstrap loader program, leaving 25 sectors on the first track and 26 sectors on the second track for a maximum system size of 51 sectors. We won't have to convert that to K bytes for now.

Still thinking in terms of sectors (just like a disk does), the map shows that the following sizes exist on the distribution disk:

Bootstrap loader	1 record
CCP	16 records
BDOS	28 records
subtotal	45 records

which leaves $52 - 45 = 7$ records for CBIOS, or 896 bytes, in decimal. That is not a whole lot of program space for adding bells and whistles. Another fact a little **E**xtra **S**neaky **P**eeking (another definition for ESP) will disclose is that when those two tracks full of CP/M are loaded into your computer, the top 640 bytes of RAM won't have been touched. We could use that space for more bells and whistles!

Other Disk Formats

That memory space was left empty because the 8-inch disk ran out of sectors on the two dedicated system tracks. We can look at other disk formats and see that sometimes there is more room on the system tracks than will fit into memory. For instance, the 5¼-inch floppies that were discussed in Chapter 8 dedicate three system tracks of 20 records each to CP/M, because two tracks are not enough. That system sets aside one 256-byte sector for the bootstrap loader, so 58 records are left over for CP/M. Take away the 44 records for CCP and BDOS, and CBIOS can hog 14 records, or 1,792 bytes. That is too much to fit into the memory available for CBIOS!

That 5¼-inch Winchester hard disk has 72 CP/M records per track, four per physical sector. Dedicate one sector to the loader, and one Winch track provides 68 records for CP/M. That is 44 for the fixed-size stuff and 24 records for CBIOS, or a whopping 3 K bytes. Try to load that into a 64 K byte version of CP/M in a 64 K byte computer, and you will run right off the top of memory. That can be a disaster using the usual indexing methods, because the extra will wrap around past location zero and garbage the sacrosanct low memory areas in your computer.

The purpose of this long-winded discussion is to impress upon all would-be system integrators that there are pitfalls awaiting the programmer who is not careful about figuring out how big the CBIOS has grown to be and how much of it can be fit into the memory and disk space available. Take it from an old pitfall faller-into-er.

THE CP/M V2.2
MEMORY MAP

Back in Chapter 7 we wrote a program to illustrate how CP/M fits into the memory space. We have now seen that CP/M on the disk does not always map nicely into CP/M in memory. When we get through with this discussion, the arithmetic will be simplified and the rough spots all smooth. Or at least smoother.

Since CCP and BDOS are fixed in size, and we want to expand CBIOS, all we have to worry about is fitting all of our extra programming into the space between the base of CBIOS and the top of memory, or RAM TOP in Figure 7.1. Since memory is so cheap these days, and all new computers come with at least 64 K bytes of RAM, we will use a 64 K RAM example, and we can start by reviewing the map in Figure 7.1 (c). It shows that we have 0FA00H through 0FFFFH = 600H bytes available for CBIOS, or 1536 bytes.

Since that is more than will fit on some disk formats, and is less than we might want to use for some systems with lots of bells and whistles, we will be looking at how to generate a system that is larger than the system tracks will accommodate. We will also see how to resize CP/M to make room for a CBIOS that is even larger than that! Believe it or not, neither task is very difficult as long as you watch the numbers.

MOVCPM AND SYSGEN

Even if you never change the size of the CP/M system in your computer, MOVCPM.COM will be used whenever you want to create a system image in RAM that you can use to merge your new CBIOS into. When that CBIOS grows too big, you may have to MOVCPM down to a slightly smaller version to make room for an expanding CBIOS. You could run a 63 K version of CP/M in a 64 K RAM computer, for example, to gain another 1 K for CBIOS. When you do that, the SYSGEN program supplied with your computer may no longer work. We will have to see how to get around that rough spot.

MOV the Same Size

Using the example of a 64 K version of CP/M loaded from an 8-inch, single-density disk, let's assume that you have generated a new CBIOS.ASM and have assembled it into CBIOS.HEX. We have already seen that a 64 K CBIOS begins at 0FA00H in RAM (Figure 7.1), and that is the address at which you ORG'd your program for the assembler. You enter a command of **MOVCPM 64 *** as the DRI manual tells you to, and after saving CPM64.COM and then entering a command of **DDT**

CPM64.COM, you end up with a memory image of CP/M that looks like this:

	RAM ADDRESS	IMAGE ADDRESS
RAM TOP:	FFFFH	257FH
BIOS TOP:	FD7FH	22FFH
CBIOS:	FA00H	1F80H
BDOS:	EC00H	1180H
CCP:	E400H	980H
BOOTSTRAP:		900H

where BIOS TOP is the highest address that will fit on the 8-inch, single-density disk system tracks.

The destination in RAM of the bootstrap loader is specific to your particular computer, and it may be larger than the 80H bytes indicated in this example. This may cause a possible error in the image addresses shown. Some customizers of CP/M deliver a MOVCPM that places the base of the CCP at a nice round 0A00H, so you may have to add 80H to all the image addresses shown above.

You can tell if you have such a nonstandard implementation by using DDT to dump the first 16 locations of the memory image of CCP. Enter **D980,98F** and your CCP start should look like:

    0980 C3 5C E7 C3 58 E7 7F 00 20 20 20 . . . .

as dumped by DDT. CCP always starts with the two JMP instructions (C3 xx xx), followed by the 7F. The next byte is at CCP+7 and is the command line character count as mentioned in Chapter 12, followed by the command line buffer. The default count is zero and the buffer is filled with 20H, the ASCII code for a space, so that CCP doesn't try to autostart anything.

Getting back to the map, you want to overlay your CBIOS.HEX into the system image at 1F80H. The .HEX file starts with an address of 0FA00H, so you have to use the DDT Read function with an offset of 2580H, because 0FA00H + 2580H = 1F80H, as either DDT or HEX-ADD.COM will show you. The DDT Hex arithmetic command (H) can be used to figure out the offset. Just enter **H1F80,FA00**, and DDT will tell you that the sum and difference are 1,980 and 2,580. Both DDT and HEXADD lose the carry out of the 16th bit when doing hex arithmetic.

So, merge in your CBIOS.HEX by entering the DDT commands:

-ICBIOS.HEX
-R2580
-G0

and when the CCP prompt reappears, execute SYSGEN to write the customized CP/M onto your disk system tracks. Then, hope it all runs right. It should if your CBIOS is no larger than the original BIOS supplied with your computer.

SYSGEN.COM has no way of knowing whether or not you have increased the size of CBIOS. Since there are now so many different disk formats, it might be possible for you to write a CBIOS that will fit into RAM but not on your system tracks. If you don't have the source code for your SYSGEN, you may not know how big CBIOS can grow and still be written onto the system tracks. We need a new technique to solve that problem.

Of course, instructions for executing all of the procedures detailed above are included in the *Alteration Guide*, and in more detail there. This is just the beginning. We want to add more bells and whistles, and they won't fit in the standard version of CP/M, so we will have to examine even more numbers and procedures. This has all been too easy up to this point.

EXTENDING CBIOS

When we add bells and whistles to CBIOS, it will grow larger, but after a MOVCPM we will always load CBIOS.HEX into the system image in RAM beginning at 1F80H. If you make small changes in CBIOS, and you have carefully counted records and know that your SYSGEN will fit the new CBIOS into your disk system tracks, you can proceed with SYSGENing a new system.

If CBIOS has gotten too big for the system tracks, however, you will have to use a new technique to generate your extended version of CP/M. The procedure is simple, using a 64 K version of CP/M for an example, as before:

1. MOVCPM as before, creating a CCP image at 980H, BDOS at 1180H, and CBIOS starting at 1F80H.
2. Exit MOVCPM and **SAVE 34 CPM64.COM**, as before.

3. Enter **DDT CPM64.COM**, as before.

4. Now, when DDT has loaded CPM64.COM into the TPA, move the CCP through BDOS image down 800H bytes lower in memory, from 980H to 180H, with the DDT command **M980,1F80,180**.

5. Now merge CBIOS.HEX into this relocated image at its new destination, 1780H, with the DDT commands **ICBIOS.HEX** and **R1D80**. Note that 1780H and 1D80H are 800H less than the values used before the relocation of the image, because we moved everything 800H lower in memory.

6. Now merge EXBOOT64.HEX into the image using the DDT commands **IEXBOOT64.HEX** and **R**.

7. Exit DDT with **G0** or CTRL C, and **SAVE 29 EXBOOT64.COM**.

8. Load and run your new system by entering the command **EXBOOT64**, following the usual CP/M prompt.

AN EXTENDED BOOTSTRAP LOADER

EXBOOT64.ASM (Listing 13.1) is a simple little program that will fit into the first few bytes of the TPA at 100H, take a complete CP/M system image beginning at 180H and move it up into its execution address (0E400H and up, for the 64 K byte example), and then jump to the BOOT entry at the beginning of CBIOS. The procedure of loading the complete CP/M image into its proper place in memory and then jumping to BOOT is exactly what the bootstrap loader in your system is doing already, but with EXBOOT, the system comes from a disk file instead of the system tracks on your disk.

What all of this means is that you can create, load, and test a new version of CP/M without disturbing your disk system tracks. This provides for a fallback if your new system does not operate correctly the first time, which is likely. In addition, EXBOOT will enable you to build a CBIOS that wouldn't fit on the system tracks anyway and will even let you create a version of CP/M small enough to fit entirely within the TPA so that you can use DDT running with your original-sized CP/M to debug the new CBIOS subroutines.

A Growing CBIOS

EXBOOT64 will work as long as your new CBIOS will fit into the 1,535 bytes available betwen the start of BIOS at 0FA00H and the top of RAM at 0FFFFH. If you add more bells and whistles or a new Winchester

Listing 13-1

```
*************************************************************
*                                                           *
*  PROGRAM NAME: EXBOOT64.ASM                               *
*                                                           *
*  LAST UPDATE:    9 MAY 84    BY: KMB                       *
*                                                           *
*  FUNCTION: BOOT CP/M FROM IMAGE AT 180H IN RAM            *
*                                                           *
*************************************************************

               ; COMPUTE CP/M ADDRESSES

0040 =            RAMSIZE EQU      64              ; SET TO RAM SIZE
FFFF =            RAMTOP  EQU      RAMSIZE*1024-1
0040 =            CPMSIZE EQU      64              ; SET TO SIZE OF CP/M
FFFF =            CPMTOP  EQU      CPMSIZE*1024-1
FA00 =            CBIOS   EQU      CPMTOP-600H+1
EC00 =            BDOS    EQU      CPMTOP-1400H+1
E400 =            CCP     EQU      CPMTOP-1C00H+1
1C00 =            MOVSIZE EQU      RAMTOP-CCP+1
0180 =            CPMIMAG EQU      180H

0100                      ORG      100H

0100 218001      XBOOT:   LXI      H,CPMIMAG       ; START WITH IMAGE
0103 1100E4               LXI      D,CCP           ; MOVE IT UP TO HERE
0106 01001C               LXI      B,MOVSIZE       ; MOVE THIS MUCH
0109 7E          BOOT1:   MOV      A,M             ; GET ONE BYTE
010A 12                   STAX     D               ; STORE IT UP
010B 23                   INX      H               ; AHEAD ONE
010C 13                   INX      D
010D 0B                   DCX      B               ; COUNT ONE
010E 79                   MOV      A,C             ; TIL ZERO
010F B0                   ORA      B
0110 C20901               JNZ      BOOT1           ; LOOP TIL DONE
0113 C300FA               JMP      CBIOS           ; THEN ENTER AT JMP BOOT

0116                      END
```

disk and its required drivers and expanded tables, you will need more room for CBIOS. Simple, just MOVCPM to a smaller size, change the CPMSIZE parameter in EXBOOTxx.ASM, leaving RAMSIZE unchanged, and when you assemble EXBOOT, all of the new CP/M addresses will be calculated for you by the assembler, as you will see from examining the new EXBOOTxx.PRN file.

There are a couple of values that the assembler will not calculate for you, but they can be found in Table 13.1. In this table you can find the read offset values required to merge CBIOS.HEX into the CP/M image in memory, along with the number of 256-byte pages required to SAVE the total EXBOOTxx.COM file once the bootstrap loader, CCP, BDOS, and CBIOS have all been assembled in RAM. As you expand

183

Table 13-1

CP/M K	BIOS START	BIOS RECORDS	READ OFFSET TO 1F80	SAVE PAGES TO RAMTOP	READ OFFSET TO 1780	SAVE PAGES TO RAMTOP
64	FA00	12	2580	37	1D80	29
63	F600	20	2980	41	2180	33
62	F200	28	2D80	45	2580	37
61	EE00	36	3180	49	2980	41
60	EA00	44	3580	53	2D80	45
32	7A00	12	A580	37	9D80	29
31	7600	20	A980	41	A180	33
30	7200	28	AD80	45	A580	37
29	6E00	36	B180	49	A980	41
28	6A00	44	B580	53	AD80	45

Table 13.1 Various sizes of CP/M installed in a 64 K RAM computer. The smaller sizes permit a larger CBIOS to fit between BIOS START and the top of RAM at 0FFFFH. Read offsets are given to permit DDT to be used to merge CBIOS.HEX with the memory images of the bootstrap loader, CCP, and BDOS. The memory image target address for CBIOS is given for the MOVCPM image with the bootstrap beginning at 900H and for the EXBOOT image beginning at 100H. The number of 256-byte pages are given for the SAVE CPMxx.COM and SAVE EXBOOTxx.COM commands. The 32 K group of values can be used to load and test a new CBIOS implementation in the TPA using a 64 K CP/M system and DDT.

CBIOS, you can pick new sizes for CP/M in 1 K byte decrements. A few K bytes less TPA space is the only price you have to pay for expanding CBIOS capability.

Just in case you have a SYSGEN that will accommodate expanding CBIOS or manage to write your own after reading the next chapter on disk drivers, the READ OFFSET and SAVE values for the system image in the original MOVCPM location (980H) are also included in Table 13.1.

Testing CBIOS in the TPA

If you MOVCPM to a 32 K size CP/M system and ORG your CBIOS accordingly, the procedure shown above can be used to generate an EXBOOT32, or EXBOOT31, etc., version of CP/M. You can then use DDT running under your original 64 K version of CP/M to load and debug your new CBIOS in the TPA. Values are included in Table 13.1 to help you with this task, which can greatly speed up the debug process. Don't forget to change RAMSIZE in EXBOOT32.ASM down to

"32," or EXBOOT will try to load memory from 6400H (the start of a 32 K CCP) all the way up to 0FFFFH!

Other CP/M Sizes

All of this discussion assumes that you have started with a 64 K version of CP/M 2.2. If this is not the case, an examination of the address differences between the entries in Table 13.1 will show you that calculating new values for other system sizes is easy. Each change of 1 K bytes results in an address change of 400H. The automated calculation of CP/M addresses that is included at the beginning of EXBOOTxx.ASM will help you get started writing your own version of the table for some other beginning size of CP/M.

AUTOMATING EXBOOT

Once you have an expanded CBIOS all debugged, but find that it won't fit on your disk system tracks, or you don't know how to make SYSGEN accept a larger CBIOS, you can automate loading the new system by plugging "EXBOOTxx" into the CCP command line buffer in your original size CP/M system, as discussed in "Program autoload" in the preceding chapter. Or, you can use some other autoload technique.

You can also automate the generation of EXBOOT by using SUB-MIT.COM and XSUB.COM. However, there is one step that refuses to be automated.

MOVCPM Won't SUBMIT

Let's assume that you need to generate a 61 K version of CP/M to run your extended CBIOS in a 64 K RAM computer. You will be repeatedly editing CBIOS.ASM, assembling it, merging it into the memory image of CP/M, merging in EXBOOT61, saving the result, and executing it to test your updates. Most of this procedure can be automated by using SUBMIT and XSUB supplied with your CP/M system. Listing 13.2 is the source code for a BUILD61.SUB file, and we will look at it step by step.

The first step is not included in BUILD61.SUB. This is to generate a memory image of a 61 K version of CP/M. The commands to do that are:

```
MOVCPM 61 *
SAVE 34 CPM61.COM
```

and if you try to include them in a SUBMIT command stream, MOVCPM will issue a "SYNCHRONIZATION ERROR" message and cause your computer to hang up. You have to perform a hardware RESET to recover from this error.

The reason for the hangup is that MOVCPM secretly checks the Digital Research serial number for your CP/M system to make sure you are not trying to steal the operating system by executing MOVCPM on a computer running some other CP/M. That checking requires an intact CCP, and SUBMIT, XSUB, DDT, or any other RSX that overlays CCP will eliminate the serial number hidden in a secret place in CCP. MOVCPM will only run under the CP/M system it was sold with, and it won't execute under DDT or any other RSX.

Therefore, to generate an expanded CP/M, you first have to manually execute the two commands shown above, following the usual CCP prompt. Once you have a CPM61.COM file on disk, you can enter **SUBMIT BUILD61** and watch your CON: screen scroll off line after line as the procedure shown in Listing 13.2 executes automatically.

The Procedure

The first line in the procedure calls for XSUB to be established as another RSX following SUBMIT. XSUB permits your .SUB file to include the commands you would otherwise manually issue to DDT. With XSUB running, you then assemble EXBOOT and your CBIOS, in this example skipping the generation of the .PRN files. Next, DDT is used to load the previously generated CPM61.COM, and the next nine lines are all commands to DDT.

DDT is commanded to move the CPM61.COM image down to 180H, merge in EXBOOT61.HEX and your CBIOS61.HEX, and then Dump three significant areas so that you can verify that the merged image is correct. The dumps appear on your CON: screen and should look like Figure 13.1. The first line shows that EXBOOT.COM got into the beginning of the TPA. The next line is the familiar start of CCP, showing that CPM61.COM made it to the right place. The third dump includes the very top of BDOS and the start of CBIOS, and will reassure you that your whole merged image is correct.

After DDT reboots the original version of CP/M, the merged image of the new version is SAVEd, and CPMMAP (Chapter 7) verifies that your original CP/M is running before EXBOOT61 is invoked to load the new version, which is then also mapped. Both maps will be incorrect.

Listing 13-2

```
XSUB
ASM EXBOOT61.AAZ
ASM CBIOS61.AAZ
DDT CPM61.COM
M980,22FF,180
IEXBOOT61.HEX
R
ICBIOS61.HEX
R2980
D100,10F
D180,18F
D1700
GO
SAVE 41 EXBOOT61.COM
CPMMAP
EXBOOT61
CPMMAP
```

Figure 13.1 BUILD1.6SUB memory dumps. As the SUBMIT program BUILD61 automatically generates an extended boot version of CP/M, DDT is used to verify on the console screen that EXBOOT61 was loaded at memory location 0100H, CCP was found at 0180H, and the new CBIOS at 1780H follows the end of BDOS (up through 177FH). The start of the BIOS jump table is obvious at 1780H, with the three-byte jump instructions each beginning with the JMP opcode 0C3H.

```
-D100,10F
0100 21 80 01 11 00 D8 01 00 28 7E 12 23 13 0B 79 B0  !.......(³.#..y.
-D180,18F
0180 C3 5C DB C3 58 DB 7F 00 20 20 20 20 20 20 20 20  .¢..X...
-D1700
1700 3A E0 ED B7 CA 91 ED 77 3A DF ED 32 D6 ED CD 45  :......w:..2...E
1710 EC 2A 0F E3 F9 2A 45 E3 7D 44 C9 CD 51 EC 3E 02  .*...*E.¼D..Q...
1720 32 D5 ED 0E 00 CD 07 EB CC 03 EA C9 E5 00 00 00  2..............
1730 00 80 00 00 00 00 00 00 00 00 00 00 00 00 00 00  ................
1740 00 00 00 00 00 00 00 00 00 00 00 00 00 00 00 00  ................
1750 00 00 00 00 00 00 00 00 00 00 00 00 00 00 00 00  ................
1760 00 00 00 00 00 00 00 00 00 00 00 00 00 00 00 00  ................
1770 00 00 00 00 00 00 00 00 00 00 00 00 00 00 00 00  ................
1780 C3 62 EE C3 33 EE C3 AC EE C3 BE EE C3 2E EF C3  .b..3...........
1790 D1 EE C3 FB EE C3 B4 EE C3 76 EF C3 3B EF C3 78  .........v..;..x
17A0 EF C3 7D EF C3 82 EF C3 9C EF C3 14 F0 C3 23 F1  ..¼...........#.
17B0 C3 6D F1 C3 8E EE D3 C0 01 00 10 21 00 D8 DB C0  .m.........!....
```

INCOMPATIBILITIES

If you follow the procedures in Listing 13.1 (or at least the last three lines) manually, skipping XSUB, of course, the first CPMMAP invocation will indeed show the normal map for your original version of CP/M. After you execute the EXBOOT, the second map will disclose that you have indeed relocated CP/M lower in memory and have your expanded CBIOS running.

The incorrect maps that result from executing the procedure under SUBMIT serve to illustrate the dangers inherent in using direct BIOS calls in programs. CPMMAP doesn't use them, but it does use a procedure that tries to find the beginning of BIOS, just like programs that try to find BIOS so that direct calls can be made. Just as CPMMAP fails when an RSX is installed, so will programs that try to find and access the jump table at the beginning of BIOS. So don't write programs like that.

This final warning message was thrown in here because this is an appropriate place to illustrate that some operations can fail under SUBMIT that execute properly when invoked by the computer operator in response to a normal CCP prompt. Where else would we put the warning message? Well, it does seem to keep cropping up . . . .

In addition to warnings, you have been given a few examples and ideas that can be used to add your own bells and whistles to CP/M. There are some examples in the preceding chapter that are very hardware-specific, and even more are to follow. To make a lot of enhancements to your system, you will need to know more and more about its hardware. That knowledge will enable you to create a super system.

chapter 14

Disk
implementations

Chapter 12 presented complete source programs for those CBIOS sub-routines that handle input/output devices. That included the implemen-tation of an IOBYT-driven CBIOS that permits swapping of each of three physical I/O devices between any of the four logical devices. All the reader needs to do to use those routines is to change the hardware port addresses and handshake bit patterns as necessary for each dif-ferent computer. The source programs in this chapter won't be quite so complete.

There are too many hardware-specific tasks that have to be accom-plished in the disk handling portions of a CBIOS for us to be able to examine universally usable source programs in this book. To implement those portions of a CBIOS from scratch, you will have to really get to know the characteristics of the ICs in your computer, and that subject could fill another book of this size. However, we can examine those tasks in general terms, and there are a few techniques presented in this chapter that you can integrate into an existing BIOS to speed up disk operation and provide more I/O flexibililty.

BOOT DOESN'T COME FIRST

The first entry in the CBIOS jump table (Table 11.1) is a jump to BOOT, but before execution gets this far, the firmware routines in your com-puter have been busy. On power up or RESET, a program stored in read-only memory somewhere in your computer has to initialize the disk controller hardware, read the bootstrap loader program from the first sector of the first track of the first drive into memory, and then execute it. Along the way, the ROM firmware may initialize all of the I/O device hardware, and may even search for the CON: device and display a sign-on message.

All of these variations exist in some combination in all microcom-puters, and we have no way of knowing just what combination you have in your computer. You may have no way of knowing, either, if you don't have the source listing for your firmware. Even if you don't have it, there are a couple of enhancements you can make to BOOT that will make your computer more usable.

The bootstrap loader from the first disk sector will load the com-plete CP/M operating system into RAM and then jump to BOOT before CP/M is entered. This gives the CBIOS author the chance to perform hardware-specific initializations that may not have been completed by the ROM firmware. It also gives you the chance to do things your way.

Finding CON:

There are certain functions that the Digital Research manuals specify must be performed in BOOT, including an initial sign-on message display on the CON: device. Before you get that far, if you have implemented the IOBYT and have more than one CON: device port available on your computer, as in the example in Chapter 12, you might want to add a search-for-CON: routine to BOOT so that you can begin computer operation from either of the two terminals.

Since we have already written console status check subroutines for both serial ports (Listing 12.5), it is a simple matter to poll the two subroutines and wait for the operator to select the terminal that will serve as CON: initially (see Listing 14.1). After the operator presses the space bar on either terminal, it will be selected as CON: and the IOBYT set accordingly. If the dual-terminal mode is desired, STAT will have to be used later to enable that IOBYT setting. Even if you do not implement this search, the initial setting of IOBYT should be part of BOOT.

Listing 14-1

```
BAE6 318000    BOOT:   LXI    SP,STAK     ; SET UP CP/M STACK
BAE9 FB                EI                 ; ENABLE REAL TIME CLOCK
BAEA 3E00              MVI    A,DDISK     ; SET DEFAULT DISK DRIVE
BAEC 320400            STA    CDISK       ;   INTO CURRENT DRIVE
BAEF DBE8              IN     S1DAT       ; CLEAR BOTH USARTS
BAF1 DBF8              IN     S2DAT       ;   FOR CON: SEARCH
BAF3 AF        BOOT1:  XRA    A           ; ZERO IOBYT
BAF4 4F                MOV    C,A         ;   SAVE IT IN C
BAF5 CD3BBA    BOOT2:  CALL   CON1S       ; FIND THE CONSOLE
BAF8 B7                ORA    A           ;   IS IT S 1:?
BAF9 C217BB            JNZ    BOOT4       ;   MAYBE CON: = S 1:
BAFC 0C                INR    C           ; IOBYT TO S 2:
BAFD CD47BA            CALL   CON2S       ;
BB00 B7                ORA    A           ; IS IT S 2:?
BB01 CAF3BA            JZ     BOOT1       ;   NEITHER, RESTART
BB04 CDD2BA            CALL   S2IN        ; MAYBE S 2:,
BB07 FE20      BOOT3:  CPI    ' '         ;   CHECK FOR SPACE BAR
BB09 C2F3BA            JNZ    BOOT1       ;   RESTART IF NOT SPACE
BB0C 3E94              MVI    A,DIOBYT
BB0E E6FC              ANI    11111100B
BB10 B1                ORA    C           ; MERGE CON: AND IOBYT
BB11 320300            STA    IOBYT
BB14 C32EBB            JMP    WBOOT1      ;   AND GO RUN CP/M
BB17 CDC4BA    BOOT4:  CALL   S1IN        ; MAYBE S 1:,
BB1A C307BB            JMP    BOOT3       ;   CHECK FOR SPACE BAR
```

Changing CON: Baud Rate

If the firmware in your computer initializes the baud rate of the serial ports to one of the slow standards like 2400 or 9600 baud, and you have acquired a new terminal that runs faster, you can add software to update the baud rate for the CON: serial port(s) early in BOOT, and certainly before the search procedure shown above. Here is one enhancement that requires intimate knowledge of your computer hardware, so we can't get into more details here. We hope you will be able to.

The other functions that are required of BOOT are spelled out in the CP/M *Alteration Guide*, and the sample programs there and in Listing 14.1 provide a framework on which to hang the enhancements mentioned above.

Listing 14-2

```
BB2E 3EC3       WBOOT1: MVI     A,JMP     ; SET UP JUMPS FOR
BB30 320000             STA     0         ;   WARM START
BB33 320500             STA     5         ;    AND BDOS
BB36 2103BA             LXI     H,BIOS+3
BB39 220100             SHLD    1
BB3C 2106AC             LXI     H,BDOS+6
BB3F 220600             SHLD    6
BB42 3A0400             LDA     CDISK     ; GET CURRENT DRIVE
BB45 4F                 MOV     C,A       ;   INTO C FOR CCP
BB46 C300A4             JMP     CCP       ;    AND START CPM
```

WBOOT GETS THINGS GOING

In a typical CP/M installation, the tasks performed in WBOOT are divided by a second entry (WBOOT1:, Listing 14.2), which is jumped into at the end of BOOT. Before that entry, WBOOT must include software that will reload those portions of CP/M that may have been overwritten by RSXs or large programs running in the TPA. That portion of the example CBIOS is not listed here because it is totally hardware-specific.

The first part of WBOOT should only reload CP/M up to the base of CBIOS and not change the settings for IOBYT or the current disk, because you want to keep running on the same terminal and the same disk at the end of any transient programs.

WBOOT Second Entry

The first part of WBOOT falls through into the second entry, WBOOT1:. After BOOT selects the CON: and initializes IOBYT and the default disk drive, it jumps into this second part of WBOOT to perform tasks that both the BOOT and WBOOT startup routines must accomplish. These include setting up the JMP WBOOT at location 0 and the JMP BDOS at location 5. Following these initialization tasks, the seond part of WBOOT will fetch the current disk assignment from location 4, put it in the C register, and jump to the CCP entry at the base of CCP. Then, and only then, CP/M is up and running.

THE CURRENT DRIVE

Historically, there has been some confusion about what disk drive is the current drive and when it should be selected. Even the early DRI manuals included the erroneous information that WBOOT should set the current drive back to A: at every warm start. This should not be done, because an operator should be able to tell CP/M once and for all that B: or C: or some other disk drive is the one that all future work will be performed on. There is nothing more frustrating than to find yourself back on A: following every warm start, whether you want to be or not.

Some programs that have to reinitialize the disk system during operation to permit writing on changed disks will alter the current disk selection during their course of events and then leave the operator stuck on the wrong drive following the program's exit through location zero. We included software in our own BEGIN: routine to prevent any of our programs from changing the current drive selection. Once the initial selection is made in BOOT no program or CBIOS function should ever change it. Let CP/M handle location 4 from BOOT on. If your BIOS keeps putting you back on A: following every warm start, you might want to move that code from WBOOT back to BOOT where it belongs.

Which Initial Drive?

Admittedly, there are systems and users that might want to return to A: at every opportunity, but when you upgrade a floppy disk-based computer to include a Winchester hard disk, you might want some other initial selection for the "current" drive. In particular, your firmware may be inflexible and might insist that the initial CP/M load must be performed

from a floppy disk as A:. Your new hard disk may have to be drive B: or
C: because you can't change the firmware. In that case you would want
the initial setting of the current drive byte at location 4 to be B: or C:
because the hard disk is where all the good software will be found. So
set location 4 to 1 or 2 instead of zero and leave it set that way at
WBOOT.

FLOPPY DISK SUBROUTINES

The disk control subroutines listed in Table 11.1 (c) can be broken down
into two subgroups: the most primitive, or first level READ and WRITE
routines that actually access the disk drives, and the second level routines HOME, SELDSK, SETTRK, SETSEC, and SETDMA that often
only set up values in memory buffers. Examples of these second-level
subroutines for floppy disks are included in the DRI manuals. We can
make some enhancements to such subroutines to speed up floppy disk
operation.

There are some general guidelines that can help you to fine-tune
the first- and/or second-level subroutines in your CBIOS. Since there is
some flexibility on organizing some functions, such as in which subroutine the actual selection of the drive and the actual seeking of the
track are performed, the code for those functions may exist in either
level subroutine. So, if you want to implement any of the following
enhancements, you will first have to find out where the functions are
actually taking place.

Drive Selection

The actual selection of the disk drive, which may produce some combination of turning on the disk drive motor, loading the read/write head,
and turning on the drive select light, may be performed in SELDSK or
in both READ and WRITE. The variations will depend on whether you
have 5¼-inch or 8-inch floppy drives, or a hard disk drive.

Our example computer (Chapter 12) includes a 2-bit latch for
floppy-disk drive selection. Write a zero to output port 0C0H (DSEL in
Listing 11.1), and both minifloppy drives are deselected, their R/W
heads unload, and their drive motors stop. Write 01 to DSEL and drive
A: is selected, or write 10 to select drive B:. Obviously, you want to
select the desired drive at the BDOS call to SELDSK. When do you
deselect both drives?

The ROM firmware in that computer initializes DSEL by setting it to zero at power up or RESET. Once a drive has been selected, it stays selected until a BDOS call to the CBIOS routine CONIN:. This ensures that the last selected floppy disk doesn't keep spinning forever after a disk access. Why CONIN:? Because almost every transient program calls CONIN: for some operator interaction after it is loaded or has performed some disk access, and CCP calls CONIN: immediately following its prompt after each warm start.

If your computer leaves the last selected disk running even when there are no disk accesses taking place, try patching CONIN: in your CBIOS with something like:

```
CONIN:  XRA   A      ; ZERO OUT TO
        OUT   DSEL   ; DISK DRIVE SELECT
        .     .
        .     .
```

provided, of course, that you can find the correct port address and value to deselect the drive.

Speed Up Track Seeks

Some CBIOS implementations rely on a disk seek error to produce a seek to track on a new drive when SELDSK switches from one drive to another. In that case, SELDSK merely selects the new drive. When a READ or WRITE to the new drive is attempted, the selected track number (established by a previous call to SETTRK) for the new drive will differ from the last track number for the previous drive that is stored in the disk controller track register. The controller will read a sector address field, determine that it is on the wrong track, and seek to the new track.

While this will produce no errors, it can slow down disk-to-disk data transfers, if they are being made one sector at a time, and will slow down many operations that compare data in a file on one drive with that in a file on another that will probably be found on a different track. The reason is that each change of drive selection will cause a seek error and reseek. That can be eliminated by saving the track number bar for the old drive and restoring it when that drive is reaccessed.

The portion of SELDSK: shown in Listing 14.3 checks for the selection of a new drive in a two-drive system. If a new drive has been selected, the track on which that drive was last positioned will have

Listing 14-3

```
BBA3 C5        SELDSK: PUSH   B        ; SAVE WORK REGISTER
BBA4 3AD2BB            LDA    DSKNO    ; GET LAST SELECTED
BBA7 47               MOV    B,A      ;   INTO B
BBA8 79               MOV    A,C      ; GET NEW SELECTED
BBA9 32D2BB           STA    DSKNO    ;   INTO DISK NUMBER
BBAC B8               CMP    B        ; DRIVE CHANGED?
BBAD CABDBB           JZ     SELD1    ;   CONTINUE IF NOT
BBB0 47               MOV    B,A      ;   ELSE SAVE NEW
BBB1 3AD3BB           LDA    OLDTRK   ; GET OTHER DRIVES TRACK
BBB4 4F               MOV    C,A      ;   AND SAVE IT
BBB5 DBE1             IN     DTRAK    ; GET THIS DRIVES TRACK
BBB7 32D3BB           STA    OLDTRK   ;   WILL NOW BE "OTHERS"
BBBA 79               MOV    A,C      ; SET NEW DRIVES TRACK
BBBB D3E1             OUT    DTRAK    ;   IN CONTROLLER REGISTER
               SELD1:  .      .
                       .      .
                       .      .
                       .      .
BBD2 00        DSKNO   DB     0        ; SELECTED DISK NUMBER
BBD3 00        OLDTRK  DB     0        ; LAST SELECTED TRACK
```

been stored in OLDTRK. The track on which the current drive is positioned is contained in the controller IC's DTRAK register. The speedup routine reads DTRAK, substitutes OLDTRK, and saves DTRAK in OLDTRK. The next READ or WRITE to the new drive will find the contents of DTRAK equal to the actual position of the R/W head on that disk, and no seek error will occur.

The floppy disk controller track register contains the number of the last track actually accessed. The desired track number (set by the BDOS call to SETTRK) is loaded into the controller's data register before a seek command is issued. If the CBIOS subroutines do not update the controller's track register after a drive change, a READ or WRITE call will result in a seek error and automatic reseek performed by the controller. No data errors will result, but operation in this mode will be characterized by a lot of trashing of the disk stepper motor and slowed disk operations.

Restoring the contents of the track register in the controller following a drive number change will eliminate the trashing and speed up disk seeks. This is most noticeable when you perform an operation such as:

ASM CBIOS64.ABC

where you are reading the source program from drive A:, writing the HEX output on drive B:, and the .PRN file on drive C:. The output pass of the assembler will begin with the R/W head of drive A: positioned at the beginning of the source program, the head of B: at the beginning of the disk space that is to receive the .HEX file, and C: at the beginning of the .PRN file space. The assembly pass will proceed with many drive changes noticeable by the flashing of the drive select lights, but few seek steps will be heard because little head positioning will be required on any drive.

The CBIOS drivers that do not update the controller track register with each drive change cause the controller to think the head for drive B: is on the track last accessed by A:, and a reseek will be performed even though the drive B: head is already on the desired track. A lot of unnecessary thrashing takes place.

This enhancement is easy to add to a two-drive system. If you have more than two drives, you will need to store OLDTRKA, and OLDTRKB, etc., and fetch the appropriate track number depending on the drive selected. In either case, the change will speed up disk operations that take place on a sector by sector basis, instead of on a buffered basis where an occasional reseek will not be noticeable.

READ AND WRITE

When the R/W head is positioned over the correct track on the floppy disk and the desired sector address field has been detected by the controller, data transfer to or from the disk begins. The computer must read or write the data one byte at a time and must do so at the speed dictated by the disk rotation. While the controller has status bits that flag "read byte ready" or "write byte buffer empty," it is all a microprocessor running at 4 MHz can do to perform the data transfers in a polled I/O mode.

In polled I/O, the CPU must repeatedly read the status bit, test it, and transfer one byte at the correct instant. For instance, a 4 MHz Z-80 can do this for a single-density 8-inch or double-density 5¼-inch disk, but a slower CPU would get behind the disk rotation and lost data would result. To operate more reliably, or operate at all with a double density 8-inch disk, the READ and WRITE subroutines must be WAIT state or interrupt-driven.

In addition, the data transfers to and from the disk can be handled through the CPU or in a **D**irect **M**emory **A**ccess mode using another (DMA) controller IC. The possible variations of polled, WAIT, or interrupt-driven direct or DMA data transfers, and the many variations on the floppy disk controller, make it impossible to include sample source programs for the READ and WRITE subroutines in this book. If they are working reliably on your computer, you don't need to change them.

All of the CBIOS disk subroutine enhancements discusssed so far can be implemented at the second level of subroutines without disturbing the time-critical, first-level coding. However, the actual drive selection or track seek operations may be part of READ or WRITE instead of SELDSK or SETTRK. In that case the code you want to change will be outside the time-critical part of READ or WRITE, and the changes can still be made.

SMART WINCHESTER CONTROLLERS

Since a typical microprocessor is barely able to keep up with the data transfer rate of a single-density floppy disk rotating at 360 RPM, it is obviously not going to be able to handle byte-by-byte data transfers from a hard disk rotating ten times that fast. That is fortunate for us, because it means that all hard disk controllers are "smart."

Through necessity, the Winchester disk controller will include its own sector buffer, and we can transfer data to and from that buffer at whatever speed our microcomputer to controller interface is capable of. Since the controller already has to handle a lot of high-speed functions, it will also have a lot of control sequences built into it that we would otherwise have to include in our CBIOS.

A feeling for this can quickly be gained by comparing the commands that can be sent to a typical floppy disk controller IC (Table 14.1) with the much higher-level commands that can be handled by a hard disk controller board (Table 14.2). In both cases the commands are usually encoded into a single byte that is written to a hardware port address. In the floppy disk controller IC, those low-level commands are received into a command register, and the host computer has to be ready to read and write a sector's worth of data at disk speed.

The higher-level command byte will be received by the hard disk controller board in a similar fashion, but the board will have its own microcontroller and will perform many low-level operations in the course of executing each command byte. Most important to us as CBIOS programmers, the board will provide data buffering, and we can fill or empty its sector buffer as fast, or as slowly, as we want.

Table 14.1

RESTORE	Move R/W head to track zero
SEEK	Move R/W head to selected track
STEP IN	Move R/W head in one track
STEP OUT	Move R/W head out one track
READ SECTOR	Read selected sector on current track
WRITE SECTOR	Write selected sector on current track
READ ADDRESS	Read next sector address field
READ TRACK	Read current track
WRITE TRACK	Write current track

Table 14.1 Floppy disk controller commands. This set of low-level commands is typical of those that can be executed by a floppy disk controller integrated circuit. While a floppy disk controller provides some automation, the host computer must still be able to handle data transfers at speeds dictated by the disk rotation.

Table 14.2

SET DRIVE PARAMETERS	Send drive characteristics to controller
TEST DRIVE READY	Check selected disk response
RECALIBRATE	Move R/W heads to track zero
SEEK TRACK	Move R/W head to selected track
READ n SECTORS	Multi-sector read (n = 1 to 256)
WRITE n SECTORS	Multi-sector write (n = 1 to 256)
COPY BLOCKS	Multi-sector copy, drive to drive
REQUEST SENSE	Read controller status block
	(a)
RUN RAM DIAGNOSTICS	Auto-test controller hardware
RUN DRIVE DIAGNOSTICS	Auto-test disk drive hardware
REQUEST ERROR LOG	Read accumulated errors
WRITE ERROR DATA	Write a bad sector for test
READ ID FIELD	Read selected sector address field
	(b)
FORMAT DRIVE	Format all tracks on selected drive
CHECK TRACK	Verify all sectors on selected track
FORMAT TRACK	Format all sectors on selected track
FORMAT BAD TRACK	Mark all sectors bad on current track
ASSIGN ALTERNATE TRACK	Spare bad track
	(c)

Table 14.2 Hard disk controller commands. This set of high-level commands is typical of those that can be executed by a hard disk controller board, which includes its own microprocessor. Disk operations (a), testing (b), and maintenance (c) functions are fully automated by the controller board, and command, status, and data transfers can be performed on a byte-by-byte basis at whatever speed the host computer is capable of.

199

Adding a Winch

If we want to add a hard disk drive to an existing floppy disk-based microcomputer, we will add new hardware to the computer and new software to the CBIOS. The existing system will remain the same. This means that we will have to break into the SELDSK, READ, and WRITE subroutines and, at the appropriate place, jump to hard disk handling routines instead of continuing through the old floppy disk software.

This actually simplifies our programming task, since we assume that a working computer with working floppy disk software is available. After plugging in the new hardware, we will use the techniques outlined in Chapter 13 to add and test the hard disk driver software. This software will probably require new sector blocking/deblocking routines and a new host buffer area, unless our existing floppies just happen to have the same sector size as the new hard disk.

Putting the Driver Together

We have already looked at blocking/deblocking (Chapter 8) and disk parameter tables (Chapter 9), and have source code examples in this book and the DRI manuals. The supplier of the hard disk drive and/or controller will have provided example driver software for command, status, and data transfers to and from the disk controller. Merging these elements into a single driver routine is not an easy task, but it is much simplified by the controller "smarts."

As you can see from Table 14.2, a single-command byte transfer to the controller can initiate a complicated action. Using a debugger like DDT, we can single-step through sending such commands to the controller and reading back status and data bytes one at a time. What is a complicated programming job can be accomplished one step at a time, and although you won't get it done in one day, the job is a lot easier than writing a floppy disk driver that has to execute in real time right from the start.

Unfortunately, since there are so many hardware variables involved, we can't include a complete sample CBIOS in this book. However, Digital Research has provided general examples, and specific ones come from the controller manufacturer. All you need to do is integrate them into an existing CBIOS, and the DRI manuals provide lots of guidelines and examples. Since those are floppy-oriented, there is one more subject we have to look at in this hard disk-oriented discussion.

MORE DISK TABLES

A complaint was raised back in Chapter 13 that the system tracks on a single-density, 8-inch floppy disk ran out of records before the last 640 bytes of RAM could be filled with CBIOS enhancements. Not all of that space would be wasted in any CP/M installation, however, because some uninitialized RAM space is always needed for disk tables.

We looked at one of the initialized disk tables, the disk parameter block (DPB), back in Chapter 8, and displayed the contents of one of the uninitialized tables, the allocation vector (ALV), using our TESTC8 program. There are other disk tables within any CP/M V2.2 CBIOS as well.

The Disk Parameter Header

The address of a DPH must be returned to BDOS by the CBIOS subroutine SELDSK:, and there is one DPH for each logical disk drive. The DPH consists mainly of addresses of other tables: a translate table (XLT) that contains the logical to physical sector mapping for skewed sectors, if used; the address of the DPB; and the addresses of three uninitialized RAM buffer areas. These areas are a 128-byte **DIR**ectory record **BUF**fer (DIRBUF), the allocation vector (ALV), and for removable media, a directory check vector (CSV).

One DIRBUF can be used for all disks. Each logical drive will need its own ALV, and removable disks need one CSV apiece. All of these areas can be in RAM that is not loaded from the system tracks, because BDOS will fill them with the correct data as each disk is accessed. The actual amount of RAM that must be dedicated to these tables depends on the capacity of each disk drive. The size of ALV in bytes is the total number of blocks on the disk divided by 8, since there is one bit per block in the disk map. The CSV needs two bits per directory entry.

Some typical values for the total sizes of disk tables XLT, DIRBUF, ALV, CSV, and the sector buffer for record blocking/deblocking are:

2 drives, 5¼″ SS SD floppy disks: 244 bytes

2 drives, 5¼″ DS DD floppy disks: 272 bytes

2 drives, 8″ SS SD floppy disks: 250 bytes

2 drives, 8″ DS DD floppy disks: 1,318 bytes

2 logical drives, 5¼″ Winchester: 984 bytes

The Winchester hard disk system used as one example in Chapter 8 includes two 5¼-inch **D**ouble **S**ide, **D**ouble **D**ensity (DSDD) floppy disks for hard disk backup and data interchange, and so the total "extra" RAM space needed by that system is 272 + 984 = 1256 bytes. Add to that the extra complications caused by mixing two different types of disk drives in one CBIOS, and you can see that the system integrators were lucky to be able to generate a 62 K version of CP/M that would fit into a 64 K byte RAM computer.

There are two reasons the hard disk tables require less RAM than those for the 8-inch DSDD floppies: the floppy uses a 1,024-byte sector, so it needs twice the blocking/deblocking buffer, and it uses a smaller allocation block size, so the ALV is not optimized.

SYSTEM INTEGRATION DECISIONS

From all of this and the discussion in Chapter 8, you can see that there are many decisions that must be made in putting together a computer system from scratch or adding new disks to an old computer. The selection of drive types and the minimization of the number of different types within one system will affect the size of the CBIOS and disk tables. Adding bells and whistles will cost TPA space.

The examples used in this book, which are all derived from actual computer systems, did not strain the limits of CP/M V2.2. One worst-case development system mixed 8-inch and 5¼-inch floppies with a hard disk, and that funny combination was still able to run a 58 K version of CP/M V2.2 in 64 K bytes of RAM.

Just as floppy disks grew in capacity from the first 92 K byte minis and 241 K byte eight-inchers, up to the multimegabytes per diskette today, the little hard disks are growing rapidly. Fifty, 100, and 400 M byte mini-Winis are starting to appear. As disks grow so do their required tables. We would run out of TPA space rapidly if it were not for bank-switched memory and CP/M Plus. Is that an invitation to read on?

chapter 15

A look at CP/M plus (version 3)

Once a CP/M programmer has written a few application programs and has added some features to CBIOS, or even written a complete CBIOS for a new computer, there are two even more complicated projects that come to mind. These are adding a hard disk drive to hold all that good programming, and implementing CP/M Plus.

A hard disk will provide not only more on-line storage but will speed up disk reads and writes. The benefits to be derived from CP/M Plus are more numerous and are obvious to any computer operator who has ever been exposed to this O.S.

CP/M PLUS FEATURES

As we saw in Table 3.1, this new version of the operating system is much larger, but it provides even more TPA space for the user when running in a bank-switched memory. So far in this book we have ignored CP/M Plus running in the nonbanked mode, although this is an option. A nonbanked V3 adds some bells and whistles not found in versions one and two, but at the cost of reduced TPA space. The nonbanked mode is useful as a stepping stone to getting the full implementation running, but it may not be too practical as an operating system in its own right, if you are used to filling up all the TPA space in your present CP/M.

In the nonbanked mode CP/M Plus provides

Support for up to 16 disk drives of up to 512 MB each

Time and date stamping of files

Advanced programming utilities that generate relocatable, linkable program modules

Provisions for attaching user-written resident system extensions.

In the banked mode, the following features are added:

Enhanced operator interfacing, including command line editing and previous line recall

Largest possible TPA space

File password protection

Greatly increased disk access speeds through the use of multiple data buffers and hashed directory access

Increased system operation speed, including instant warm starts with CCP reloaded from a memory image

Banked Memory

In addition to providing a place to store most of BDOS and CBIOS, a multibank memory provides storage for the CCP image so that it can be reloaded into the TPA instantly at all warm starts. The extra memory space can also provide optional data buffers for multiple disk sectors to speed up disk accesses.

These buffers are swapped to and from disk on a least-recently-used priority basis, so that data and programs that are continually accessed will reside in the RAM buffer and won't have to be fetched from disk a sector at a time. As new disk data is called for, old, unused sector images in RAM will be flushed to the disk if they have been written to or just erased if they were accessed only for read.

Another use for RAM buffer space is to provide a hashed directory index table, where RAM lookup can be used to find an index into the sector containing a desired directory file control block. This enables the direct fetching of the desired directory sector without having to search the entire directory sequentially to find a particular file.

Mass Storage Features

Directory hashing will greatly speed up disk access on hard disk systems using large directories. There are other features of CP/M Plus that are also hard disk-oriented. You can place all of your system files in the USER 0 directory, and as long as they are tagged SYS (Figure 10.1), they can be read by any other USER number. This means that all permanent programs, like the assembler, editor, and other utilities, can exist in a single copy on drive A: USER 0, but all other users working on any logical disk can call on them for execution.

Another tag bit shown in that figure was the archive attribute, which aids in backing up updated files from the hard disk to whatever backup device you are using. While this is useful in a floppy disk-based computer, it is vital for hard disk operation.

RELOCATABLE MODULAR PROGRAMMING

ASM.COM and LOAD.COM no longer exist on CP/M Plus system disks. They have been replaced by RMAC.COM and LINK.COM. The major differences are that RMAC produces relocatable programs or program segments. LINK can be used to create a binary .COM file ORG'd at 100H to execute in the TPA just as LOAD did, but it can also be used to link individual program modules into a larger transient program or resident system extension.

We have been using modular programming in this book, but all of our program modules have to be merged into a single source file before being assembled. This can become awkward as program sizes increase. A reasonably commented assembly language source file will be at least 15 times as large as the resulting binary .COM file. A 32 K byte application program, therefore, came about from the assembly of about half a megabyte of source code.

RMAC   The **R**elocatable **MAC**ro assembler supplied with version 3 is upward compatible with earlier versions of RMAC that were optionally available for CP/M 2.2 at extra cost. RMAC produces a relocatable (.REL) object file that is slightly larger than the .HEX file produced by ASM.COM. The major difference is that .REL files have no specified absolute load address. Program modules can be individually assembled, stored away in a library of .REL files, and LINKed into a single program as required.

This flexibility is not without its cost. All intermodule references have to be explicitly declared as externals in the module source programs. The .PRN files for each module show all program addresses relative to the beginning of the module so that when the program is linked, you have no printout showing where in memory each operation is located. This complicates debugging.

SID   The **S**ymbolic **I**nstruction **D**ebugger supplied with CP/M Plus is necessary for working with relocated and linked programs. The program generation process produces .SYM files containing lists of the program symbols (labels, like BEGIN:) and the absolute addresses where they can be found after the program is loaded into the TPA. The absolute memory addresses can then be fetched from the .SYM file and referenced by SID symbolically during the debugging process.

Just as DDT could be used to **D**ump 100H to see the object code of BEGIN:, so can SID be commanded to **D.BEGIN** to produce the same display without the programmer knowing the absolute address of BEGIN: until SID finds it. Similarly, traps can be set using symbolic rather than absolute addresses, and all of the other DDT functions duplicated by SID can operate this way as well.

This mode of programming and debugging is not as easy to get used to as the good old-fashioned methods we have been using. In order for you to write your own CP/M Plus BIOS, you will have to learn to use these new tools, because the system generation process for version 3 demands it.

A MODULAR, TABLE-DRIVEN BIOS

In Table 11.1 we took the liberty of breaking up the BIOS jump table into logical blocks, and we have seen the use of some tables so far in this book. CP/M Plus formalizes the modularization of the BIOS and creates more and larger tables for system control.

All of the little odds and ends of values like the current disk byte, the IOBYT, and the device names we changed in Chapter 12 have all been moved into easily modifiable tables in version 3. Greatly expanded I/O capabilities have caused the 8-bit IOBYT to be replaced by two bytes of I/O device redirection for each logical device, so you can have a dozen consoles to select among, if you wish. Also, new I/O controls permit commands that change baud rates as well as devices.

Of course, you will still have to do all of the CBIOS programming at the primitive device driver level, but those tasks have been divided among five modules and two tables. A brief description of each follows.

BIOSKRNL   This module is supplied by Digital Research and is the executive for the BIOS. At cold boot it will call initialization routines for each I/O device and disk controller, using the appropriate tables to decide what devices you have incorporated in your computer. This **BIOS KeRNeL** will handle the decoding of the IOBYT-equivalent words and will call the appropriate individual I/O device drivers.

BOOT   The V3 boot module is similar to the BOOT routine in earlier versions and includes system initialization routines and the CCP loader.

MOVE   A separate module is provided for you to program with all of the memory-to-memory and bank-to-bank block moves that are required. Block moves can be made faster by your own programming taking advantage of the extra facilities of the Z-80, if your computer runs this microprocessor.

CHARIO   This module includes the kind of device drivers we found in Table 11.1(b). Now there may be more devices, but for just getting things started, a single CON: driver may be programmed into

CHARIO. Since the BIOS is so modularized, adding more devices later is simplified, because only CHARIO would then need to be updated and reassembled.

DISKIO   Only READ and WRITE from Table 11.1(c) will be included in this disk driver module, along with new routines to log in a disk and initialize the controller. HOME, SELDSK, SETTRK, SETSEC, and SETDMA are now all handled within BIOSKRNL, so this module could possibly be even smaller than the equivalent in earlier versions, depending on the number of different controllers and drives in your system. As was true for CHARIO, you could start your system generation process easily by beginning with a single disk drive.

SCB   The **S**ystem **C**ontrol **B**lock gathers together in one table all of the various bytes, words, and flags that need to be referenced by any of the driver modules, as well as the addresses of routines that have to be called by other modules. SCB also includes bytes containing the current time and date, if your system includes a calendar clock.

DRVTBL   This disk **DR**i**V**e **T**a**BL**e includes an expanded disk parameter header for each of up to 16 disk drives. The expansion of the old tables is required by new features like data buffering and directory hashing.

Writing CBIOS Modules

Just as we used the subdivision of Table 11.1 to break up the writing of a V2.2 CBIOS into manageable chunks, the generation of V3 BIOS modules can proceed step by step following the now formalized outline. As has been true for any CP/M version, you can start easily by writing drivers for one disk and one console. Now, however, there are more routines that have to be written, including initialization of each device.

Since the new BIOS has been so nicely modularized, there are many table entries that must be initialized even for a minimum system. Aiding in the tasks is documentation that is much easier to read and follow than earlier versions, and there is also built-in automation of the system generation process.

AUTOMATED
SYSTEM GENERATION

In Chapter 13 we wrote a SUBMIT file to aid in automating the generation of a customized version of CP/M. As you can imagine from the proliferation of V3 BIOS modules, the task is now much more complicated. The CP/M Plus *System Guide* includes pages and pages illustrating the operation GENCPM, because there are now so many options that must be considered in generating the operating system.

Will your system have bank-switched memory? Do you want directory hashing? How wide is your terminal? (Don't answer "12 inches.") How big is your memory? These are only a few of the options that must be defined before a CP/M Plus system can be put together and loaded into your computer.

A BIG JOB

The first part of this chapter should have stimulated your interest in the ultimate 8-bit version of CP/M, but that last half may have given you the idea that installing V3 on your computer is a difficult task. That is not too far from the truth. There is much that needs to be learned before you can even get started, including the operation of a new assembler, linker, and debugger. The hardware and software options are many times those that faced the V2.2 system programmer. Although the task is not easy, it is not impossible.

It would not be possible to go into more details of the CP/M Plus system generation process here, because the Digital Research *System Guide* alone is about the same size as this book. What has been attempted here is to show you that the job is much bigger than any you have faced before, but it is well organized, well documented, and the end result is well worth the effort.

The CP/M operating system has always suffered in comparison to its more exotic competitors because too many reviewers have failed to note that earlier versions were designed to be small in size and simple to implement. Bells and whistles have their costs, and if you want to install CP/M Plus on your own computer, you will have to pay the cost in terms of time and programming effort.

If you have been able to perform all of the exercises in this book, including some from this section, then tackling the big Plus may be for you. It won't be easy, but when you finish your smile may be as wide as your terminal.

Appendix A

American Standard Code for Information Interchange (ASCII)

————— Nonprinting (control) codes ————

Control	Key-stroke(s)	HEX code	Function-standard usage (CP/M, BASIC, etc., usage may differ)
NUL	CTRL @	00	Null (blank)
SOH	CTRL A	01	Start of header message
STX	CTRL B	02	Start of message text
ETX	CTRL C	03	End of message text
EOT	CTRL D	04	End of transmission
ENQ	CTRL E	05	Enquiry, i.e., "Did you get that?"
ACK	CTRL F	06	Acknowledge, i.e., "Yes, I did."
BEL	CTRL G	07	Bell, operator alert
BS	CTRL H/BS	08	Backspace one character
HT	CTRL I/TAB	09	Horizontal tab
LF	CTRL J/LF	0A	Line feed
VT	CTRL K	0B	Vertical tab
FF	CTRL L	0C	Form feed
CR	CTRL M/CR	0D	Carriage return
SO	CTRL N	0E	Shift Out, to alternate character set
SI	CTRL O	0F	Shift In, back to standard characters
DLE	CTRL P	10	Data Link Escape to alternate functions
DC1	CTRL Q	11	Device Control 1, XON
DC2	CTRL R	12	Device Control 2
DC3	CTRL S	13	Device Control 3, XOFF
DC4	CTRL T	14	Device Control 4
NAK	CTRL U	15	No Acknowledge, i.e., "I didn't get that."
SYN	CTRL V	16	Synchronization character
ETB	CTRL W	17	End of transmitted block
CAN	CTRL X	18	Cancel previous message
EM	CTRL Y	19	End of message
SUB	CTRL Z	1A	Substitute incorrect character
ESC	CTRL [	1B	Escape to alternate functions
FS	CTRL \	1C	File separator
GS	CTRL]	1D	Group separator
RS	CTRL ^	1E	Record separator
US	CTRL —	1F	Unit separator
DEL	DEL	7F	Delete, or rubout

Key	HEX code	Key	HEX code	Key	HEX code
SPACE	20	@	40		60
!	21	A	41	a	61
"	22	B	42	b	62
#	23	C	43	c	63
$	24	D	44	d	64
%	25	E	45	e	65
&	26	F	46	f	66
'	27	G	47	g	67
(	28	H	48	h	68
)	29	I	49	i	69
*	2A	J	4A	j	6A
+	2B	K	4B	k	6B
,	2C	L	4C	l	6C
-	2D	M	4D	m	6D
.	2E	N	4E	n	6E
/	2F	O	4F	o	6F
0	30	P	50	p	70
1	31	Q	51	q	71
2	32	R	52	r	72
3	33	S	53	s	73
4	34	T	54	t	74
5	35	U	55	u	75
6	36	V	56	v	76
7	37	W	57	w	77
8	38	X	58	x	78
9	39	Y	59	y	79
:	3A	Z	5A	z	7A
;	3B	[	5B	{	7B
<	3C	\	5C	|	7C
=	3D	]	5D	}	7D
>	3E	^	5E	~	7E
?	3F	—	5F		

Appendix B

General Purpose Subroutines

The following is a list of general purpose subroutines found in this book, arranged by function. The subroutine entry point label is listed, followed by the subroutine function. The .LIB file or program listing where the source of the subroutine is to be found is listed in the right-hand column.

Buffered Console Input Subroutines

CIMSG:	Input a line from the CON: device	CONBUFFI
GETYN:	Get a yes or no response from the CON:	CONBUFFI

Numeric Input Subroutines

LI8HEX:	Get an 8-bit hexadecimal value from the CCP command line buffer	HEXNUMBI
CI8HEX:	Get an 8-bit hexadecimal value from the CON: device buffered input	HEXNUMBI
BI8HEX:	Get an 8-bit hexadecimal value from any designated ASCII line buffer	HEXNUMBI
LI6HEX:	Get a 16-bit hexadecimal value from the CCP command line buffer	HEXNUMBI
CI6HEX:	Get a 16-bit hexadecimal value from the CON: device buffered input	HEXNUMBI
BI6HEX:	Get a 16-bit hexadecimal value from any designated ASCII line buffer	HEXNUMBI
LI8DEC:	Get an 8-bit decimal value from the CCP command line buffer	DECNUMBI
CI8DEC:	Get an 8-bit decimal value from the CON: device buffered input	DECNUMBI

BI8DEC:	Get an 8-bit decimal value from any designated ASCII line buffer	DECNUMBI
LI6DEC:	Get a 16-bit decimal value from the CCP command line buffer	DECNUMBI
CI6DEC:	Get a 16-bit decimal value from the CON: device buffered input	DECNUMBI
BI6DEC:	Get a 16-bit decimal value from any designated ASCII line buffer	DECNUMBI

Console Device Display Subroutines

CO:	Send the character in A to the CON:	BEGIN
SPACES:	Display the number of spaces in A	BEGIN
CCRLF:	Display a CR, LF (new line) sequence	BEGIN
TWOCR:	Display two CR, LF sequences	BEGIN
SPMSG:	Display the message text terminated by zero immediately following the call	BEGIN
COMSG:	Display the message text terminated by zero pointed to by H,L	CPMIO
SHOLN:	Display the message text terminated by CR pointed to by BFPNT	FINDSTRN

Numeric Display Subroutines

CO8BIN:	Display 8 bits from A in binary	SHOWNUMB
CO6BIN:	Display 16 bits from H,L in binary	SHOWNUMB
CO8HEX:	Display 8 bits from A in hexadecimal	SHOWNUMB

CO6HEX:	Display 16 bits from H,L in hexadecimal	SHOWNUMB
CO8DEC:	Display 8 bits from A in decimal	SHOWNUMB
CO6DEC:	Display 16 bits from H,L in decimal	SHOWNUMB
CO8BHD:	Display 8 bits from A in binary, then hexadecimal, then decimal	SHOWNUMB
CO6BHD:	Display 16 bits from H,L in binary, then hexadecimal, then decimal	SHOWNUMB
CO8HD:	Display 8 bits from A in hexadecimal, then decimal	SHOWNUMB
CO6HD:	Display 16 bits from H,L in hexadecimal, then decimal	SHOWNUMB

Disk System Display Subroutines

DLOGI:	Display the disk logged on	SHOWDISK
DSIZE:	Display the disk and block sizes	SHOWDISK
DMAP:	Display the disk allocation vector	SHOWDISK
DSHOW:	Display the disk logged on, then the disk and block sizes, then the disk map	SHOWDISK
FSHOW:	Display the file name/file type from the designated file control block	FINDASMS
TSHOW:	Display the file name/file type from the transient file control block	FINDASMS

Disk Access Subroutines

DLOGI:	Log on the designated disk and display the disk designator	SHOWDISK
NEWBUF:	Read the next record into the double record buffer	FINDSTRN

READR:	Read the next record into the buffer pointed to by H,L	MISC-SU
SINFL:	Find a string in a file pointed to by the transient file control block	FINDSTRN
SINXT:	Find a subsequent string in a file	FINDSTRN
SINLN:	Find a string in an input buffer	FINDSTRN

Program Control Subroutines

OPINT:	Check for operator interrupt, abort to DONE: if CTRL Z	BEGIN
CHKHEX:	Check for a valid hexadecimal character, convert to binary if good	NICOMMON
CHKDEC:	Check for a valid decimal character, convert to binary if good	NICOMMON
LIMITS:	Check for A equal to or greater than C and less than or equal to B	NICOMMON
COMHD:	Compare H,L to D,E	MISC-SU
HFIELD:	Find the first valid hexadecimal character in the input buffer	NICOMMON
DFIELD:	Find the first valid decimal character in the input buffer	NICOMMON

System Status Subroutine

RAMTOP:	Find the address of the top of contiguous random access memory	CPMMAP

System Generation Routines

EXBOOTxx	Move the CP/M system image from 180H up to its destination in memory	Listing 13.1
BUILDxx	Generate an xx size CP/M system	Listing 13.2

CBIOS Subroutines Driven by IOBYT

Index

A

Address field:
  disk sector, 93, 134
  disk track, 123, 134
Address:
  absolute, 206
  physical, 90
  symbolic, 206
AFIND:, 131
Allocation block size, 119
Allocation vector, 98, 101
Allocation, resource, 11
ALV, 101, 201
Ambiguous file name, 130
Attribute:
  archive, 129, 205
  R/O, 129, 134
  SYS, 129, 205
Autoload, program, 152, 171
AUX:, 5, 163

B

Background, 13
Bank switch, memory, 18, 205
Base, number, 58
Batch processing, 11
Baud rate, console, 192
BDOS, 16
BDOS call, 22, 33
BEGIN:, 49
BEGIN.LIB, 49
BI6DEC:,83
BI6HEX:, 73
BI8DEC:, 83
BI8HEX:, 76
Binary, 58
Binary display, 60
BIOSKRNL, 207
Block:
  size, 119
  allocation, 90, 95